# The Economics
# of VAT

# The Economics of VAT

**Preserving Efficiency, Capitalism, and Social Progress**

**Richard W. Lindholm**
University of Oregon

**LexingtonBooks**
D.C. Heath and Company
Lexington, Massachusetts
Toronto

**Library of Congress Cataloging in Publication Data**

Lindholm, Richard Wadsworth, 1914-
  The economics of VAT.

  1. Value-added tax—United States. I. Title.
HJ5715.U6L54        337.2'714'0973        80-8428
ISBN 0-669-04111-4

Published simultaneously in Canada

Printed in the United States of America

International Standard Book Number: 0-669-04111-4

Library of Congress Catalog Card Number: 80-8428

# Contents

# List of Figures
# and Tables

## Figures

## Tables

# Preface

The explanation of the value-added tax (VAT) presented in this book is not simply a description of how VAT is collected, although that is done. The analyses developed here are much broader. They look at VAT as a needed basic aspect of the functioning of a democratic, capitalistic, industrial nation.

Much of what is discussed directly relates to H.R. 7015, the proposed federal Tax Restructuring Act of 1980. The analyses point to a broad consideration of what could be expected from the introduction of a major national VAT. The VAT is analyzed in relation to the very serious, long-run fiscal crisis of the federal government as well as the needs of a sound national economy. In this discussion we examine both the philosophical aspects and the nuts and bolts of the VAT concept.

This book explores the broad economic impacts of the tax programs existing in the United States and the rest of the Western world. The reality of the demand for government expenditures to finance many vital programs is accepted. The failure of the federal tax system to provide stable and substantial tax collections that encourage savings and investment in the private sector is seen to be a principal cause of the existing and continuing economic crisis.

Because it is a time of crisis, both wise and bold actions are needed to reach our high economic, social, and political potentials. Answers are provided to the legitimate questions: Why now? Why VAT? What would happen to me? Most important, the discussions lead to reasonable solutions to basic economic difficulties, for example, financing social security and maintaining a competitive international economic posture.

# Introduction

The value-added tax (VAT) is levied as a percentage of the receipts from a transaction or a sale. The tax due from each business firm is reduced by the VAT paid by the firm on raw materials, capital goods, components, and services purchased from other businesses. A VAT calculated in this fashion is called a subtractive type of VAT. Approximately the same total tax base can be developed by adding the amounts paid as wages and as net interest and rents to what is earned as profits. This procedure results in an additive type of VAT.

All the VATs in Western Europe are the subtractive type. Also, all the VATs in use avoid double taxation of capital goods (investments) by allowing immediate credit for the VAT paid, for example, when a machine is purchased. The machine becomes a portion of the cost of sales of the firm, and therefore the capital-goods price becomes a portion of the VAT base at this later date.

Transactions are the source of all realized income. The source of all private-sector payments made to complete transactions is income remaining after tax payments. The income available for purchases is reduced by income taxes, and this reduces the goods and services that the private sector can purchase. The same reduction of the purchasing power of the private sector takes place when a tax based on the value of a transaction is collected.

The basic economic (and perhaps philosophical and social) difference between a transactions tax and an income tax to raise revenues required by government if it is to provide expected services is this: *A tax on transactions can be personally decreased by saving more, and an income tax can be decreased by earning less.*

The VAT works to reduce the core rate of inflation by increasing the productivity and decreasing the waste of both business and government. The stability of the tax revenues that a VAT provides government increases the efficiency of public-sector operations. The collection of VAT from businesses avoids modification of the most efficient allocation of the factors of production as established in the marketplace. The VAT is an economic neutral.

The use of VAT means that taxes are paid regularly by businesses along with other normal costs of operation. The relatively stable inflow of revenues protects government from violent and wasteful swings in the level of spending and borrowing. In addition, the availability of savings and the resulting stability of capital-formation planning reduce risks and therefore the cost of loanable funds to the private sector. As a result, the core rate of inflation is reduced through the increased productivity arising from the normal impacts of a major national VAT.

# The Economics
# of VAT

# 1  Facing up to the Financing of Government

## Overview

The Introduction describes the boundaries of this book and defines basic concepts, such as tax, regressive tax, and the appropriateness of counter-cyclical fiscal impacts.

The next section is concerned with a basic new fiscal development—the relationship between tax reform and the rapidly expanded and expanding level of social expenditures. The modernization of revenue sources to meet current citizen expectations of government expenditures is seen to be further along in Western Europe than in the United States. With government expenditures at the current high level, the types of taxes used become very important. In the 1930s programs were introduced to stimulate the economy through countercyclical spending and tax programs. The need to change this approach to the economic relationship existing between the public and private sectors is demonstrated to currently exist.

The third section describes the financing of personal income security and its effect on the balance of payments.

The fourth section describes faltering spending and employment policies. The relatively slow growth of U.S. productivity shown in table 1-1 and the low level of savings shown in table 1-2 are linked to the economic instability and inflation inherent in the federal government's reliance on taxes that use a base which fluctuates widely.

The fifth section discusses the nuts and bolts of VAT. The VAT is often called nothing but a complicated sales tax. This characterization is not helpful in understanding how the tax operates. The VAT is a tax on the gross receipts or gross income of a firm. However, the firm can deduct the VAT which it paid directly to selling firms on its purchases. This deductibility makes VAT a tax on net turnover or on net payments in wages, interest, and dividends.

Although VAT has its complexities, it is relatively simple when compared with a progressive income tax or a corporate profits tax. The VAT calculated on the subtractive basis is used in Europe with great success; the VAT calculated under the additive approach is used in Michigan under the name *single business tax* (SBT).

The sixth section provides background material about the economic roots of VAT. The idea of having all businesses contribute to government a

1

fixed percentage of the value of their goods and services sold goes back to
the 1920s and the first serious gathering of gross national product (GNP)
data. People in the United States and the Germans have most actively
researched and discussed VAT, but the French were the first to develop
VAT as a national tax. The VAT gathered great momentum when countries
in the European Economic Community (EEC) decided that, in order to harmonize member state tax systems, all would be required to adopt a relatively
uniform VAT which included the retail level. The French must be given
credit for realizing that VAT possessed international-trade advantages that
were important and could be realized only if VAT were used at the national
level. People in the United States had generally thought of VAT as appropriate at the state or provinical level of government. Table 1-3
demonstrates how a simple subtractive VAT would be calculated. The
Danish law most nearly meets this ideal approach.

The seventh section explores in some detail the findings of the Fiscal
and Financial Committee of the EEC, which recommended in 1963 that
member states adopt a relatively uniform and substantial VAT. The report
is often called the Newmark report, after the German tax specialist who
headed the group. The findings and recommendations were adopted by the
EEC. These resulted in a major expansion in the harmonization of the tax
systems of the EEC's member states and speeded up the general acceptance
of a VAT. The Newmark committee favored a VAT over expansion of a
retail sales tax. The reason given for the position was that the "fiscal
technicalities" related to a major use of a national retail sales tax ruled out
its adoption. Basically the committee was interested in enjoying the trade
benefits that France was enjoying from a VAT which had been in place for
nearly ten years at that time.

The eighth section describes the state legislative VAT proposals and the
actual use of a VAT-type tax in Michigan between 1953 and 1967 and from
1976 to the present. Only Michigan has adopted and used a tax that can be
called a VAT, although a VAT has been seriously considered in West
Virginia, Hawaii, Oregon, Alabama, and Iowa. The Michigan VAT is
called a single business tax (SBT). The rate of the 1980 tax is 0.0235. It is an
additive type of VAT.

The final section describes the background of the British VAT. The
study by the Richardson committee in 1964 concluded that VAT was not a
useful tax procedure and that the United Kingdom would be wise to leave it
alone. The rapid adoption of VAT by the EEC member states at about this
time plus Britain's desire to become a member of the EEC caused a new
study to be commissioned. The study completed by the National Economic
Development (NED) office recommended the use of VAT even if the United
Kingdom did not join the EEC. The decision rested largely on the
international-trade usefulness of VAT, as well as the usefulness of VAT in

providing revenues to substitute for those lost as the highly progressive British income taxes were reduced to stimulate savings and investment. Currently VAT is providing about 15 percent of the British tax collections.

**New Economics**

On August 15, 1971, the shortcomings of huge federal government deficits closed the U.S. gold window. The devaluated U.S. dollar was the result of large foreign holdings of liquid dollar balances, increased domestic costs, and reduced receipts from exports. Conditions have not really improved since 1971.

In 1971 the annual carrying cost of the federal debt was $25 billion; by 1980 it had risen to $80 billion. The huge debt carrying cost plus growing social costs of all kinds sharply cut the productivity of expenditures from the public sector. As a result, rising prices developed a sensitivity to expecting inflation that destroyed the usefulness of the old policy relationships among federal deficits, increased employment levels, and economic growth. The new conditions require new policies in many areas, particularly in the manner in which governments at all levels collect as taxes about one-third of GNP.

*Current Conditions*

Resolution of the quandary existing in the U.S. fiscal pattern of operation seems to point toward some basic tax legislation and not just a switching around of income tax favors. Europe's good experience with VAT makes VAT a logical choice to become the core of the new approach. For the United States, VAT makes a lot of sense at this juncture. A substantial VAT would stimulate movement away from taxes that discourage savings, expanded effort, and productive investment.

The existing emphasis on progressive income taxes, on double taxation of corporate earnings, and on higher labor costs through payroll taxes discourages efficient use of land, labor, and capital. As a stable revenue provider with a base as broad as GNP, VAT permits an efficient, capitalistic, market-dominated production-and-distribution system to work even though taxes are one-third of GNP.

In this discussion of taxation we frequently quote tax data and refer to a tax as being regressive. Both the terms *tax* and *regressive* need defining at the very start. When this is done, some of the confusion so common in taxation discussions is avoided.

*Defining a Tax*

The principal criterion used in determining whether a government revenue is a tax revenue is that it is a compulsory payment to general government. Another criterion is that the levies are not associated with the enjoyment of a particular service. The major exception made in the application of this criterion is the treatment of social security contributions. These are counted as taxes even though the revenues are, to a greater or lesser extent, related to benefits received. In some instances, social security payments are partially voluntary. This voluntary portion is excluded from the tax-revenue total.

Compulsory payments to non-general-government agencies, such as labor unions and churches, are also excluded. General government includes national, state, and local governments and their independent agencies, but public enterprises are excluded. The profits arising from the operation of economic activities by government are not included as taxes even when compulsion and monopoly control exist. Depending somewhat on one's point of view, the total includes a double counting, for taxes paid by one government unit to another are included in the tax total. The largest item in this category is the payment of payroll taxes by one government as an employer to another government that manages a pension system.

*Defining* Regressive

The term *regressive*, when used in reference to taxation, frequently is thought of in connection with the word *regression*. *Regression* is defined in the dictionary as meaning going back to previous place or state. Popularly, the word means going backward, that is, that things are becoming worse. In taxation, *regressive* is used correctly in referring to tax payments that decrease proportionately with an increase in the tax base. A regressive sales tax would require reduced payments as a portion of sales as the value of sales increased. For example, a sales tax with a higher rate on a small purchase than on a large purchase meets the requirements needed to be called a regressive sales tax. Also, a property tax that applies more nearly to the full value of a modest rather than a luxury residence is correctly labeled a regressive property tax.

The term *regressive*, as applied to tax policy, does not contain the concept of regression. The idea of going backward, in terms of either shifting the economic burden to the producer rather than forward to the buyer or reducing well-being or forward progress, is not a portion of the meaning of *regressive* as applied to taxes.

Frequently the unmodified word *regressive* is used in a tax discussion when family or personal income payments are being referred to. A person who smokes a lot of cigarettes but has a low income is said to be subject to a regressive cigarette tax. Of course, this is not the case because the tax per package of cigarettes does not increase as fewer cigarettes are purchased. Rather, because cigarettes are subject to a special tax, a purchaser pays more of this tax if his or her consumption pattern includes purchase of quite a few cigarettes instead of only a few.

## Countercyclical Budget

The famed built-in, cyclical stabilizing impacts of the corporate income tax and the individual income tax operate as economic destabilizers rather than as stabilizers. They do not affect the economy, as had been taught in economic classes through the years. Foreign and domestic investment managers see the U.S. tax system as forcing the Federal Reserve to again and again abandon its tight monetary policy too rapidly, requiring a later sharp tightening. The construction industry finds the Treasury bidding away savings to cover its deficit, causing a shortage of financing for new housing at the very time when labor and material resources are available for housing expansion.

To put it bluntly, the countercyclical budget policy, once the darling of economists Walter Heller, Herbert Stein, and the big business association called the Committee for Economic Development (CED), has lost much of its former allure. It is incompatible with a monetary policy that wants, above all, to avoid feast and famine. Milton Friedman's recommendations of a steady expansion of money at a 4 percent rate may be dead, but the desire to play it safe—monetarily speaking—has become very attractive.

The corporate profits tax is even faulted on a fiscal-policy basis during prosperity. The large tax-collection increases of prosperity stimulate government spending when the private economy is already demanding all available resources. The countercyclical balanced-budget policy causes a cyclical stimulating-spending budget. It also prevents private investment from carrying out its full potential for stimulating private-sector economic growth.

## Needs of Capitalism

A nation can be capitalistic and a democracy and still collect in taxes as much as 50 percent of GNP. However, if these very large taxes are collected, care must be taken in the type of tax used if the basic roots of capitalism and democracy are not to be destroyed.

Tax collections at the level prevailing in Western industrial nations cannot be concentrated on profits and savings and expect investment to be sufficiently strong to aggressively innovate and increase capacity. The use of taxes aimed principally at profits, capital equipment, and savings were all right when taxes in the United States approximated 18 percent of GNP, as in 1940, rather than about 33 percent, as it is today. Today's fiscal conditions require a broader tax base if expectations of the government's expenditure level are to be met without destroying the economic-growth base required for a growing economy. Citizens of capitalistic democracies know in a general way that private-sector growth depends on wise government tax and expenditure policies. However, the realization has not been sharp enough in the United States to bring forth the use of a tax base at the federal level which approximates GNP in its breadth and stability.

*Conclusion*

Old ways of doing things and the justifications that support the accepted procedure are difficult to shift under all conditions. A change is particularly difficult in a federal democracy loaded with checks and balances. To add to this difficulty, taxation is an area in which both politicians and social-science teachers have treaded with extreme care, if at all. As a result, slogan-type words and phrases possess the power to affect tax actions of those who otherwise behave quite rationally.

## Developing Role of VAT in Financing
## Income-Maintenance Programs

The relative international position of the United States in the level of expenditures needed to finance its social security program remains about as shown in table 1-1. Substantial pressures for more revenues exist currently because U.S. personal income security support has increased sharply, and the fund or actuarial concept of financing social security has been largely abandoned.[1]

The U.S. level of fiscal 1970 income security spending was $43,073 million, up about $6 billion from 1969. In fiscal 1974, spending jumped to $108,610 million, some $55 billion above the 1970 level. During the next five-year period, the increase in income security expenditures was again substantial. The total reached $190,948 million in 1980. During the same ten-year period, federal health-related expenditures went from $13,051 million to $56,563 million. The all-item consumer price index for the same ten-year period increased from 116 to 230.[2]

These U.S. social-expenditure increases are much greater than those experienced in other industrial democracies, but the current portion of total

**Table 1-1**
**Annual Growth in GNP per Employed Worker in Major Industrial Countries, 1963-1979**
*(percentage change per year)*

| Country | 1963 to 1973 | 1973 to 1979 |
|---|---|---|
| United States | 1.9 | 0.1 |
| Japan | 8.7 | 3.4 |
| Germany | 4.6 | 3.2 |
| France | 4.6 | 2.7 |
| United Kingdom | 3.0 | 0.3 |
| Italy | 5.4 | 1.6 |
| Canada | 2.4 | 0.4 |

Source: International Monetary Fund, *Government Finance Statistics Yearbook 3* (Washington, D.C., 1979).

central-government expenditures allocated to social purposes remains below the average (see table 4-1). If it is assumed that, because of the aging population and other trends, the U.S. social security spending level will reach the level prevailing in Western Europe, then substantial additional financing will be required.[3]

At the same time as social security expenditures have been increasing, requiring additional taxes unless other portions of the national governments's budget are cut, international economic and political conditions have been deteriorating. Higher taxes mean additional costs and a reduced international competitive position. Exports become higher-priced, and imports become more competitive with products of domestic businesses. Changes in relative costs have had a greater economic impact than would have been true in the 1950s because tariffs and international trade barriers were sharply reduced in the 1964 Kennedy round of trade liberalization. This worldwide trade liberalization was completed in 1979 under the auspices of the General Agreement on Tariff and Trade (GATT). These tariff reductions have developed an intensively felt need to finance expensive social security programs without affecting a nation's international economic posture.

*Tax-Policy Ideas*

The publication *EFTA Today and Tomorrow* (1964) indicated an awareness of the likelihood that the dismantling of trade barriers and protective customs' duties would be circumvented by international taxes having a protective effect. The growth of VAT in Europe after the Kennedy round of tariff reductions (1964) was just such a development. The United States demonstrated a low awareness of what was taking place and did not mount a strong protest or develop a counterprogram except to move a bit toward greater action under the U.S. antidumping legislation first enacted in 1921.

The 1966 CED publication *A Better Balance in Federal Taxes on Business* advocated the introduction of VAT to stimulate investment through a simultaneous reduction of the corporate profits tax. The CED failed to consider VAT's international-trade strengths except to point out that VAT would not apply to foreign production of U.S. firms. The failure of this influential business research and policy group to realize that VAT acted as a protective shield to nations with rapidly expanding social security programs cannot be explained.

E.G. Horsman, writing in *Lloyds' Bank Review* of January 1972, said, "Once a country's trade rivals have VAT, the tax's intrinsic merits and failings cease to be the dominant consideration." Horsman's statement took as a given that prices of a country using VAT are not higher by the VAT percentage than the prices existing in countries not using VAT. The VAT is seen to be translated into higher prices to no greater extent or no more evenly than other taxes. The funds for the payment of VAT, just like those of any tax, must be taken largely out of prices charged.

Only a tax on land can be expected to not result in the allocation of the costs of government to purchasers of goods and services. Both strong and weak economic units will be raising prices as costs (including taxes of all kinds) increase. To assume that this does not take place—admittedly often haltingly—is to accept the proposition that prices before introduction of the tax were *not* set at the level that maximized profits, that is, that economic units are not profit maximizers.

The financing by government of transfer payments to support the aged, needy students, widows, and dependent children results in higher prices unless productivity can be expanded. What is required is a tax that meets the revenue needs without decreasing the efficiency of the market in allocating funds for investment out of normal levels of retained profits and individual savings. It is in meeting these basic revenue-related requirements of sound economic policy that VAT finds favor.

William E. Simon, former Secretary of the Treasury, said in the foreword to *Blueprints for Basic Tax Reform*, "It is time to start over from scratch and develop a new tax system in the United States. . . . We must design an entirely new tax system."[4] The need for basic reform of the U.S. tax system is obvious. The current system raises inadequate and uneven revenues while discouraging saving and domestic investment, the source of added production.

The two reforms developed in *Blueprints for Basic Tax Reform* stay basically with the concept of individual economic well-being. The tax base and rate variation are related to personal economic well-being as measured under the law. The reforms fail to abandon the basic position of the federal income tax, that is, that tax rates and the taxable base are allocable to individuals. A new tax system starting from scratch must question the desirability of staying with the personal effect of taxes rather than moving to an impersonal type of taxation. *Blueprints for Basic Tax Reform* does not do what is promised.

If the United States adopts a major VAT, it will have made some very basic decisions. First, the United States will have changed how the public sector is to acquire its revenues. Second, it will have abandoned tax collections as the major approach to greater economic equality. Third, it will have moved toward a harmonization of the U.S. tax system with the revenue systems in use in other major industrial nations.[5]

The use of large deficits by the federal government to finance activities normally being provided out of largely balanced budgets by the governments of the world's major and high-personal-income nations is no longer acceptable, for a numer of reasons. One is that the deficit approach of the United States creates an annual-interest-cost burden and a capital-market impact which are becoming more and more difficult to manage. The more than $100 billion of new (federal) government borrowing forecasted in 1980 for the next eighteen months will do little to stimulate additional economic activity. The principal impact is being registered in renewing inflation and high-interest-rate pressures. In addition, annual interest payments on the federal debt have risen above 10 percent of aggregate federal receipts and will reach the $80 billion level in fiscal 1981. Interest payments alone equal in nominal dollars the total budgetary receipts of the federal government in 1956.

## Modernization of Revenue Sources

Congress and the President have been reluctant to intensively consider the introduction of VAT in the United States. The hesitancy is understandable. There would be many trying and difficult complications. The federal fiscal system currently relies for more than 70 percent of its gross revenues on collections from assessments on wages, other personal income, and profits as defined by legislation and for 15 percent on borrowed funds. A tax restructuring based on a 10 percent VAT would develop a balanced-budget situation and a 25 percent decrease in the emphasis on wages, other income, and profit taxes. This would include a 40 pecent reduction of planned social security tax collections. The shift would be a dramatic one, and it is desperately needed.

*Type of Tax Makes a Difference*

When one considers the productivity of the public and private sectors, the dependence of each on the other becomes obvious. Thus the manner in which the public sector gains support from the private sector has a substantial impact on business efficiency. In addition, the efficiency of the public sector is affected, for example, by the stability of revenues. The type of taxes used to raise a given level of government revenues is very important in establishing the level of economic activity and the per capita consumption levels which increased productivity permits.

The introduction of a major VAT would harmonize the U.S. tax system with tax systems of other industrial nations. The investment of U.S. savings and foreign earnings of the U.S. companies would be affected much less by tax considerations if the United States were to adopt a major VAT than is currently true. This would increase the availability of domestic and foreign capital for private purposes in the United States, the potential productivity, and thus the real income level of U.S. wage earners. These are rather substantial and worthwhile pluses not generally considered in deciding which revenue sources should be used by government. These benefits are now being enjoyed by Germany and other industrial nations using VAT.

The U.S. federal public sector currently uses incomes and produces services and goods equal to approximately 22 percent of GNP. The very fact of the sector's size causes the way revenues are raised to possess the potential of seriously harming the efficiency with which day-to-day economic activities are carried out. Much is said of the desirability of cutting the spending of the federal government; however, any realistic evaluation largely accepts current expected government-expenditure levels. Therefore, financing sources should be looked at with an eye toward carrying an expenditure load at about the current level and doing it in a manner which would best serve the general welfare, and not special interest groups.

If the tax system sharply reduces after-tax profits, many investments with considerable potential become uneconomic. Also, when a tax system increases the cost of hiring a worker considerably above the negotiated wage rate, the inducement to hire more workers is reduced. In addition, if a tax fails to increase the price of imports through use of border taxes, so that import prices meet full-production-plus-tax costs of domestic goods, production for the domestic market tends to migrate to foreign-based firms. Finally, if private savings are absorbed in government deficits, high interest rates and the supply of inflationary money grow, and unemployment develops.

*Orientation toward Private Enterprise*

Each of the basic elements of a successful private-enterprise-oriented federal revenue system deserves serious reflection when one considers modernization of the U.S. tax system to better meet the needs of our kind of society. The shortcomings of the taxes in use and the overreliance on deficit finance, of which we are all aware in a general way, become specific when measured against the shortage of investment capital, the unemployment of labor, the deficit in the trade-account portion of the international balance of payments, and the export of domestic savings. In addition, our reliance on income taxes causes U.S. multinational firms to hesitate to repatriate their profits. Also, large federal government deficits are part and parcel of this fiscal policy. The combined effect reduces the level of U.S. productivity and economic growth. The introduction of VAT would improve the economic environment by reducing the inequality of the treatment of income sources.

The United States' fiscal cyclical need is for a major tax that collects a constant portion of total production sold in the market. Income taxes of all types, and particularly those with graduated and progressive rates, fail to do this. In both Western Europe and Michigan VAT proved capable of doing a pretty fair job.

*Harmonization*

Today, with federal government spending equal to about 22 percent of GNP, it is necessary to consider taxation in a much broader sense than was required when the level was one-tenth or even one-fifth of GNP. Also, rapid transportation and communication has increased the proximity of nations. This, in turn, requires greater consideration of the difficulties arising from a failure to harmonize national tax procedures used by major industrial nations.

The multinational corporation (MNC), which became feasible because of new commercial and technical relationships, is an institutional arrangement that needs worldwide tax uniformity if it is to avoid investment and marketing inefficiencies and serious international frictions. The United States is the home of a very large portion of the MNCs of the world; yet its adjustment to their tax-harmonization needs has been half-hearted.

More serious consideration of MNC tax liabilities is needed. Particularly close attention is required of the way in which taxes affect the economic processes of capitalism and the resulting efficiency of the immense worldwide markets in which MNCs function. Basically, domestic fiscal legislation should be aimed at making additional federal borrowing more difficult and tax adjustments easier. Because of its potential for providing large revenues with small tax-rate changes without affecting the existing market-determined relationship among wages, profits, interest, and rents, VAT appears to develop the political and economic impacts required of fiscal policy in today's world of shortages, unemployment, high interest rates, and inflation.

*Conclusion*

As a mature economy, the United States is destined to rely more and more on the skills of its people, the capital goods of its industries, and an attitude of looking to government as a cooperating agent. A major element of the government's role is the manner in which it collects taxes and the quantity of borrowed funds it uses to finance its functions. Ability to pay and related concepts of economic justice will always determine, to some extent, the tax approach used, and economic conditions will affect the quantity of funds borrowed. However, when economic pressures unfavorable to the efficient use of labor and capital develop from the tax approaches used to raise revenues, the procedure needs to be modified. This is basically the position in which the United States finds itself today.

## Faltering Spending and Employment Policies

The many special income-tax-relief provisions of the revenue acts of the 1970s are evidence of the pressures arising to increase tax deductions from earnings and to reduce the tax rate applied to nominal incomes. To reduce these taxes without providing for alternative revenues or a reduction of expenditures increases the size of the interest-bearing federal debt. This practical arithmetic is sometimes denied. There are those who say that tax reductions increase tax collections and that reduced federal expenditures can be taken from the "fat." Therefore, deficit spending will not be needed to continue vital services.

*Rising Interest Costs*

Currently, annual federal expenditures of between $10 billion and $35 billion are being financed with new debt. The increasing interest-bearing debt combined with higher interest rates results in interest-cost increases just about equal to the deficit. A considerable portion of the interest paid on the federal debt goes to foreign investors, which expands the international supply of dollars. In turn, this pushes down the international value of the dollar, causing imports (including oil) and the cost of borrowed funds to rise in price. Much of this upward interest and price movement could be avoided with the introduction of a substantial national VAT. Reliance on VAT to meet the costs of government would reduce the tax burden on savings and on returns from investment. The result would be to increase the attractiveness of investment opportunities. Thus this shift would result in expanded investments, and the multiplier from this turn of events would result in a dynamic economy.

*Comparison of the Payroll Tax and VAT*

The federal government has not enacted a basic new tax since the 1930s, when the social security payroll tax was adopted. The use of special excise taxes and the excess-profits tax of World War II reintroduced the concept of war taxes used during the Civil War and World War I. The growth of the payroll tax and the continuation of the development of the personal income tax as a tax paid by the receivers of very modest incomes have combined to cause substantial double taxation of U.S. wage incomes. The income receiver under the system is required to pay a payroll tax that makes no allowance for dependents and is not deductible from taxable income and, in addition, to pay an income tax with graduated rates that has reached lower and lower real incomes during the past ten years of inflation.

If a value-added tax of 10 percent were introduced in the United States, other taxes could be reduced sharply. The payroll tax could be brought down to levels existing in other nations. In addition, interest receipts from a modest amount of savings could be exempted from the income tax. This is basically what the Tax Restructuring Act of 1980 accomplishes.

A considerable portion of the philosophical opposition to the introduction of taxes to meet the costs of government has been related to the belief that the level of employment was increased by government deficits and the related inflation. In the 1960s, this seemed to be a tenable position in developed countries such as the United States and England, even though inflation and unemployment had expanded together in the less developed countries of the world. Current thinking that is based on U.S. data concludes that under current conditions of inflation expectation, additional money supply does not reduce interest rates. Instead, prices are increased, and real savings are decreased.

*Liquidity Uses*

In 1979 and 1980, with the economy ravaged by inflation and the liquidity of many financial and nonfinancial firms at very low levels, a belief that economic expansion can be hastened through the accumulation of huge inert government deficits requires faith that the private demand for funds to increase personal security will be great enough to overcome the weakness of the demand for money as a store of value. This position also requires confidence that, once the normal liquidity needed for personal security is reached, private spending of all types will increase in a normal manner to stimulate production and sales and will not be used to accumulate inventories or to bid up prices of natural resources, will not be transferred abroad, or will not be used to purchase gold.

*Impact of Federal Deficits*

The serious inflation experienced worldwide is often attributed to the huge U.S. budgetary deficits since 1968. The failure to finance the Vietnam war with a tax increase created a $25 billion deficit in fiscal 1968 that clearly kicked off the series of events which has led to the destruction of the Bretton Woods arrangement, the U.S. stock-market crises of 1969-1970 and 1974, and continuing destructive levels of inflation.

The economic advice of the 1965-1975 period, which proved to be so terribly wrong, was typified by economic analyses that were in one way or another dominated by the idea of a tradeoff between the rate of inflation and the level of unemployment.[6] Economists, who have come to be known as the Brookings Group, popularized a naive model called the "full employment balanced budget."[7] This economic environment has not been suitable to the development of a revenue program by the federal government providing for a new substantial source of tax receipts which would permit the politically required level of spending without an inflationary expansion of the money supply and a federal debt with a current annual carrying charge of some $80 billion. Interest on the federal debt amounts to an average family cost forever and ever of $750 to $1,500 a year for each of our 60 million family units. Each twenty-year family generation must now dedicate $15,000 to $30,000 of earnings to pay the interest on an ever-expanding national debt.

Too much good has been seen to exist in rising prices, an inflationary money supply, an expanding federal debt, and a tax system that avoided the use of production and sales as a tax base. Often all these have been justified on the basis of the need for an adequate demand to forestall unemployment.

Full employment as an overriding goal is attainable, according to what has come to be called the Phillips curve, through an appropriate inflation rate. The Phillips curve is constructed by plotting the percentage of money wage increase (vertical axis) against the pecentage of the labor force that is unemployed (horizontal axis). When this is done, a curve fitted to the points slopes downward to the right.[8]

*Phillips Curve*

The Phillips curve demonstrates that a tradeoff exists between the degree of inflation and the degree of unemployment; that is, the benefit of less unemployment requires the disadvantage of more inflation. However, although the historical record shows, for example, that a 1 percent increase in the rate of inflation decreases the rate of unemployment by 1 percent, it does not provide assurance this will happen in the future. The basic reason for this lack of assurance is that the Phillips-curve analysis does not provide an explanation of exactly what caused the historical relationship between the inflation rate and the unemployment rate.

One economist, at least, has speculated that as our economy becomes more affluent and can "support" more unemployed, it will take more unemployment "to keep inflation down to any specific rate."[9] It is argued this is so because being unemployed will involve a small reduction of purchases when unemployment benefits are substantial. If purchases are not reduced when unemployment increases, the inflationary pressures are not reduced through unemployment. In fact, increasing unemployment could expand inflation, causing stagflation. Higher prices and costs arise because unemployment expansion increases the pressures for reduced hours of work without a compensating reduction of pay and triggers unemployment-benefit payments. Fewer hours of work at the same pay decreases productivity per dollar of wages. Actually, except for the steel and automobile industries, blue-collar workers have been in short supply. It is college graduates that have kept the unemployment rate above 6 percent. Therefore, the expansion of construction and manufacturing activity does not directly decrease the unemployment pool. Instead, the increased demand for blue-collar workers in the areas already in short supply pushes up costs and prices.[10]

*Relating Taxing to Spending*

The highway program and the social security program are two examples of major government expenditures financed with tax collections paid into dedicated trust funds. Both the gasoline tax and the payroll tax are, perhaps, also income-regressive taxes. Another similarity of the two taxes is that the base taxed is rather directly associated with the expenditure financed.

The regressivity of the gasoline tax is largely hidden in the impact which it has on the prices of nearly all goods and services. The quantity of the product, gasoline, purchased is determined more by the section of the country in which the buyer lives than by his or her income level. Also, gasoline is a joint product whose use creates a very large satisfaction surplus. The existence of this surplus and the lack of a close substitute combined in the past to make the gasoline tax an OK tax that financed productive investment. But OPEC-determined high prices for oil have now lessened the potential of this public-sector production stimulant.

The payroll tax has benefited from the matching payment by the employer. In a way, the employee got $2 for 1$. The relationship between wages earned and provision for old age has also seemed proper. As a result, the tax has not needed to be supported by a provision for progressive rates, a dependency deduction, or the inclusion of all income in the base. This relationship continues to be strong, but the more rapid increase in the prices of necessities than in the general price level has reduced the soundness of the payroll tax-financing procedure, even when the wage ceiling increases at the same rate as general inflation.

The relationship between revenue source and expenditure benefit from highway and social security programs in the past has been sufficiently close to make the revenue-expenditure package acceptable. In both instances, the need for tax revenues to finance what was to be done and the relation of the revenue source to expenditure enjoyment were understandable to the electorate.

In the case of general government expenditures, this basic fiscal logic provided by the relationship of the tax to the expenditure satisfaction does not exist. This has not always been the situation. Formerly general expenditures of the federal government were expected to be met with tax receipts, as is largely the current practice among the states. The abandonment of the practice arose somewhat from the Congressional Committee Organization which is now partially remedied. Economic teachings related to the cyclically balanced budget, excess-savings doctrines, the full-employment balanced budget, and the Phillips-curve concept combined to weaken the practical citizen's conviction that what is bought must be paid for.

*Conclusion*

The current economic crisis highlights several basic shortcomings of fiscal-policy conventional wisdom developed during the past forty years under quite different conditions. In developed as well as in less developed countries, the expansion of liquidity can be inflationary even though the level of unemployment is relatively high. Also, savings are discouraged by the current economic environment. The intuitive realization of the accuracy of these two basic observations of the current scene is sharply reducing voter confidence in the helpfulness of federal deficits and the usefulness of government tax reductions to stimulate the economy and to increase productivity and the level of savings. The data of table 1-1 and figure 1-1 provide a summary of the productivity and savings trend.

**Nuts and Bolts of VAT**

The rates legislated and the tax base to which the legislated rates apply have a substantial effect on the economics of the use of a VAT system. The

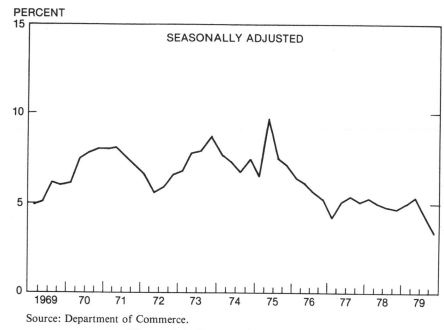

PERCENT

SEASONALLY ADJUSTED

Source: Department of Commerce.

**Figure 1-1.** Personal Saving Rate

federal VAT legislation (H.R. 7015) introduced in the Ways and Means Committee by its chairman, Al Ullman, in the spring of 1980 provides for a VAT that would earn a rating of 4, on a scale of 1 to 10, with 10 being the most complex. However, one must offer a caveat. In 1980, neither H.R. 7015 nor any other federal VAT legislation has gone through the legislative process. Therefore, the impact of amendments to grant favors to certain groups and products has not been felt.[11]

*Tax-Collection Variation*

Four different VAT rate-application procedures have developed out of European experience. Three are included in the original provisions of H.R. 7015. These VAT rate-application procedures come under the headings of taxable, exempt, rate variation, and zero-rated.[12] With the exception of rate variation, all are included in H.R. 7015.[13] In addition, there is the additive-type VAT. The application of rates under this approach is discussed in the explanation of the Michigan single business tax (SBT), a modified VAT.

When a product or service is exempt, the VAT is not applied to the retail price of products or services sold, but the seller must have paid the VAT included as a portion of the invoices of products and services purchased from other businesses. H.R. 7015 does not use rate variation. Only one rate, a 10 percent rate, is used. In Britain, the conservative government elected in 1979 amended the VAT to a single rate of 15 percent. This is a return to the single-rate approach previously used by the United Kingdom.

Zero rate means sales are exempt and the VAT paid on purchases is refunded. Zero rate is always given to exports. In H.R. 7015, zero rate is also extended to transactions of charities, public and private nonprofit educational institutions, mass transit, housing, capital investments, and sales to government. Under the proposed VAT for the United States, a border tax of 10 percent on the Customs Insurance Freight (CIF) price of imports would be imposed where a lower tax rate or exemption is not deemed to be in the best interests of the country. This is the same procedure that is followed in Europe and generally wherever VAT is used. In Europe, sales to government are not generally zero-rated, as is proposed in H.R. 7015.

*More Detail on VAT Tax Rate and Base*

The banks are exempt from VAT in all European countries, and this is also true in H.R. 7015. Banks and other financial institutions are given the exempt status because the banking industry is subject to special taxation. In addition, because financial incomes of all kinds are not included directly in VAT, the exemption of interst paid and received by banks is a tax position consistent with the general philosophy of VAT. In the United States, banks are not taxed in a particular fashion, but are treated generally as are all other businesses. Nevertheless, H.R. 7015, because of the general treatment of financial incomes under VAT, exempts banks and financial institutions generally. Special treatment is provided for insurance companies.

The exempt status for U.S. financial institutions more than likely is more generous than it need be. Financial institutions are treated as though they only receive deposits and extend loans. In fact, they also perform many advisory and safe-keeping services. This favoritism is partially rectified because exemption means that all VAT paid on utilities, supplies, and capital equipment cannot be deducted except as an ordinary expense. Thus, for VAT purposes, these financial institutions become end users and pay VAT on purchases without receiving funds from collection of VAT on sales.

*Government Services*

In Europe, government services are generally subject to the same VAT rate as similar services or products produced and/or marketed within the private sector. Under H.R. 7015, governments are zero-rated. Government is treated like food, medical care, and housing. Education, public and private nonprofit, is given a zero rating under H.R. 7015. In Europe, only room and tuition fees are generally given the exempt status. Book and supply sales are taxable.

The invoice approach used in Europe is called the consumption or subtractive type of VAT. The amount of VAT paid is given on the invoice that is deductible from VAT due on sales of the firm. This approach provides a self-enforcement feature. An invoice that includes VAT paid which has not actually been paid can be identified with ordinary commonsense auditing. Therefore, taxes not shown as paid on the invoice provide a sound procedure to recoup the unpaid tax at the next level of business activity.

## Additive Approach

The Michigan SBT adopted in 1975 applies a rate of 2.35 percent on the gross income of all businesses. From 1953 to 1967, Michigan used a business activity tax (BAT), a modified VAT.[14] The repeal of BAT was largely the result of a vendetta of Governor Romney of Michigan, a former president of American Motors. American Motors, a low-profit company, fared better under a corporate income tax than under a VAT. By 1975, Governor Romney was gone, but Michigan's need for increased investment and stable revenues continued. The legislature turned back to the use of VAT. The base of the Michigan SBT is calculated on the income side. This makes SBT an additive VAT. Table 1-2 summarizes the manner in which the Michigan SBT base is calculated.

## Michigan

The people of Michigan with their fourteen years of experience with a VAT calculated on the subtractive basis opted in 1975 for a VAT calculated on the additive basis. Actually many businesses in Michigan were permitted under the earlier VAT to calculate their base on the additive basis.

The main advantage of the additive-VAT procedure, as learned in Michigan, is its simplicity and comprehensibleness in the U.S. tax environment.[15] The additive procedure is also believed to push up prices less than the subtractive approach. In addition, the additive approach makes it easier to include financial institutions within the general value-added tax. Interest treatment under the additive calculation method is reversed: interest paid is deducted from the tax base, and interest received is added to the tax base.

At the national level, a considerable portion of the usefulness of VAT arises from the way it can be used to stimulate exports and retard imports.

**Table 1-2**
**How to Compute the Michigan Value-Added Tax**

Add: Total compensation = salaries and wages (W-2), FICA payments, unemployment insurance tax, worker's compensation premium, health insurance pre-
mium, pension, profit-sharing cost.

*Subtotal*

Add:   Taxable income from federal return
Add:   Net interest (paid less received)
Add:   All depreciation taken on federal return for assets purchased before 1/1/76
       All depreciation taken on federal return for assets purchased after 1/1/76

*Subtotal: Gross tax base*
Subtract:   28% of depreciation on federal return for assets purchased before 1/7/76[a]
Subtract:   Full value of real and personal-property capital acquisitions

*Subtotal: Adjusted gross tax base*
       Apportion by three-factor formula to determine Michigan tax base

*Subtotal: Michigan tax base*
Subtract:   Small-business low-profit exclusion, if eligible

*Subtotal: Adjusted tax base*
Subtract:   Gross-receipts limitation, if eligible
Subtract:   Labor-intensity deduction, if eligible[b]

*Total tax base*

*Multiply by tax rate, 0.0235*

*Tax Liability*

Source: Office of Revenue and Tax Analysis, Department of Management and Budget, State
of Michigan (1978).
[a]Applies to 1976 tax year; deduction increases to 50 percent in 1977 and 60 percent in subsequent years.
[b]Calculated on the gross tax base above.

The calculation of VAT under the additive approach would endanger these
important advantages. This probable difficulty provides a supportive
justification of the adoption of a consumption-subtractive VAT, as provided in H.R. 7015.

The additive approach to VAT sharply reduces the flexibility of the tax
in providing for special exemption and lower rates on certain goods.
However, adjustment for size can be readily made. This is good in the sense
that the VAT base is apt to remain broader and the calculation of the tax
due less complex. These same characteristics reduce the attractiveness of the
additive VAT to those wishing to use the tax to reach certain social and subsidy goals above the raising of revenues in an economically neutral manner.
An additive VAT can be more easily applied across the board than a subtractive VAT.

*Base*

The base subject to VAT rates is bound to be a compromise between the need for a broad base, to provide required revenues through the application of reasonable rates, and the large number of special situations that could provide greater benefits to society if the taxes on their sales were lower. The typical procedure used in making these adjustments under a subtractive VAT is to exempt or apply a lower rate on the selling activity and largely ignore the purchaser. The seller is granted a benefit; it does not matter who the purchaser may be. Of course, the other side of the tax-based discussion is to use a tax rate as a percentage of total investment or gross income, without any consideration of the type or source of the income.

*Secondhand Goods*

One area of continuing difficulty in taxing current sales is the base to be used on secondhand sales and how to treat trade-ins.[16] The problem is even more difficult under the retail sales tax (RST) than under VAT. This is true because under VAT much of the tax has already been paid and therefore the allowance of an excessive amount for trade-ins does not have the capability of reducing the tax beyond the retail markup. Under this treatment, trade-ins are taxed when sold.

In Europe, VAT is collected on all used equipment sold by businesses. However, sales of used items by individuals are not included in the VAT tax base. This has had the effect of inducing individuals to sell their own used cars rather than trading them in. The dealer's offer is likely to be low because he must take account of the fact that his sale will be included in his VAT base. Under H.R. 7015, the European approach has not been followed. All sales of used property by a taxable person is reduced by the amount that the property was taxed when originally purchased.

*Rent Payments*

The leasing of tangible property is another area where relatively minor differences in tax philosophy can have an important tax-administration effect. Under H.R. 7015, the payment of housing rent is zero-rated. The composition of the costs covered through the rent payment does not affect the VAT liability.[17] The extra financing cost included in the payment when the property is purchased under a lease arrangement does not affect the VAT due in all Western Europe or under H.R. 7015, but it does in the United Kingdom. In the United Kingdom, the financing portion of the payment under the contract is exempt from VAT.

*Small Businesses*

The Michigan and European experience with VAT has demonstrated VAT's usefulness in encouraging small business. The base exemption because of the size of the business in the Michigan legislation was $36,000 in 1977. Provision is also made in Michigan for an additional deduction with an increase in the number of working partners or stockholders of a Subchapter S corporation. The general practice in Europe follows similar lines. If sales of property and services are not greater than $20,000 per year, H.R. 7015 makes provision for exemption. This must be judged to be too low.

The administrative ability of VAT legislation to encourage small and labor-intensive business is a substantial plus for the tax. In addition, because VAT is not limited to profits, unprofitable businesses can benefit from VAT exemptions and lower rates. On the other hand, corporate income tax favors from the use of an investment tax credit to lower tax payments are limited largely to profitable businesses.

*Tax Inclusive or Exclusive*

As it is collected on sales of goods and services passing through the production and marketing process, VAT can either become a portion of the base on which the tax at the next stage is collected or be excluded. That is, the VAT rate can apply to a tax inclusive or a tax exclusive. The French have used the tax-inclusive basis. This can be done without making VAT a gross turnover tax and bringing about the cascade effect. The cascade effect is avoided because the tax paid at previous stages is deductible from the tax due. As a result, the application of the rate to a larger base increases the amount deductible by the same portion of the total at all levels of economic activity.[18] For example, when the French-legislated VAT rate was 16 2/3 percent, the effective rate was 20 percent. The formula used to turn a legislated rate into an effective rate under the tax-inclusive procedure is

$$\frac{T}{100 - T} = \frac{16\frac{2}{3}}{100 - 16\frac{2}{3}} = \frac{0.1667}{0.8333} = 20\% \quad \text{(effective rate)}$$

Tax exclusive is now widely accepted as preferable to the "tax on tax," or tax-inclusive, approach. The amount of the tax in the tax-exclusive approach is kept out of the price of the goods or services subject to VAT. Also, the tax rate applied is the same as the legislated rate. These characteristics of a tax-exclusive approach reduce confusion and expand taxpayer and voter understanding.

*Conclusion*

The VAT has been thoroughly tested in Europe and Michigan as a tax to supply stable and substantial revenues required by an advanced industrial society to meet rising social expenditures. The proposed H.R. 7015 differs in some respects from the developed Michigan and European practice. This is to be expected since U.S. political and social priorities vary somewhat from those of Europe. Michigan's practice is greatly different because the base is developed on the income side.

## Economic Roots of VAT

The roots of the value-added tax are embedded in U.S. economic theory and data. The theoretical support of the concept of value added as a tax base, usually using the additive approach (that is, the sum of wages, interest, rent, and profits), came from U.S. fiscal analysts. The VAT was initiated by U.S. economists with a desire to generate a neutral tax that would provide substantial revenues without reducing the effectiveness and efficiency of the market system in allocating capital, labor, and land. The United States, was, and remains even more so today as a result of consumer-group efforts and the 1972-1973 price-control fiasco, the great free-market nation. Therefore, it was very appropriate that the early examining, explaining, and advocating of VAT be done in the United States. U.S. economists have been more interested in business statistics and analyses based on these data than their European counterparts. German interest in VAT has always been considerable, but the concept did not attract German tax scholars as it did U.S. fiscal experts. German industry, typified by Wilhelm von Siemans of the German steel industry, studied and supported the use of VAT.

*Data-Based Economics*

After World War I, VAT was seriously considered as the replacement for special World War I excise taxes and the excess-profits tax introduced to siphon off war profits. The U.S. heritage of VAT is forgotten or being neglected when VAT is called a "foreign tax," as is often done by those familiar with only the actual application of the tax by a major nation. The VAT is as American as apple pie; it was used successfully by Michigan from 1953 to 1967 and was readopted as the single business tax in 1975. In fact, U.S. economists originated the whole business of gathering economic statistics to calculate national income and GNP, that is, income of the factors of production and goods and services produced for the market. At the turn of the century, even as is true today, sound economics, that is, economics that dealt with realities, found the University of Chicago intellectual climate stimulating. Thorstein Veblen and his students, particularly the brilliant Wesley Claire Mitchell, the founder of the National Bureau of Economic Research (which continues as a substantial research organization and the official declarer of when a recession starts and when it ends), developed the statistics that made possible the calculation of national income and GNP.[19]

Once total current production and the incomes of the factors of production became measurable as a sum of the value added by major industries, their use as the base for a general business tax became inevitable. And it was in the United States that economics first broke away from the armchair philosophizing of Marx and Ricardo. The field of economics was started on the long road to becoming a real social science, and the concept of VAT was developed. At its inception, VAT was seen as a tax on total production, which means a tax that becomes a part of the cost of all consumption of goods and services purchased in the market. Another result of the national data-gathering activity about income was to quantify the expenditure shortfalls that caused depressed economic conditions. In both cases, the early U.S. development was to be grasped and utilized more effectively in Europe than in the United States.[20]

The VAT has become a principal tax of twelve Western European nations (France, Denmark, Germany, the Netherlands, Belgium, Luxembourg, Norway, Ireland, Italy, Great Britain, Sweden, and Austria). In addition to its reintroduction in Michigan in 1975, VAT has been proposed by a number of states, including Alabama, Hawaii, Oregon, and West Virginia. The federal government, in 1965 and again in 1972 and 1980, gave serious consideration to introduction of VAT.

Also, the fundamental business-cycle work of Wesley Mitchell, a U.S. economist, has not been pursued in the United States. Economic planning combined with government budgetary, revenue-source, and central-bank policy is fundamental in most Western European nations, but has never been wholeheartedly accepted in the United States.[21]

*Consideration of GNP as a Tax Base*

In 1932 and 1933, the Brookings Institution recommended the adoption of VAT in Alabama and Iowa.[22] In 1964, a little over thirty years later, Brookings published the proceedings of a conference entitled "The Role of Direct and Indirect Taxes in the Federal Revenue System." The conclusion of the conference was that VAT would not be helpful to the United States in developing sound domestic fiscal policy or an improved international economic balance. Finally today, more than fifteen years later, Brookings, our chief fiscal-policy research center, is taking another serious look at VAT as a major federal tax under existing conditions.

Dr. Gerhard Colm, a German-trained fiscal expert who became a leading tax specialist in the federal government and of the American Planning Association, in 1934 published in *Social Research* an article entitled "The Ideal Tax System." It was an article recommending and describing VAT.[23] In 1940, Paul Studenski, certainly one of the most distinguished U.S. business-taxation scholars, concluded that VAT was the ideal business tax. His general ethical and philosophical foundation for VAT bears the short title "Cost of Services Varient."[24] He saw VAT as a neutral tax because it did not change the relative payments for wages, rent, interest, and profits or the return to the factors of production, labor, land, capital, and entrepreneurship as set in the marketplace. After the payment of VAT, the payments to each factor continued at the same relative height. Studenski saw government services benefiting each of the factors of production largely in proportion to income received; therefore, the payment of the VAT became a collection for government services enjoyed.

Studenski's support of VAT was an expression of a generally felt attitude toward VAT by knowledgeable U.S. students of taxation in the 1940s. The early favorable reception given to VAT by the tax profession goes back to the writings by T.S. Adams, the father of the 1913 individual income tax legislation. His article in the *Quarterly Journal of Economics* supported VAT as the best approach to the taxation of businesses.[25] He had previously supported the basic concept of VAT in 1911. This U.S. awareness of VAT led to the introduction of Senate Bill 3560, on March 11, 1940, in the 76th Congress, Second Session, by Senator C. Joseph O'Mahoney. It was a legislative proposal for the introduction of VAT by the U.S. federal government.

After the defeat of Japan in World War II, the United States sent a group of tax experts to Japan to assist in the development of a democratic Japanese tax system.[26] The mission was headed by Carl S. Shoup of Columbia University. The U.S. taxation mission to Japan, the Shoup mission, recommended that Japan adopt the VAT. The Shoup mission presented its recommendations to the Japanese government in 1949. In 1950, the Japanese Diet adopted a local-government VAT. A variety of circumstances prevented the legislation from being activated, and it was later repealed. Legislation somewhat similar to the Shoup-inspired Japanese proposals is currently being used very effectively in Brazil.

Michigan's modified VAT was adopted in 1953. It was successfully utilized until 1968.[27] It was called the business activity tax (BAT). A number of Michigan tax specialists praised the tax. Included in the group were A.L. Cornick from Ford Motor Company and Harvey Brazer from the University of Michigan.

All these U.S. developments took place *before* the French introduced their VAT in 1954. The French VAT is called *taxe sur la valeur adjoutée* (TVA). In introducing TVA, the French were taking a U.S. and German tax idea based on modern national income accounting and using it to meet a serious French fiscal crisis.[28] The VAT was adopted by France at first as a limited reform of a badly functioning tax system. Later it became the basic characteristic of French fiscal policy. The first French economic writer to seriously evaluate VAT was M. Lauré in 1952.[29] In 1921 Wilhelm von Siemens, of the great German steel family, wrote of the desirability of VAT.[30] And VAT, by 1952, had been a portion of the business taxation bibliography in U.S. university courses in public finance for at least twelve years.

## French Origins

The French general consumption or gross-turnover tax grew quickly out of a luxury tax introduced in 1917 in the form of a sales stamp, as part of the highly organized French stamp duty system.[31] As time went on, it was observed that this general gross-turnover tax rested too lightly on "industrial and business services included in processing and distribution as such."[32] The result was the introduction of a single-stage production tax (*taxe à la production*) in 1936. This production tax used value added as its base and demonstrated a tendency to cover a broader and broader sweep of French production activity. Between 1953 and 1955, with April 10, 1954, given as the official date, the French production tax became TVA, a genuine value-added tax, albeit with quite a few exemptions, including retailing. In 1966, retailing was added. The French originators of TVA in 1954 saw it as a portion of a philosophy of an economic development plan.[33] The TVA grew out of a popular desire to allocate for government use a stable portion of the new productiveness of French business enterprise.

## Concept of a Neutral Tax

There is no doubt that the concept of a tax using the GNP base grew out of the U.S. economic and business environment. National income and GNP, which are calculated by adding the market value of effort measured on the income or product sides at each stage of production have become the basic measurement of economic well-being. This is also how the base of VAT can be calculated and the tax rate applied.

A basic characteristic of VAT is that it treats all economic activity similarly. It does not dictate the use of savings, and it does not treat the profits of success more harshly than wage or interest income. Also VAT does not attempt to favor partnerships over corporations. When VAT legislation has abandoned this uniformity, political pressures have gained priority over economic considerations.

It is an indisputable fact that the concept of a tax on national income and GNP is a native U.S. product, not a foreign import. A realization of this should somewhat reduce the illogical U.S. opposition to this tax development which has been received with much enthusiasm in Western Europe.[34] It is also indisputable that the practical use of VAT by the French arose from a desire to place a basic tax on the new productiveness of French enterprise without at the same time retarding the continuation of the economic development being enjoyed. This relationship between the desirableness of VAT and the enjoyment of economic development continues to be fundamental.

The degree of U.S. rejection of VAT varies, as would be expected. The September 1970 report of the President's Task Force on Business Taxation included a minority report favoring immediate adoption of the VAT. It was filed by two members out of the total membership of fifteen. The thirteen other members of the task force recommended that "should the need ever arise for substantial additional Federal revenues, the government should turn to the value-added tax or some other form of indirect taxation rather than to an increase in rates of the corporate or personal income tax."[35] The task force did not consider financing an expanded medical and social security program through the use of VAT nor did they consider indexing the income tax and increasing real revenues with a VAT.

In 1971, the international economic shortcomings of the U.S. approach to business taxation was recognized in congressional legislation establishing the Domestic International Sales Corporation (DISC). This legislation delays indefinitely 50 percent of corporate profit taxes arising from exports if the taxes saved are used to expand exports. In so doing, DISC has moved one step toward giving our exporters the tax-refund assistance enjoyed by Europeans under VAT.[36]

*International Development*

West Germany introduced its VAT in the fall of 1965. The VAT replaced the gross-turnover tax and permitted reductions in the corporate and individual income taxes. In 1978 VAT provided 12 percent of West Germany's central-government revenues.

In addition to its domestic revenue-gathering appropriateness for industrial nations, VAT has an international adjustment (competition) face that is very pleasant. The tax can be readily rebated on goods exported, and its correct compensatory rate on imports can be accurately set and justified. *The use of the tax by one major trading nation requires that all others adopt the tax or accept one of a number of unpleasant alternatives, unless the nation using the tax is willing to abandon its international commercial impact.* The unpleasant alternatives include hidden export subsidies, devaluation, higher tariff rates, and an incomes policy sufficiently tight to reduce inflation below the world rate. To a degree these are currently being experienced in the world and particularly by the United States.

## Calculation of Subtractive VAT

A usable, subtractive value-added base for the application of a percentage appropriate to revenue needs can be relatively simple. A possible base that allows for some of the traditional deductions developed in the administration of the U.S. corporate income tax provides for investment stimulation, by following immediate deduction of capital purchases, is shown in table 1-3.

## Conclusion

The use of national income and/or GNP as the base to be used in the taxation of business is not a new idea. It came along as a tax concept with the development of national income accounts and the realization that government was going to be an important element in the day-to-day affairs of businesses.

Some active political support for VAT exists in the United States, but it has been insufficient to bring VAT close to adoption. On the other hand, in Western Europe, the favorable French experience caused a revolution in the indirect tax system in use. The potential for this to happen in the United States exists. The current inflation rate and the loss of the availability of federal government deficits to finance estalished expenditures point in this direction. In November 1979, hearings were held on H.R. 5665 which provided for a subtractive VAT with revenues dedicated to replacing individual and corporate income taxes plus a rollback of the social security payroll tax.[37] These hearings and other discussions resulted in modifications included in H.R. 7015 introduced in April, 1980.

## Living Together with Big Tax Collections

The adoption of H.R. 7015 would introduce tax reductions equal to revenues expected from a comprehensive VAT with substantial rates. The

**Table 1-3**
**Calculation of Subtractive VAT**

| | | |
|---|---|---|
| Total sales of goods and services[a] | $ _____ | |
| *Plus* total interest, dividends, rents, and royalties received | _____ | |
| *Plus* inventory expansion | _____ | |
| Total | _____ | |
| *Less* the total of | | |
| Corporate income taxes | _____ | |
| All other taxes, including payroll taxes | _____ | |
| Purchases of materials, services, and power from other firms or credit for VAT paid on these purchases | _____ | |
| Dividends, interest, rents, and royalties paid to other companies | _____ | |
| Inventory reduction | _____ | |
| Purchase of capital goods | _____ | |
| Contributions and gifts allowed | _____ | |
| Total | _____ | *(B)* |
| Value-added base after adjustments | _____ | *(A − B)* |

[a]The problem of sale and purchase of used goods was not considered.

economic, social, and political effects would be a combination of tax-reduction stimulants and new tax-introduction restraints. This was expected to result in not a standoff, but a generally improved U.S. economic environment. The VAT, the new tax, would improve the U.S. internationnal competitive position and stimulate supply. The tax reductions would strengthen inducements to produce and save.

The decision to reject or adopt H.R. 7015 or similar U.S. legislation is akin to the problem faced by the EEC when they decided to adopt VAT. Tax uniformity among the industrial neighbors was seen to be a necessary if sound private investment and production decisions were to be made. A tax levied on net turnover, that is, VAT, was selected as best hope for helpful progress toward the enjoyment of tax harmonization.

The next few pages describe in some detail the thinking behind the original EEC decision to require member states to adopt a substantial and uniform VAT which included the final end-use sale, that is, retail sales, in its base. The discussion is largley based on the detailed report entitled *Tax Harmonization in the Common Market*, developed by an international group of tax specialists. The chairman was Fritz Neumark, a German tax scholar. The study, often referred to as the Neumark Report, became the basic policy document used in the development of a relatively uniform VAT in Europe. It remains the authoritative analysis in this area of taxation policy.

*Fiscal-Policy Goals*

The general aim of European Economic Community's financial policy as it is included in fiscal policy is to eliminate differences in tax and expenditure policies "which lead enterprises and, consequently, capital, labor, and business to choose to establish in locations other than which would be naturally or technically the most favorable." Among other things, this includes the elimination of both tax havens and tax discrimination based on nationality and often fiscal domicile.[38] The analysis of the tax and expenditures are sufficiently similar in the aggregate, at least, that they do not provide important obstacles to the development of a common market. However, the Fiscal and Financial Committee (FFC) of the EEC emphasizes that "in ascertaining possible dislocations of competition which may result in trade between states from public-finance measures, one must take into consideration . . . the additional effects . . . resulting from the use of tax revenues. . . ." The types of state expenditures generally considered most influential in improving the competitive position of a nation are those made for research and for stimulating exports.

The FFC concludes that although "the total amount of taxes are approximately the same in two countries, a structural difference in fiscal systems . . . can . . . influence the competitive conditions. . . ." Nevertheless, some structural tax differences must be accepted because they are deeply rooted in the social or economic habits of the country. The inability to remove these structural differences in the way that the tax revenues of the different member states are raised need not prevent establishing tax conditions which do not materially affect competition. The competitive impact of the disparities in the structure of taxes in countries can be greatly relieved "if one were to retain the principle of the country of destination. . . ." Basically, this means that all taxes on goods exported would be levied by the country of import; the exporting country would exempt exports of all taxes. However, a major goal of FFC is the elimination of fiscal frontiers, and this requires abandoning the principle of the country of destination.

The FFC accepts "fiscal transparency" as one of the basic requirements of taxation which promotes sound competitive relations among nations. The term *fiscal transparency* means that the way in which the tax system works is readily understood. The FFC also recommends that all member states use a special company tax which, at the time of the report, existed in all countries except Belgium. Effective January 1, 1963, a distinct corporate income tax was initiated in Belgium.

*Business Taxes*

The FFC analysis considers corporation taxes, particularly with regard to "different tax treatment of company profits retained for the purpose of self-financing.'' The general conclusion is that an approximation of similar treatment is very important in this area to prevent international companies from concentrating their reserves in those countries "having the lowest fiscal burden." The reasons for avoiding a concentration of international-company reserves are not given, but certainly the difficulty which this could create in maintaining a balance-of-payments equilibrium would be one very real danger.

The FFC kept the turnover tax in the foreground of its discussion of tax harmonizations because it was considered the tax having the greatest "direct influence on price formation and, therefore, on competition." The first basic decision was that all member states having "multistage gross turnover taxes" should abolish them. Abolition was recommended for the stock reason that the tax was believed to distort domestic commerce and artificially promote concentration of enterprise. The principal international-competition shortcoming given was that an exact overall burden could not be calculated and that, therefore, the amount of countervailing levies or refunds "was uncertain." It may be that this phrase, in addition to uncertainty, also meant that the turnover tax was not a match for France's value-added tax in establishing favorable international competitive conditions.

*Fiscal Frontiers*

The FFC has as one of its major goals the elimination of fiscal frontiers. The fiscal frontier must continue to exist as long as taxes, and particularly turnover taxes of either the net or gross type, are levied on the basis of the country of destination rather than the country of origin. When these taxes are levied on the basis of the country of destination, neither the country of destination nor that of origin is assumed to be particularly concerned with the tax rate because the rebate of the tax on exports and the levy of a compensating tax on imports eliminate any direct impact of rate differences. When the net- or gross-turnover tax is levied on the basis of the country of origin, as are income taxes under the present GATT rules, then the goods taxed and the rates become important, because rebates on exports and compensatory levies on imports are abolished, and the relative international competitive position *is* directly affected. It is also true that when the net- or gross-turnover taxes are levied on the basis of the country of origin, fiscal frontiers can be abolished and a major goal of EEC tax harmonization is met. A basic requirement for the adoption of the country-of-origin basis in the area of turnover taxes then becomes the initiation of a relatively uniform rate and coverage turnover tax, by each of the EEC member states. The FFC recommendations face up to this and recommend the use of a uniform net-turnover tax "with the same or almost the same rates." The recommendations on coverage are less precise.

The area of agriculture is not carefully analyzed, but is taken care of by being described as a "most delicate and complex field" which is being studied by other EEC committees. The liberal professions and independent craftsmen are considered as another possible area of differences, and could be exempted under the net-turnover tax, that is, the value-added tax. It is concluded that craftsmen should not be given special treatment, but that it might be desirable to apply a gross-turnover tax to independent craftsmen.

*Retail Sales Tax*

The goal of eliminating fiscal frontiers and still making considerable use of indirect taxation could be accomplished by levying retail sales taxes. This alternative solution is discussed and disposed of with this sentence: "Since for a long time it will not be feasible to impose as the sole form of the turn-over tax a single tax at the retail stage, due to practical reasons of fiscal technicalities (particularly considering the very large number of small retail merchants, most of whom are unable to keep exact books), a decision in favor of the principle of the country of origin is in principle tantamount to a decision in favor of an all-stage tax on net turnover ('net value-added tax' or *taxe sur la valeur ajoutée*)."

More than likely, there are other reasons for discarding the retail sales tax than "fiscal technicalities." One might be that the high rate required to raise the revenue needed would become apparent to the buyer and would develop an undesired antitax complex. Another might be that this would not give the EEC member states, when trading outside the EEC, the advantage of tax rebates on exports, for goods exported are typically exported before the retail sale.

Finally, it is quite likely that the FFC members had in their minds some general theory of incidence which concluded that domestic prices would rise less rapidly when providing the same government revenue from a value-added tax than from a retail sales tax. That these features of a single-stage retail sales tax were considered important by the FFC members seems to be borne out by their observation that a retail sales tax levied at moderate rates was appropriate.

*Miscellaneous Taxes*

The FFC accepted the continued use of special excises, such as those on alcohol and tobacco, on the basis of the country of destination. Therefore, fiscal frontiers would continue to exist after the acceptance of the common value-added tax by all EEC member states. The FFC recommended that all EEC member states consider the levy of a net-wealth tax limited to natural persons the uniformity of treatment as to deductibility from the income tax. The problem of special treatment of real estate is mentioned, but not considered in detail.

Death taxes are not seen to be large revenue raisers, but could create problems by affecting the domicile of capital. Here the need for "tax transparency" is emphasized, and the problem of the impact of the capital's nationality of "situs" on tax liability is included with the recommendation that member states apply the same criteria.

After considerable consideration of how the between-member-state competitive position of a country with a relatively low net-turnover tax rate would be affected, the FFC concluded that "it is necessary to reach complete equality in rates for a tax on net turnover taken as a base tax, if distortions of competition caused by the turnover tax are to be avoided." The only member country of EEC then collecting a net-turnover tax was France. The French rate was 20 percent "tax on tax." If the EEC had recommended that the common net-turnover tax of EEC be levied on the "basis on basis" method, the French, to avoid a revenue loss, would have required a 25 percent rate. Because this was the one net-turnover rate then existing and because it was much easier for member states to decrease the rates and coverage of other taxes than for France to find revenue sources to replace lost TVA collections, the net-turnover tax rate of all member states is apt to be 20 percent "tax on tax" or 25 percent "basis on basis."

The FFC is on the side of the gods in believing that taxes, and particularly indirect taxes (and the former U.S. interest equalization tax would be included in this category), should not affect the movement of capital among EEC member states. The administration of the income tax and other taxes should not, for example, determine whether a company expanding operations in a member state opens a branch or a subsidiary. The FFC recommendation is for final abolition of all taxes on capital transfers within the EEC.

In view of the position of the American Automobile Manufacturers Association that road taxes are highly discriminatory, it is of interest that the FFC concludes they do not "disturb competition" or are not of sufficient importance to "influence purchasers of automobiles and trucks." (Of course, only sales of EEC-produced automobiles were under consideration.) However, the FFC is a bit worried that differences in vehicle taxation may cause commercial users to concentrate registrations in the low-cost member state if agreement is not reached on relatively uniform tax rates. The FFC considered petroleum taxation too complicated an area for definite recommendations and suggested the establishment of a special committee to study the problem.[39]

Although transportation is an industry that sells the value it adds, like all other businesses, the FFC does *not* recommend that transportation be treated under the net-turnover tax like other industries. The harmonization between EEC member states is recommended in the area of transportation by "calculating this tax according to the number of kilometer tons traveled within the particular country or according to such share of the compensations for transportation as is attributable to the individual country" as well as equal treatment in all states of particular types of transportation.

*Principles of Direct Taxes and Destination*

The FFC sees a similarity in determining who should tax income, the country of source or taxpayer's domicile, and the country of origin or destination principles in the levy of indirect taxes. To consider this similarity vital is stretching the direct-tax situation considerably. Actually, direct taxation has the same origin and destination aspect as indirect taxation and in addition has the same problems of country of origin and country of taxpayer's domicile. The FFC believes that the destination principle, because "there is no practical possibility of calculating for each product the amount which would be paid by a compensatory tax levied on imports or by a refund paid on exports" is inapplicable "to income tax or to tax on companies." The FFC position seems to be stronger than appropriate; the problems involved in using the country-of-destination principle do not appear to be of a much different order than those experienced for years in applying the cascade turnover tax in this fashion, but certainly are much greater than in applying the value added tax.

The FFC concluded that harmonization of income taxes on wages and social security tax rates is not needed; they believe this to be true because they saw the movement of workers among member states as being determined by other factors. However, they were of the opinon that differences in the income and social security taxes would have a greater effect on competition among the member states "as during the course of integration gross earnings in the member states become aligned and as the psychological and legal hinderances to the free movement of labor are eliminated."

The taxation of the incomes of highly mobile consultants, scientists, and artists and of the recipients of property income from foreign sources is quite another matter from the taxation of wage income. Here the FFC concluded that the best course of action is the harmonization of income-tax-withholding rates on property and service and consulting-contract income at high levels. This action would be accompanied by a provision for refunding citizens of member states who paid a higher overall tax than applicable under domicile income tax legislation contemplated.

It is a matter of growing concern that provisions for the avoidance of double taxation on personal income of the various international tax treaties, many initiated by the United States, are seldom utilized because the income recipient is avoiding entirely the tax liability of the country of domicile by not reporting foreign income. If the foreign-income receiver were to make use of the treaty provisions for avoiding double taxation, the source and amount of foreign income would become a matter of record. By failing to do this, the total tax burden is limited to the income tax withheld at the source. The FFC does not recommend the extra step of requiring income sources to report the income paid to tax authorities of the country of domicile of the income receiver, but does note this may be possible in the future. By taking this nonaction, the expanding international underground economy is allowed to grow and prosper.

## Tax Rebates

Much of the problem of the taxation of foreign business operations arises from the portion of the total taxes paid by the firm that is measured by income and by sales and the different traditional incidence assumptions of net income and transaction taxes. If it could be assumed that transaction taxes decrease net profits as much as net income taxes, or, to put it the other way around, that the firm is able to shift net income taxes as completely as transaction taxes, then the tax authorities of the country of domicile could take a much more relaxed attitude toward the taxation of foreign operations of domestic business interests. However, this is not the traditional position, and therefore a nation which taxes net income at a lower rate attracts investment and the location of production facilities from higher-rate countries, even though the total tax payments by the firm are equal to or greater than those in the country of lower net income taxes or lower taxes on capital gains. The FFC, in discussing this aspect of international tax harmonization, concludes that "From a realistic viewpoint, one will have to assume . . . that a *graduated* tax on industrial and commercial income cannot, or at most only in part, be passed on, particularly when dealing with a buyers' market. This conclusion regarding incidence of direct taxes paid by businesses excludes the *flat-rate* income taxes of the large corporations.

When considering company taxes of large corporations, FFC writes that ". . . income tax and the tax on companies and general charges with respect to which it is to be presumed that their international differences will, to a great extent, be leveled out by the rate of exchange." and need not be harmonized. This is a peculiar statement to make regarding corporate income taxes when it had not been previously made of indirect taxes. If indirect taxes were considered to have "to a great extent [been] leveled out by the rate of exchange," then the case for the use of rebates on exports and border tax on imports equal to domestic indirect taxes, particularly when rates are not increased, is largley destroyed. However, the FFC does not believe that this is the manner in which the economic burden of indirect taxes is distributed, and thus its concern with indirect tax rebates on exports and compensatory indirect border taxes on imports finds justification.

In its consideration of the harmonization of EEC member states' company (corporate) income taxes, the FFC recommends the following actions:

1. ". . . The tax on companies be levied at an equal [or almost equal] rate, at least in regard to the taxation of undistributed profits."
2. ". . . The amount of this tax [company undistributed profits] should not be too different from the maximum rate for income tax . . ."
3. ". . . The tax applicable to the part of the profits distributed in the form of dividends, etc., should amount to about half the tax applicable to undistributed profits and should in no case be less than 15 percent."
4. The withholding rate on profits distributed to persons outside the EEC or to bearer shares should be at least 25 percent and "would be the same in all member states."[40] This rate shall also apply "if the dividend recipient is a company which has its seat outside the EEC."[41]
5. Exemption from the undistributed profits tax for the EEC company receiving the dividends is provided if they are distributed to natural persons within "two to four years from the time when the dividends are received."[42]
6. "The state in which the withholding is done [should] reimburse the state where shareholder has his domicile, if the shareholder is domiciled outside the first state."

The basic point that the FFC seems to consider functional in dealing with double taxation is to change member-state tax systems so that "an approximation of national laws" exists in all tax areas "where double taxation occurs." These are also the same areas of corporation taxation which frequently serve to induce businesses to locate activities for tax reasons rather than true economic reasons.

The basic considerations to be applicable in the tax treatment of capital gains are not taken seriously by the FFC. By their very nature, the recommendations for harmonization in the income tax area assume that either capital gains will be included in the definition of taxable income or capital gains will be carefully defined and exempt from the income tax. The taxation of capital gains at a considerably lower rate than income, with capital gains rather broadly defined, is not included in the world of taxation to be harmonized by the FFC.

*Conclusion*

The area of harmonization in which the greatest progress has been made by the EEC since 1962 is the development of a common value-added tax. It was the area of central interest to FFC and the one type of tax harmonization for which a timetable was developed. (The original timing provided for passing and promulgating a common VAT system before December 31, 1967, and the entry of the system into force could not be delayed beyond December 31, 1969.) Now that this harmonization of turnover taxation is completed, a limited EEC tax union exists alongside the EEC customs union.

Whether the failure in other areas of tax harmonization will eventually destroy that achieved in developing a common VAT is not predictable. The gains made are important, and the United States, by moving in the same direction through consideration and adoption of legislation such as H.R. 5665 (October 1979) or H.R. 7015 (April 1980), can reduce friction now becoming apparent in U.S. legislative actions and industry advocacy of antidumping provisions and to use them whenever domestic industry meets strong domestic competition from foreign producers.[42]

Individual member states are apt to find the pressure resistible only if the EEC requires of its member states that turnover taxes be levied on the country-of-origin principle, and the application of this principle is tolerable only if the tax is of the same type in all member states and the rates are uniform.

Finally, consensus seems to exist that the French type of net-turnover, or value-added, tax is preferable to some variety of cascade turnover or single-level retail sales tax, the alternative transaction taxes available.

Tables 1-4 to 1-7 summarize the principal sources of tax revenues of four major industrial European nations. The portion provided by VAT is

**Table 1-4**
**France: Comparative Tax Usages**
*(billions of francs, year ending December 31)*

|  | 1974 | 1975 | 1976 | 1977 | 1978 |
|---|---|---|---|---|---|
| Total tax revenue | 428.70 | 484.28 | 587.95 | 660.26 | 756.11 |
| Personal income tax | 46.44 | 50.25 | 66.66 | 78.71 | |
| Social security contributions | 169.53 | 210.01 | 250.90 | 293.06 | |
| Employees' portion | 36.59 | 45.21 | 56.53 | 68.07 | |
| VAT | 115.57 | 126.51 | 156.19 | 157.37 | |

Source: International Monetary Fund, *Government Finance Statistics Yearbook 3* (Washington, D.C., 1979), p. 141.

**Table 1-5**
**Germany: Comparative Tax Usages**
*(billions of Deutsche marks)*

|                              | 1973   | 1974   | 1975   | 1976   | 1977   |
|------------------------------|--------|--------|--------|--------|--------|
| Total tax revenue            | 231.47 | 247.99 | 260.45 | 290.67 | 315.47 |
| Individual income tax        | 39.26  | 44.27  | 43.04  | 48.34  | 54.34  |
| Social security contributions| 115.21 | 127.28 | 139.20 | 157.47 | 169.18 |
| Employees' portion           | 49.21  | 53.91  | 59.19  | 67.05  | 72.31  |
| VAT                          | 32.17  | 32.24  | 34.15  | 37.47  | 39.04  |

Source: International Monetary Fund, *Government Finance Statistics Yearbook* (Washington, D.C., 1979), p. 152.

twice that of the individual income tax in France and less than one-third of the British total. In Sweden, VAT is about equal to individual income tax collections, and in Germany, VAT collections are about three-quarters as great as individual income-tax assessments.

### State Experience with VAT

The value-added tax has been considered an ideal business tax for use by states from its first development by the Brookings Institution in the 1930s. The 1954 introduction of the French national VAT, called TVA, demonstrated its usefulness as a national tax. The advantages of VAT as a state tax have resulted in considerable study of VAT as a possible state business tax reform, and VAT legislation was adopted in Michigan. *The desirability of VAT as a state or provincial tax compared with its use as a national tax was sharply reduced in the 1950s when the French were able to persuade GATT to accept TVA as an indirect tax. This made VAT eligible for refund on exports and to be assessed as a border tax on imports.*

**Table 1-6**
**United Kingdom: Comparative Tax Usages**
*(millions of pounds sterling)*

|                              | 1974   | 1975   | 1976   | 1977   | 1978   |
|------------------------------|--------|--------|--------|--------|--------|
| Total tax revenue            | 29,913 | 37,664 | 45,353 | 51,365 | 55,661 |
| Individual income tax        | 10,176 | 14,710 | 17,010 | 17,494 | 17,896 |
| Social security contributions| 5,000  | 6,540  | 8,230  | 9,339  | 10,006 |
| Employees' portion           | 2,016  | 2,477  | 3,013  | 3,425  | 3,676  |
| VAT                          | 2,595  | 3,299  | 3,834  | 4,238  | 5,030  |

Source: International Monetary Fund, *Government Finance Statistics Yearbook 3* (Washington, D.C., 1979), p. 368.

**Table 1-7**
**Sweden: Comparative Tax Usages**
*(billions of kronor)*

|                              | 1974  | 1975  | 1976   | 1977   | 1978   |
|------------------------------|-------|-------|--------|--------|--------|
| Total tax revenue            | 80.52 | 95.74 | 125.67 | 144.28 | 159.31 |
| Individual income tax        | 13.52 | 17.15 | 27.17  | 28.76  | 25.00  |
| Social security contributions| 20.89 | 27.79 | 36.73  | 45.22  | 56.94  |
| Employees' portion           | 5.50  | 6.51  | 4.22   | 1.73   | 2.01   |
| VAT                          | 13.93 | 14.68 | 18.20  | 21.26  | 26.58  |

Source: International Monetary Fund, *Government Finance Statistics Yearbook 3* (Washington, D.C., 1979), p. 342.

### Business Personal Property

In a 1953 study, the National Tax Association's (NTA) personal-property taxation committee recommended the adoption of VAT legislation. The study favored removing the property tax on business personal property and replacing the revenues with a VAT.[44] The NTA committee held fast to the idea that the VAT was a business tax paid by businesses very much as the property tax on personal property is a business tax paid by businesses.[45] Both taxes were seen to cause business operational adjustments to permit payment out of operating receipts.

The shortage of funds for capital modernization and new investments in 1980 makes any tax that selects business personal property as its base for taxation a particularly bad tax. Its effect is similar to a low level of depreciation allowance. An investment shortage was just developing in 1953 when the NTA study and recommendations were made. Therefore, their support of the VAT as a replacement for business personal-property taxes had to rest on the basis of increased equity and decreased administration difficulties. Today such a recommendation could utilize inadequate investment as a strong prop. Since 1953, personal property consisting of inventories has generally become exempt or taxed on less than 100 percent of the base or exempt if in transit. The number of states exempting machinery and tools of business personal property is growing. Currently the exemption is in effect in major industrial states such as Pennsylvania, New York, and Delaware.[46]

### West Virginia

In 1970, the West Virginia legislature adopted VAT. The VAT enacted was an additive-type VAT and was actually titled a "value-added income tax." The governor, through a veto, prevented the legislation from going into force.[47]

The base of the West Virginia VAT was (1) interest payments except those made by financial institutions on savings accounts; (2) rentals or other payments required to be made for continued use or possession; (3) compensation paid for personal services rendered by employees and officers; (4) all taxes imposed that are measured by income except portions of social security paid by business; and (5) contributions to employer-provided trusts and profit-sharing funds.

West Virginia is today, and was in 1970, a heavy user of retail sales taxes. In 1977 these taxes provided 22.2 percent of its state and local revenues. The national average was 12.7 percent. This heavy transaction-tax emphasis of the existing West Virginia tax system required that the new VAT be given the appearance of an income tax. More than likely, this fact largely accounts for West Virginia's development of an additive VAT. The Oregon revenue system is similar to that of the federal government in that it does not use a general tax based on transactions. Therefore, it was appropriate for Oregon to adopt a VAT emphasizing sales receipts reduced by purchases from other businesses. For the same reasons, a VAT of this type is also more attractive to the federal government. In addition, the national government's responsibilities in keeping the dollar strong and U.S. businesses competitive make the subtractive approach more attractive to a national government than to a state government.

When the federal government puts a major VAT into effect, the states with substantial retail sales taxes will be tempted to substitute the VAT base arising in their state for their retail sales tax base. The few states without a major transaction tax would find use of a federal subtractive VAT base a simple procedure for broadening their tax base, and in this way permit a reduction of individual and business income and property taxes. This opportunity arising under a federal subtractive VAT could be very attractive to states. Any state not making use of this new situation would encounter difficulties in financing an acceptable level of service while remaining competitive in attracting and holding industry.

*Oregon*

The Oregon legislative assembly, in regular sessions of both 1969 and 1971, introduced legislation that provided for a modified subtractive-type VAT. In both cases, the sponsors of the legislation included Representatives Eymann and Roberts. The bills were seen as a method for initiating additional taxation of transactions in Oregon without enacting a retail sales tax. Oregon still does not have a retail sales, a general excise, or a business gross-receipts tax. Portland, the major industrial and commercial center of the state, has a business-receipts tax. It is called a business income tax, and the rate is 0.6 percent. It was adopted in 1976 to replace a business license tax with a narrower base and a 1.5 percent rate.

The 1969 legislative proposal (House BIll 1888) imposed a net-turnover tax on persons doing business in the state. A 2 percent rate was applied to the adjusted receipts from business activities. The adjustment made to the receipts is the deduction of all materials and services, including taxes paid. The bill allowed as a deduction from the taxable base a reasonable allowance for the "depreciation, exhaustion, wear and tear, and obsolescence of property used in the business." Provision was also made in the law for determining the portion of total receipts that should be allocated to Oregon of a firm located inside or outside Oregon but doing business in Oregon.

This type of VAT, by not allowing direct adjustment of the taxable base by deduction of capital equipment purchased, violates a basic aspect of the subtractive-type VAT as developed in Western Europe. Also, the possibility of avoiding the problem of calculating appropriate depreciation levels is lost.[48] The proposal provided for a financial-institution excise tax law as a way to avoid the problems associated with the use of the subtractive VAT to tax financial institutions.

The proposed VAT legislation of 1971 (House Bill 3054) provided for dedication of collections to the Department of Education in carrying out its education programs. Also, the rate was raised to 3 percent, while increasing the exemptions and introducing the use of reduced percentages of the base to which the VAT rate is applied.

The construction industry's gross receipts subject to VAT were reduced by 90 percent; used retail goods, by 70 percent; businesses with taxable gross receipts of less than $100,000 per year, by 60 percent; and the agriculture base, by 50 percent. The tax applied only to business done in the state by persons engaged in business in the state. A use tax of 1 percent was assessed on goods or services sold in Oregon on which a VAT had not been previously paid. This later legislation made no distinction between capital goods purchased and sold and all other transactions.

An Oregon tax analysis group carried out several studies under the general title "A Description and Analysis of Oregon's Fiscal System." One of these was a study of the VAT completed in January 1971. The tone of the conclusions of the study was that because Oregon did not already have a general transaction-type tax, its VAT should be completely a transaction-type tax and should not include elements of an income or additive-type VAT except in the taxation of financial institutions, where an additive VAT was recommended. The study also concluded that sales by Oregon firms outside the state should bear the VAT on these gross receipts and that goods and services coming into the state should be subject to a use tax equal to the Oregon VAT rate. In other words, the VAT recommended for Oregon would be a modified destination-principle tax (that is, a tax paid where consumption takes place) and a modified origin-principle tax (that is, a tax paid where production takes place). This approach works out to give Oregon additional revenues from the export of its timber and provides some protection to Oregon's developing consumer-goods industry.[49]

## Hawaii

Hawaii has developed the general transaction-tax base to a greater degree than any other state, with the possible exception of Washington and the resort-gambling-dominated state of Nevada. The general excise tax, or the gross-receipts tax or the gross-turnover tax, possesses serious weaknesses that, to a considerable degree, VAT overcomes. As a result, a number of legislative recommendations and studies conclude that Hawaii should replace its general excise-tax system with a tax that more or less follows the principles of the VAT.

Both the VAT and the Hawaiian general excise tax (GET) system go beyond a retail sales tax and the taxation of only the receipts from retail transactions. The VAT and the GET are multistage business tax collection procedures.[50] The basic difference between VAT and GET is that under VAT, sales between businesses are netted out of the total of transactions, leaving only sales to end users; under GET, only certain types of receipts, such as returned sales, can be deducted. The rates of GET vary depending on whether the sale is at wholesale or by a manufacturer or whether the transaction is subject to a special excise tax; as is true of cigarettes, for example.

A simple tax on gross receipts like the GET of Hawaii has built within it pressures for two types of reforms: The tax impact should be made equal among taxpayers in terms of some general idea of the profitability of the activity, and the tax payment should be made independent of the way the business is organized and controlled.

At the national level, commentators often say VAT is a national retail sales tax collected in a manner that leaves taxpayers unaware that they are paying the tax. There is little justification for this description of VAT at the national level. It acts to reduce the general understanding of the tax. At the subnational level, by assessing a tax rate on all businesses and not just on those selling to the final user, VAT is collecting a cost of government services roughly measured by sales less purchases from other businesses.[51] The basic justice of VAT is quite different from that of the retail sales tax (RST). On one hand, the RST assumes that government services are best paid at the point of consumption, and not along the line as the service or good is produced and marketed. On the other hand, VAT assumes it is best to levy taxes as the production of goods and services is marketed.

## Alabama and Iowa

The Brookings Institution in the 1930s saw VAT to be a tax suitable for use by subnational governments and that calculation should be through sales procedures rather than through adding incomes. The name given was *net-value product*, and its use was recommended in tax studies carried out at the request of Alabama and Iowa. These two studies were completed in 1932 and 1933, the period in which rapid declines in farmland values caused considerable tax legislative activity aimed at developing revenue substitutes.[52]

The VAT was not adopted by either Alabama or Iowa. The fiscal crisis of the 1930s, combined with the educational costs generated by the post-World War II birth bulge, made the United States a nation using the retail sales tax at the state and local levels as a method of taxing the transaction base, and not a VAT user. However, there was one exception—Michigan.

## Michigan

In 1953 Michigan introduced a VAT to the family of state taxes. The tax was called the business activities tax (BAT), and it remained in effect until 1967. From 1967 until 1975, Michigan did not use a VAT, but in 1975 new legislation called the single business tax (SBT), a VAT-type tax, was enacted. The legislation was amended rather substantially in 1977. Fiscal 1980 collections from SBT reached $899 million. The SBT has become the state's second largest revenue raiser. During the severe depression of the automobile industry in 1980 VAT proved to be a more stable revenue producer than the income and profit taxes used by neighboring states.

The BAT was repealed in 1967 largely because a personal income tax had been enacted and the revenues from this tax reduced the need for BAT. In addition, it seemed appropriate to introduce a corporate income tax to accompany the personal income tax. This new corporate income tax became the business tax to replace the BAT. Michigan tax policy was dominated at this time by those favoring "ability to pay."

By 1972, it was becoming clear that the corporate income tax (CIT) retained its old instability shortcomings. When car sales were down, CIT revenues fell sharply, forcing sharp cutbacks in state programs and searches for additional revenues. When car sales were strong, revenues increased sharply, inducing the introduction of new programs. It also became clear that the CIT was reducing Michigan's attractiveness to high-technology and high-profit industries. So VAT was reintroduced, but in a form quite different from the legislation repealed in 1967. The first payments of the new SBT were for fiscal 1976-1977.

The new Michigan VAT goes a step further than the BAT in being a full-fledged additive VAT. Calculation of the SBT base starts with the calculation which the firm has made in meeting federal tax requirements. From this federal income tax base the following can be deducted in arriving at the SBT base: dividends, interest, royalties received, and capital purchases. The treatment of dividends is particularly attractive to the many Michigan corporations engaged in international activities. You add to the remainder interest, royalty, depreciation, and wages.

After establishing the base to which SBT is applied, the taxpayer, if eligible, can make other deductions in arriving at a taxable base. These deductions plus the special exemptions reduce expected collections so much that in 1977 the tax rate of SBT had to be raised from 0.02 to 0.0235. This adjustment brings to the front two advantages of VAT. First, revenue shifts of a substantial nature can be made without substantial rate changes; second, changes in treatment of various portions of the base can be used to stimulate identified desirable business decisions.

It is preferable that the origin basis be used by subnational governments rather than the destination basis, which is used in the VATs of Western European nations. The origin basis establishes that the payment of the VAT is being made to the goverment which made available to the firm the services needed for its operations.

The Michigan VAT is called the SBT because its initiation was accompanied by the repeal of a series of Michigan business taxes.[53] It has already been mentioned that the corporate income tax was repealed. In addition, the following taxes on business were repealed: a special financial institutions tax, a corporate franchise tax, a portion of the intangibles tax, a savings-and-loan privilege tax, a tax on inventory, and the individual income tax on unincorporated businesses. Most of the shift in taxes paid on the adoption of SBT was from profitable manufacturing, banking, and utility businesses to service and professional firms. These professional and service firms were perhaps undertaxed prior to the SBT. The increase merely raised their tax liabilities to the prevailing level.

*Conclusion*

The established use of the retail sales tax and some experience with gross-receipts taxes (that is, a gross-turnover tax) have resulted in a state tax environment not particularly conducive to the introduction of VAT. The RST appears to be easier to pass forward to the customer than a VAT. Businesses not selling at retail do not feel that they are bearing a tax burden under the retail sales tax, but they would under VAT, because they make VAT payments on their addition to the value of goods and services passing through the production and marketing process.

Not a single state has abandoned its retail sales tax to introduce VAT. Michigan, the only state using a VAT, has kept an RST rate of 4 percent. More than likely, the RST rate would be higher if a VAT were not being used. Also, the use of an RST is a portion of the reason why Michigan adopted an additive VAT. Adding income going to the factors of production does not directly complicate the administration of an RST.

Oregon commissioned a study which recommended that exports out of the state be subject to VAT with imports subject to a use tax equal to the VAT rate. The use of VAT to encourage industries in an open economy does not have the potential existing in a semiclosed economy, but some possibility does exist. This would be true also of a state add-on to a federal VAT.

### British Analysis of Usefulness of VAT[54]

British tax writers and analysts failed to participate in the early European and U.S. consideration of the VAT. This aloofness vanished in the early 1960s. A.R. Prest led the way when he included a consideration of VAT in his very authoritative *Public Finance: In Theory and Practice*, published in 1960. Arthur Dale, another influential British tax expert, picked up the ball in his book *Tax Harmonization in Europe*, published in 1963.[55] In addition, the *British Tax Review* dedicated its 1963 fall issue to the consideration of VAT.

This British reconsideration of their traditional position was stimulated by the adoption of a VAT by the member states of the Common Market. The British application for Common Market memberships had already become a hot topic, and foreign-trade data being released showed over and over that British producers were finding it difficult to meet foreign competition. Some people thought a VAT could help. In addition, Britain needed more tax revenues to finance income security and military expenditures. The conservative government of Sir Alec Douglas-Home in its last days in power, before Labour led by Harold Wilson came in for the first time, commissioned a study of VAT. It was released in 1964 as the Richardson Report.[56]

### Analysis of the Richardson Report

The report was more a vendetta against the French, the only user of VAT at that time, than an analysis of VAT. The attitude was a reflection of the political scene. France had just vetoed Britain's bid for Common Market membership. The report concluded that a profits tax neither raises prices nor discourages investment. Dan Throop Smith, a former president of the American National Tax Association, with tongue in cheek concluded that this makes "it [tax on profits] indeed an ideal revenue source and one which should be relied on to the utmost."[57]

The stated purpose of the study was to conduct an analysis of how a shift from the corporate income tax (CIT) to a VAT of equal productivity would promote economic development, expand exports, and affect the fairness of the British tax system.[58] It was a noble group of purposes, but badly carried out.

The report did not really zero in on the stated purposes. Instead it was largely a summary of descriptive materials related to rates and tax-administration procedures. Practically no effort was made to estimate how the tax had affected French exporters or British exporters engaged in the French trade. The different approaches of a VAT and a CIT to depreciation were not discussed. Yet, the stimulation of exports and investments were the two areas singled out as of great importance in considering the effect of taxes on economic growth. Since France was the only nation using a VAT, the impacts of VAT in France on investment levels and exports should have been the major emphasis of the study. Maybe this was not done because at that time the French economy was very strong indeed.

At the time, the British were relying very heavily for their revenues on a purchase tax collected at the wholesale level on a group of designated commodities from about 65,000 businesses. The introduction of a VAT with substantial rates would undoubtedly be a replacement of this tax. The Richardson Report, however, largely limits itself to a low-rate VAT that would replace the CIT. This is justified by devoting considerable space to demonstrating the superiority of the purchase tax to a VAT. The finding rests nearly entirely on a calculation of the larger number of businesses that would be taxpayers under VAT. The conclusion is: Why go to the extra fuss of introducing a VAT when we have the good old purchase tax and a very unusual no-burden CIT?

The study failed to examine VAT in terms of the objectives of the study because it failed to carefully examine the impact of VAT on the French economy. Important questions that were left unexamined are: Will the use of a VAT cause a larger portion of the tax burden to be shifted backward than a tax at the wholesale level on a few designated items? Is a VAT that covers most of GNP more just than a tax on a few selected commodities? Will the reduction or elimination of the CIT encourage investment and economic growth? What would be the impact if VAT revenues were used to reduce individual income tax withholdings on ordinary wage income? Will social security financed directly or indirectly with a VAT have a more desirable economic impact than payroll taxes? How helpful would har-monization of British taxes with Western European taxes turn out to be?

*Price Levels*

The Richardson Report doggedly and dogmatically insists that general price levels will increase by the amount of a VAT. The report concludes that this will happen even though the VAT is introduced largely as a replacement of former taxes along the lines of the proposed U.S. Federal Tax Restructuring Act of 1980. The report relies on a general and unproved relationship between transaction taxes and prices that does not exist between income or wealth taxes and prices. The report states, "When a generalized tax such as a turnover or value-added tax is imposed on *all* goods and services, the tax is likely to be passed on in full: the consumer cannot evade the burden by shifting demand to nontaxed substitutes."[59]

In taking this position, the report denies that general price levels are a reflection of monetary policy and relative prices a reflection of costs including all taxes. If there is not enough purchasing power to float taxes off in higher prices, then taxes must cause lower costs; and this is brought about through reduced sales at existing prices. If money is not easy or if demand is weak, a tax increase is shifted backward in lower payments to suppliers unless suppliers are able to completely adjust supply to the new situation. If old taxes on wages are replaced with a tax such as a VAT, no general price change in the short term seems to be the best general expectation.

*National Economic Development Office Study*

Despite the defeat of the Conservative Party, British entry into the Common Market continued to be an issue. Also, the Labour Government was not able to cure British economic ills. Balance-of-international-payments problems remained, as did inflation, low investment levels, and public-revenue shortages (this is a good approximation of current economic conditions in the United States). British tax theorists also continued to write about VAT.

Douglas Dosser began to write about the advantage of tax harmonization of Britain with the EEC.[60] E.B. Butler published in two issues of *The Bankers Magazine* a careful analysis entitled "Britain and the Continental Value Added Tax."[61] There were many other British-originated studies and Canadian as well as U.S. spin-off discussions. The VAT had not been laid to rest. This new spate of analyses was topped off by a much more careful British government study in 1969 by the National Economic Development (NED) Office. The published study was titled *VAT*.[62] The use of the title *VAT* by a major English-language study laid to rest the use of TVA in referring to a tax on GNP as it arose from the sale of produced goods and services. The use of the additive rather than the subtractive VAT was not seriously considered.

**Environment in 1969.** The NED study continued to emphasize the administrative difficulties of a VAT, as had the Richardson Report. This British attitude persisted despite reports from the Netherlands and Germany, as well as from Michigan, that the administration of a VAT was not difficult or expensive.[63] Part of the reason for this British attitude was due to tardiness in the introduction of modern computer systems by H.M. Customs and Excise Staff.

**NED Study Findings.** In most respects, the NED study is a careful conservative analysis of the desirability of adopting VAT even though Britian does not become a member of the Common Market. The NED finding is a qualified yes. As the study takes pains to point out, the VAT is a tax and not a fiscal philosopher's stone, that is, a subsidy which yields net revenues.

The NED study envisages a substantial VAT with a major portion of the collections used to replace revenues lost through elimination of the purchase tax and the selective employment tax (SET). A major VAT would be levied on the subtractive basis with most of the revenues going to replace payroll and transaction-tax collections lost through tax-repeal legislation.

The big difference in the basic position of the Richardson and the NED studies is the treatment of the corporate income tax (CIT). The NED study does not see VAT as largely a substitute for CIT, as the Richardson study does. The revenues of the VAT envisaged by the NED study would permit a more liberal CIT and lower individual income tax rates, but the big tax switch would be the elimination of the purchase tax and the SET.

This represents a substantial shift in the British understanding of the usefulness of VAT.[64] The very strong, long-standing preference of the British for income and profits taxation and transaction taxes consisting of special excises was not quickly overcome. The taxation of general production to finance government costs was a big hurdle to overcome for people raised in the English, as well as the U.S., fiscal cultural tradition. It is even more difficult for those still living on the "tight little island" than for those of British culture living in Australia or the United States. Nevertheless, the NED study findings demonstrated rapid progress in British thinking during a five-year period. *Taxation needed to be considered a general cost of producing GNP and not an excess received by some that could be funneled off to meet government costs.*

**Analyses of NED Study of VAT.** The NED study included calculation of Gini coefficients of income inequality. Inequality was measured in percentage terms after the direct benefits and personal income tax depending on whether a purchase tax or a VAT exempting food or a VAT not exempting food was used to provide a given level of government revenues. The exercise used childless households up to households with four children. The three alternative methods of raising 100 pounds sterling were found to cause "insignificant differences in the Gini measure of income inequality."[65] The study did not consider the relative effect of a personal income tax with rising real rates due to inflation. Of course, this study, like all tax-burden studies, must make certain tax-burden assumptions.

*The findings demonstrate that the income-distribution change arising from direct provision of government benefits is much more important than the type of tax used.* The use of taxes to redistribute income is always hindered by the stronger economic bargaining power of the wealthy and the skilled.

The main emphasis of the NED study was on the general desirability of a greater use of indirect taxation. A second aim was the measurement of the impact of the replacement of the purchase tax and the SET with a substantial VAT. The study concludes that VAT, when compared with CIT and the purchase tax, results in a relative encouragement of exports and a greater capital-intensiveness of industry.[66]

The authors of the NED study generally agree with those who find the domestic impacts of a substantial VAT about the same as those of other indirect taxes and less burdensome than CIT. They finally come down in favor of a VAT largely because of international considerations. They consider the tax much less destructive of exports and capital investments than the alternatives.[67]

### Influence of Common Market Tax Requirements

The authors of the NED study were well aware that the United Kingdom was mounting another effort to become a member of the Common Market. They also knew that the effort would be successful. The immediate policy decision, therefore, was whether the United Kingdom should negotiate delays in introducing a VAT. More than likely, for a brief time, the EEC would accept a movement toward a VAT meeting the general characteristics adopted by the member states.

The NED concluded that VAT, along the EEC pattern, should be adopted on its own merits. The incidence (economic burden) of the tax is seen to "depend upon the state of competition in particular markets, upon the powers of particular taxpayers to vary prices, and upon what associated changes are introduced in other taxes at the same time."[68] This is a sound economic position which varies substantially from the one-sided Richardson Report.

In June 1971, ten years after Prime Minister Harold Macmillan filed the United Kingdom's first EEC membership application and after two vetoes by Charles de Gaulle, President of France, all points of discussion were resolved. In January 1972, the Treaty of Accession was signed. On January 1, 1973, the United Kingdom became a formal member of the European Economic Community [also called the Common Market, or European Community (EC)]. The British VAT became operative on April 1, 1973, and registration for VAT got underway on October 1, 1972, as provided in the Finance Act of 1972.

Between the publication of NED's analysis of VAT in August 1969 and Parliament's passage of the Finance Act of 1972, there was considerable additional professional and political analysis of VAT in the United Kingdom.

*The Green Paper of 1971*

In March 1971, the government's "Green Paper" was released. It became the basis for the later announcement by the Chancellor of the Exchequer that VAT would be introduced as a major tax for 1973. The Green Paper took the position generally accepted in Western Europe that an RST rate above 7 percent is very difficult to administer. Because the revenues needed were seen to require a rate above 7 percent, an RST was eliminated as a possible alternative to VAT.[69]

The Green Paper identifies and accepts a number of other basic public-finance positions developed by the NED study. The VAT was seen to avoid administrative shortcomings of both selective excise taxes and a gross-turnover tax. In addition, the economic impact of VAT was seen to be basically good and better than that of existing transaction taxes.[70]

The Green Paper accepted the administrative experience of the EEC member states and recommended a subtractive VAT based on sales. The price base to which the VAT rate was to be applied was to include all duties and taxes other than VAT.[71] The effect of this procedure is to make the costs of government other than those financed with VAT a portion of the VAT base. The European practice of largely excluding financial operations was also accepted. This was rationalized on the basis that "VAT, which is an appropriate method of taxing flows of goods and services, is not appropriate for taxing flows of money and paper representing money."[72] In addition, a subtractive-type VAT is difficult to apply to this area of business activity. Here the European tradition of separate taxation of financial institutions was followed.

*Journalistic, Academic, and Government Analyses*

The decision in the Green Paper to adopt a major VAT was influenced by academic and journalistic discussions of 1970. *The Times* pointed out that the "more viable alternative [to a spendings tax] would be a deliberate switch of the main impact of taxation onto a general sales tax."[73] *The Times* warned that VAT was regressive and that its use required income-maintenance efforts.

The Fabian Society expressed the anti-VAT position of the European labor movement.[74] They were supported by another analytical article by A.R. Prest, who concluded that VAT reduces itself to a tax on wages and salaries.[75] Philip Lawton concluded that profits were also a portion of the base to which the VAT rate was applied.[76]

The possibility that economic rent and inflation caused higher capital values that would become a portion of the VAT base was not neglected. Sturroch discussed this aspect of VAT in relation to the agriculture industry.[77] Finally, the *Economist* assured the nation that a VAT is neutral and then added that because it is refunded on exports, "it will in no way enter into the cost of exports."[78] Actually it is the additive-type VAT which is neutral; it applies a uniform rate to payments received by all the factors of production.

The VAT had its opponents as well as its supporters in 1970. In addition, attitudes toward EEC membership often affected the attitude toward a VAT. Basically the tax stood on its own and came off strong enough to make an acceptable case for itself as a needed tax reform, EEC membership or not. A Canadian writing in 1969 of the possibility of introduction of a VAT in the United Kingdom pointed out the need of revenues in a welfare state and the weaknesses of SET as a tax. From this background experience, he concluded it is better for the United Kingdom to gain the funds needed by taxing expenditures rather than earned income.[79]

In a 1971 study, the government revealed that its attitude toward a VAT had shifted from negotiating with the EEC for a delay in the introduction of a VAT to one favoring action at as rapid a pace as consistent with sound tax administrative practice. Subsequently, in the 1971 budget, the Chancellor announced a VAT would be introduced in 1973 "as a means of improving our [own] tax system."[80] The opposition to VAT, based on a belief it would push up prices, continued into 1971. Upward price movements were also being forecasted to accompany United Kingdom membership in the EEC without the adoption of VAT.[81] None of the analysts, of course, realized that OPEC national policies relative to the marketing of oil would soon push prices and costs upward at a rate experienced before only during war and its aftereffect.

As the government of the United Kingdom made up its mind to introduce VAT prior to full EEC membership, VAT's press improved. The *Daily Telegraph* joined the *Economist* and *The Times* in favoring a general-expenditure tax approach to Britain's revenue-collection needs.[82] *Lloyd's Bank Review* noted that "while few countries were initially attracted to

VAT, once the EEC had adopted it, the pressures for its introduction elsewhere rose sharply. Once a country's trade rivals have VAT, the tax's intrinsic merits and failings cease to be the dominant consideration."[83]

Economists in the United States have frequently argued that the VAT refund on exports and the collection of a border tax up to the domestic VAT rate do not strengthen the international economic position. European business leaders and economists have not generally accepted this position.

Nicholas Kaldor had advocated a VAT for the United Kingdom that was nearly entirely aimed at correcting the weak British international-trade position.[84] This road became inappropriate as the result of mounting revenue needs, the prospects of EEC membership, and the tax-harmonization provision of the Treaty of Rome which established the EEC.[85]

As the implementation of the original single-rate 10 percent British VAT approached, the explainers as well as the providers of equipment and soft goods had a field day. Gray areas were found in the legislation, and the concept of zero rate compared with exemption caused confusion.[86] Also VAT, in its treatment of who was covered, operated just opposite from the long-established procedure under the income tax. Under the new VAT legislation, every commercial activity was covered unless specifically exempt. Under the United Kingdom income tax, only that income identified is taxable.[87]

The British found the treatment of club dues a vexing problem, and it finally turned out that trading stamps were to be neither a good nor a service "and so outside the scope of VAT."[88] Nevertheless, VAT develped quickly into a substantial revenue raiser, without being a major source of additional inflation or tax injustice. And as Cripps wrote, "a tax must not only be fair, it must be seen to be fair."[89]

*VAT as a British Tax Restructuring Tool*

The budget introduced by the Conservative Party after winning the election of June 1979 included returning the VAT to a flat rate and using exemption and zero rates as provided in the original 1972 legislation. The VAT legislation in effect at the time of the election applied an 8 percent rate to items designated as nonluxury and a 12½ percent rate to the remainder of transactions not included under the exemption or zero-rate designation. This tendency of political leadership to move toward greater multiplicity of VAT rates has gone further in France than in any other EEC country. Denmark has been able to resist exemption and multiple rates most effectively.

The use of multiple rates opens a pandora's box of pressure groups desiring favorable treatment. More than likely, this "me too" attitude was influential in returning to a flat-rate VAT in the United Kingdom. It is estimated that VAT is levied directly on about one-half of British consumer expenditures.

The Thatcher government's 1979 budget raised the VAT rate to 15 percent. The rate is uniform except where exemption and zero rating existed and continue. The VAT rate on nonluxury transactions was raised by 87.5 percent, and the VAT rate on designated luxury transactions was raised by 24 percent.[90] As a result of this action, VAT collections will increase by about 60 percent.

The increased VAT collections, in combination with receipts from sales of government property, are expected to finance cuts in income taxes. Within very few years the top tax rate on workers' income will be down to 25 percent from the 33 percent rate of 1979. Its top marginal income tax rate on dividends and other property-sourced income is being reduced to 60 percent, down from 75 percent and 83 percent levels, respectively. The top income tax rate applicable to earned income is expected to be set at 50 percent.[91] Some 700,000 people will be taken out from under the income tax.

This restructuring of the British tax system is an important step toward reviving the economy by stimulating savings and investment. The VAT will be important in a policy to roll back socialism.[92] The failure to index the income tax combined with the higher VAT rates result in a budget level adequate to support a British society with a government-sector activity level decreased by only about 5.5 percent.[93] Tax collections emphasizing VAT have been turned to as the appropriate revenue source to be expanded as investment-, savings-, and earnings-related taxes are reduced. Table 1-6 summarizes the trend of VAT collections in the United Kingdom during the 1974-1978 period:

| Year | 1974 | 1975 | 1976 | 1977 | 1978 |
|---|---|---|---|---|---|
| Amount | 2,595 | 3,299 | 3,834 | 4,238 | 5,030 |

In 1974 VAT collections were about 9.4 percent of total United Kingdom tax revenues. By 1978 this percentage had risen to around 10.1 percent. The 1979 United Kingdom budget contemplates a sharp increase in the VAT-provided portion of tax revenues of the central government.[94] The higher VAT rates are expected to add an original 3½ percent to the price index.

These data demonstrate, first, that VAT is a steady and major revenue provider and, second, that *the introduction of VAT does not lead to a wild and unbridled expansion of government tax collections.*

## Conclusion

The VAT was considered in great detail by many segments of British society. The relationship of VAT to prices compared with that of other revenue sources continues to be an area of conflict. A resolution to the satisfaction of all parties is not likely, but the relatively good inflation records of the major users of the VAT have acted to reduce the stridency of the claims of the sharp-price-increase believers. The new role of the British VAT in turning around the British economy promises to be a social engineering project of great interest to U.S. policymakers.[95]

## Notes

1. Al Ullman, "Foreword," in Richard W. Lindholm, *Value Added Tax and Other Tax Reforms* (Chicago: Nelson Hall, 1976), 7, 8; Russell B. Long, "Foreword," in Norman B. Ture, *Value Added Tax: Facts and Fancies* (Washington: Heritage Foundation, 1979), 5.

2. *The Organization of Economic Cooperation and Development Observer*, December 1972, pp. 16-17. Other sources of comparative tax data include Eurostat, *1973 Tax Statistics Yearbook*; The Organization of Economic Cooperation and Development, *Revenue Statistics, 1967-1971*; OECD, *Company Tax Systems in OECD Member Countries*, 1973; International Monetary Fund, *Government Finances* (Washington, D.C., 1979).

3. IMF, *Finance Statistics Yearbook*, vol. 3, 1979, p. 25.

4. Department of the Treasury, *Blueprints for Basic Tax Reform* (Washington: GPO, 1977), 113-144.

5. Eitan Berglas, "The Effect of the Public Sector on the Base of the Value Added Tax," *National Tax Journal* 24, no. 4 (December 1971):459-464.

6. *Economic Report of the President*, 1975, 94-97.

7. Arthur M. Okun and Nancy H. Teeters, "The Full Employment Surplus Revisited," *Brookings Paper* (Washington: Brookings Institution, 1970), 77-110. The problems encountered in working with the concept of revenues and expenditures under a full-employment budget assumption are discussed in the *Economic Report of the President*, 1975, 62-65.

8. The basic analysis of the relationship between inflation and employment is found in A.W. Phillips, "The Relation between the Level of Unemployment and the Role of Change of Money Wage Rates in the United Kingdom from 1862 to 1958," *Economica*, November 1958, 283-29; G.L. Perry, *Unemployment, Money Wage Rates and Inflation* (Cambridge, Mass.: M.I.T. Press, 1966).

9. Abba P. Lerner, "Employment Theory and Employment Policy," *American Economic Review* 57 (May 1967):1-18.

10. Robert E. Hall, "Labor Markets in Recession and Recovery," *National Bureau of Economic Research 1979 Research Conference: A Summary*, pp. 5-7.

11. Committee on Ways and Means, *Hearings Announcement on the "Tax Restructuring Act of 1979"* (H.R. 5665), October 22, 1979, 10-12; and *Explanation of the "Tax Restructuring Act of 1980"* (H.R. 7015).

12. American Institute of Certified Public Accountants, *Value Added Tax* (New York, 1975), 13-15.

13. *Congressional Record*, April 2, 1980, H2481-2486. Also see Appendix B of this book and Ways and Means Committee Print, April 10, 1980 (96-56).

14. Advisory Commission on Intergovernmental Relations, *The Michigan Single Business Tax* (Washington, 1978), 5-15.

15. Richard W. Lindholm, *Value Added Tax* (Chicago: Nelson-Hall, 1976), 27-36.

16. Clara K. Sullivan, *The Tax on Value Added* (New York: Columbia University Press, 1965), 214-262.

17. Eric Schiff, *Value Added Taxation in Europe* (Washington: American Enterprise Institute for Public Polling Research, 1973), 21-42.

18. Norman B. True, *The Value Added Tax: Facts and Fancies* (Washington: Heritage Foundation, 1979), 49-67.

19. Wesley Claire Mitchell is best known for his empirical work associated with the development of an explanation of business cycles.

20. John Maynard Keynes, *The General Theory of Employment, Interest and Money* (New York: Harcourt Brace, 1936).

21. The Council of Economic Advisers has never been given the responsibility of identifying what must be done to avoid unemployment.

22. Brookings Institution, *Report on a Survey of the Organization and Administration of State and County Governments of Alabama* vol. 4, pt. 3 (Montgomery, Ala.: Wilson Publishing Co., 1932), pp. 341-398, and *Report on Survey of Administration in Iowa: The Revenue System* (Des Moines, Iowa: State of Iowa, 1933), 120-154.

23. Ibid., 319-342.

24. Paul Studenski, "Towad a Theory of Business Taxation," *Journal of Political Economy* 48 (October 1940):621-654.

25. T.S. Adams, "Fundamental Problems of Federal Income Taxation," *Quarterly Journal of Economics* 35 (August 1921):527-556.

26. Martin Branfenbrenner and Kiichira Kogiku, "The Aftermath of the Shoup Tax Reforms," *National Tax Journal* 10 (September 1959):236-254.

27. James A. Papke, "Michigan's Value Added Tax after Seven Years," *National Tax Journal* 13 (December 1960):350-363.

28. Harvard Law School International Tax Program, *World Tax Series, Taxation in France* (Chicago: Commerce Clearing House, 1966), 991, 1003.

29. Maurice Laure, *La Taxe sur la valeur ajoutee* (Paris: Recueil Sirey, 1952).

30. Wilhelm von Siemens, *Verdelte Umstatsteuer*, 2d ed. (Liemenstadt, Germany: private, 1921).

31. Gunter Schmolders, "Turnover Taxes," in *Developments in Taxation since World War I* (Amsterdam: International Bureau of Fiscal Documentation, 1966), p. IV-17.

32. Ibid., p. IV-18.

33. Note from Clara Sullivan, October 2, 1965.

34. *Business Taxation: The Report of the President: A Task Force on Business Taxation*. (Washington: GPO, 1970).

35. Ibid., 61.

36. U.S Department of the Treasury, *DISC: A Handbook for Exporters* (Washington: GPO, 1972).

37. *Tax Restructuring Act of 1979* (H.R. 5665), *Hearings*, Committee on Ways and Means, 96th Cong., November 8, 14, 15, 1979, pt. I, Serial 96-50.

38. Portions taken from the English translation of the Neumark Report reprinted with permission from *Tax Harmonization in the Common Market*, published and copyrighted by Commerce Clearing House, Inc., Chicago, Illinois. The membership of the FFC committee included: Chairman, Fritz Neumark, Frankfurt am Main; members: Willy Albers, Kiel; Alain Barrere, Paris; Cesare Cosciani, Rome; Joseph Kauffman, Luxembourg; Maurice Masoin, Brussels; Bernard Schendstok, The Hague; Carl S. Shoup, New York; G. Stammati, Rome; George Vedel, Paris.

39. *French Automotive "vignette" and "Special Taxation" Discrimination* (Washington: World Trade Department, Automobile Manufacturers Association, 1963).

40. Neumark, *Tax Harmonization*, p. 58.

41. The Europeans utilize the concept of company seat, meaning headquarters' office, as a principal determiner of tax liability. The United States does not make use of this concept, and tax liability is based on fact of incorporation. Therefore, a foreign corporation controlled and owned by a U.S. corporation is treated as a foreign business under U.S. tax legislation, but is a portion of the controlling corporation under European practice.

42. Neumark, *Tax Harmonization*, p. 70.

43. Oswald H. Brownlee, *Taxing the Income from U.S. Corporation Investments Abroad* (Washington: American Enterprise Institute, 1980).

44. "Report of the Committee on Personal Property Taxation," *Proceedings of the National Tax Association for 1953*, National Tax Association, Harrisburg, Pennsylvania, 388-389.

45. Ibid., 392-393.

46. Advisory Commission on Intergovernmental Relations, *Federal-State-Local Finances* (Washington: GPO, 1974), 214-218.

47. American Bar Association, "Evaluation of an Additive-Method-Value-Added Tax for Use in the United States," *The Tax Lawyer*, Spring 1977, 579.

48. Advisory Commission on Intergovernmental Relations, *The Value-Added Tax and Alternative Sources of Federal Revenues* (Washington: ACIR, 1973), 23.

49. Richard W. Lindholm, "Area II, Value-Added Tax" in *A Description and Analysis of Oregon's Fiscal System* (Eugene: University of Oregon, 1971), p. 35.

50. Arthur D. Little, Inc., *Hawaii's Federal Excise Tax* (Cambridge, Mass., 1968), p. 5.

51. Robert D. Ebel, *An Evaluation of a Value Added Tax for the State of Hawaii*, (Honolulu: University of Hawaii, 1973), 25-27.

52. Brookings Institution, *Report on the Survey of the Organization and Administration of the State and County Governments of Alabama*, vol. 4, pt. 3 (Montgomery, Ala., 1932), pp. 342-398, and *Report on a Survey of Administration in Iowa: The Revenue System* (Washington, 1933), 120-154.

53. Advisory Commission on Intergovernmental Relations, *The Michigan Single Business Tax* (Washington: GPO, 1978), pp. 25-27.

54. This section was previously published in about the same form in *The Tax Executive* 32 (January 1980):133-143 and in *Hearings of H.R. 5665* (96-50):188-194.

55. A.R. Prest, *Public Finance: In Theory and Practice* (London: Weidenfield and Nicholson, 1960), pp. 343-357; Arthur Dale, *Tax Harmonization in Europe* (London: Taxation Publishing Co., 1963), pp. 47-56.

56. *Richardson Report of the Committee on Turnover Taxation*, Cmnd. 2300 (London: Her Majesty's Stationery Office, 1964).

57. Compendium of Papers on Excise Tax Structure Submitted to the Committee on Ways and Means on June 15 and 16, 1964, vol. 2 (panel discussion before the Committee).

58. Fairness is related to the concept of minimum sacrifice. Gunnar Myrdal, the great Swedish Noble Prize-winning economist, claims that the entire framework of economic justice used to support the progressive income tax is faulty. It is faulty because the analysis works at the margin and marginal utility. To be appropriate, total dissatisfactions should be compared. Myrdal concludes that "even if subjective value theory could evolve a political rule, this would have to aim at maximization or a just distribution of *total utilities* and not of marginal utilities." Gunnar Myrdal, *The Political Development of Economic Theory* (London: Rutledge and Kegan, 1953), p. 185.

59. *Richardson Report*, 63.

60. Douglas Dosser and S.S. Han, *Taxes in the EEC and Britain: The Problem of Harmonization* PEP European Series no. 6 (London: Chatham House, 1968). The European Economic Community (EEC), the European Community (EC), and the Common Market all refer to the same grouping of Western European nations.

61. E.B. Butler, "Britain and the Continental Value Added Tax, I and II," *The Bankers Magazine* 205 (May-June 1968):274-279, 348-358.

62. National Economic Development Office, *Value Added Tax* (London: Her Majesty's Stationery Office, 1969).

63. Rudolf J. Niehus, "The German Added Value Tax—Two Years *After,*" *Taxes, The Tax Magazine* 47 (September 1969):554-566; Clarence W. Lock, "An Administrator's Point of View on the Value Added Tax," in *Alternatives to Present Federal Taxes* (Princeton, N.J.: Tax Institute of America, 1964), 55-63; E. Beekmna, *De Invlved van de BTW op de Administratie* (Deventer, The Netherlands: A.E.E. Kluver, 1968).

64. G.S.A. Wheatcroft, "Inequity in Britains Tax Structure," *Lloyd's Bank Review* 93 (July 1969):11-21. Wheatcroft concludes that gradual reform of the British tax system should be made by collecting the greater part of revenue from two main taxes: a general sales tax or added-value tax on all expenditures at a single rate and a progressive income tax and a modified capital-gains tax and estate duty.

65. NED, *Value Added Tax*, 60.

66. Ibid., 70.

67. Ibid., 67.

68. Ibid., 18.

69. Chancellor of the Exchequer, *Value-Added Tax* (London: Her Majesty's Stationery Office, 1971), 4. The United Kingdom does not use a general retail sales tax at the local-government levels as was true in France and is true in the United States.

70. Ibid., 4, 5.

71. Ibid., 11.

72. Ibid., 18.

73. *The Times* (London), April 13, 1970.

74. Alf Morris, *Value-Added Tax*, Fabian Research Series no. 264 (London: Fabian Society, 1970).

75. A.R. Prest, "Taxation and Growth," *The Political Quarterly* 42 (January-March 1971):66-74.

76. Philip Lawton, "Value-Added Tax," *British Tax Review*, 1971, 171-178.

77. F.G. Sturrock, "The Effect on Efficiency of Introducing a Value-Added Tax to Agriculture," *British Tax Review*, 1970, 112-121.

78. *Economist*, April 3, 1971, 60.

79. A.R. Ilersic, "Value-Added Tax for the United Kindom?" *Canadian Tax Journal* 17 no. 6 (November-December 1969):446-451, 448.

80. *The United Kingdom and the European Communities* (Cmnd 4715) (London: Her Majesty's Stationery Office, 1971), 34.

81. Britain and the European Communities: An Economic Assessment, (Cmnd. 4289) (London: Her Majesty's Stationery Office, 1970). Samuel Brittan opposed VAT because it "would give costs and prices a further up-

ward twist." S. Brittan, "Cuts in Government Spending and the Tax Illusion," *The Political Quarterly* 42 (January-March 1971):7-19, 17.

82. Douglas Dosser, *The Daily Telegraph*, September 30, 1971.

83. E.G. Horsman, "Britain and Value-Added Taxation," *Lloyd's Bank Review*, no. 103 (January 1972):25-36.

84. Nicholas Kaldor, "A Memorandum on the Value-Added Tax," *Essays in Economic Policy*, vol. 2 (London: Gerald Ouchworth, 1964), 266-299.

85. Article 99, *Treaty of Rome* (EEC).

86. H.H. Mainprice, *VAT: A Concise Guide* (London: VAT Planning and Publi, Limited, 1972).

87. *Accountancy* 83 (May 1972):14-16.

88. R.S. Nock, "Value Added Tax—Amendments and Regulations, II," *British Tax Review*, March-April 1974, pp. 108-115.

89. Jeremy G.A. Cripps, "Stirring the VAT," *Financial Executive*, October 1973, pp. 88-91, 116-117.

90. Walter Eltis, "The Tory Government's Budget," *Wall Street Journal*, June 14, 1979, 24.

91. Ibid.

92. Editorial, *Wall Street Journal*, June 14, 1979, 24.

93. *Business Week*, October 15, 1979, 50.

94. "Big Risks, Small Mistakes," *Economist*, June 16, 1979, 63-75.

95. J.A. King and M.A. King, *The British Tax System* (Oxford, England: Oxford University Press, 1978).

# 2

# Stranglehold of Income Tax

## Overview

The second section explores the effectiveness of revenue raising and income and wealth redistribution of the progressive personal income tax and a tax on corporate profits. The complexity that one encounters in calculating economic income for a period or the portion of business gross receipts that are profits is only referred to. An example of the complexity is not given.

Congress asks for additional income and profit tax simplicity and passes legislation that increases the complexity. More than likely, the current impasse is telling us that the income, payroll, and profit types of taxes are overloaded. Nevertheless, the basic justice of tax payments according to ability remains a noble aim and politically, at least, cannot be abandoned. As studies demonstrate, (1) the progressive income tax rates do not mean progressive tax collections, (2) the underground economy is apparently experiencing an explosive growth, and (3) the ability of the tax expenditure to increase the enthusiasm for reliance on income and profit taxes is declining. This is true in both Europe and the United States. These topics are discussed in the third section.

In government administration *justice* is the key word. In business administration *efficiency* is the key word. This difference in emphasis between the two giants of our production system creates conflict as goals and plans are developed for implementation. Taxation policy is definitely not an exception.

The ability of the taxation of profits or the progressive income tax to even theoretically minimize tax-payment sacrifices of taxpayers has been challenged by Gunnar Myrdal. He says we are continually changing the definition of taxable income and thus the political meaning of the relation of income to tax paid. Others, such as C. Battistella, an Italian economist, would permit the cost of replacing the taxpayer to be a cost deductible from taxable income.

The fourth section takes a look at how the personal income tax could be changed substantially to improve welfare directly as well as the environment in which saving and investment are taking place. The reforms considered do not abandon the relation of the tax to the personal condition of the taxpayer, as do sales and production-type taxes.

The negative income tax (NIT) is a procedure that causes the income tax system to make payments as well as collect taxes. Income taxes are collected at about a 50 percent rate on incomes above a certain size. Collections are used to make payments to the poor to bring their incomes close to the level where the 50 percent income tax rates start to apply. The NIT reduces economic inequality by transfering funds directly as a right to those with incomes not up to a set minimum level.

The expenditure tax (ET) is closely associated with the name of Kaldor, a British economist, and more recently with the U.S. Treasury's *Blueprints for Tax Reform*. The aim is to make a tax on expenditures a personal tax. This is to be done without going through the administrative difficulties involved in counting and giving a value to all expenditures made by an individual or a family in a year. The central difficulty is how to treat changes in the asset holdings of the taxable spenders so that the tax base can be adjusted to reflect expenditure levels. Expenditure levels are taxed at progressive rates. A big earner and a small spender pay much lower taxes than a big spender, even if his income is low.

Both NIT and ET have grown in favor as (1) savings and supplies have shown signs of becoming inadequate and as (2) adequate income for all to live above the poverty line is accepted as a basic aim of modern industrial societies. To a considerable degree, of course, items 1 and 2 are inconsistent.

The general subject of the fifth section is the difference in the price effect of two different taxes raising equal revenues. A tax, whether personal or impersonal, amounts to a wedge that is driven between cost and selling price, or income and spendable resources.

A purchase of a private-sector good or service involves a tie-in purchase of government spending. The availability of funds for use by the government may be the most productive and useful portion of the purchase. However, in all cases the use of your resources by the government was not the activating element in your determination to make the expenditure or earn the income. Government uses of resources are not freely determined by the wishes of those making resources available for a particular use by government. Therefore, in this strict sense, funds used by government are taken and are not received in exchange for goods and services offered.

Taxes have an *income effect* when the tax collection induces a person to work harder so that he can maintain his level of personal consumption. The *substitution* effect of taxes is operative when a taxpayer decides to take things easier because so much of what is earned is siphoned off in taxes. When taxes are not levied on a person, such as is true of VAT, both the substitution and income effects become less useful concepts in understanding how taxes affect individual economic decisions.

Term *incidence* refers to the final location of the economic burden of a tax. The corporate income tax in the past forty years has gone from a tax considered to be paid out of surplus business income to a tax seen to be added to unit selling prices, as are property, sales, payroll, and value-added taxes. The location of incidence is difficult to determine for all taxes, but perhaps most difficult in the case of the corporate income tax.

The sixth section continues with the analysis of the corporate income tax (CIT). The CIT formerly dominated business federal taxes, but its revenue-raising level has fallen below the portion of social security contributions paid by the firm. Neither of these taxes is available as refunds on exports or to justify border taxes on imports.

The CIT lost much of its economic support when its characteristics no longer supported what is seen to be desirable economic policy. For example, savings are no longer in surplus, and CIT reduces savings; sharp shifts in tax collections with changes in the business climate are now seen to be counter-productive rather than a desirable countercyclical quality; finally, prices are seen now to be set by the large profitable firms and not by the no-profit marginal firms.

The continued substantial use of CIT as a tax not integrated with the individual income tax and being collected at substantial rates on profits returned from abroad hurts the U.S. international posture. At the same time, as the introduction of VAT would shift CIT's application, it would stimulate employment and investment in the United States.

## Limited Legitimate Function of the Progressive Income Tax

It is generally accepted that the federal income tax crossed the Atlantic from the United Kingdom to the United States as "the result of a great equalitarian movement generated by two prolonged post-war depressions of great severity."[1] The income tax was adopted to collect taxes from those enjoying substantial income surpluses. Twenty-five years later, however, Goode quotes with approval the *Internal Revenue Bulletin* when it reports the 1913 income tax to be a response to "the general demand for justice in taxation, and to the long-standing need of an elastic and productive system of revenue."[2]

The ordinary voter of 1913 saw the income tax to be a tax of the rich. It was not envisaged as a tax on the large middle class—the farmers, small businessmen, and skilled workers. As Goode points out, to a degree the voter saw the income tax as more just than duties on imported sugar, for example. The voter's basic understanding of the income tax did not include countercyclical characteristics, as Goode seems to believe.

The *Internal Revenue Cumulative Bulletin* of 1959 also attributed to the voter a greater desire for tax justice and tax economic-level sensitivity than the facts appear to justify. The income tax had proved itself as a war tax during the Civil War. Now it was to be used as a peacetime tax that would be directly paid by only 1 percent of the population. To a degree the income tax continued as a tax "extra," and not a basic, substantial, broad-based tax. In fact, not until the World War II withholding was introduced did the income tax reach down to include 5 percent of the population.

The Constitution envisaged the national government collecting its revenues from indirect taxes—excises and import duties. The states and local governments had all tax bases available to them (there were only restrictions on import duties), but they were expected to rely on direct taxes. This is the way things actually worked out, except during wars, until the income tax withholding introduced in 1943 during World War II was continued as a basic aspect of the income tax and a very major portion of expanded federal government revenue collections. The income tax continues as a tax based to a substantiated extent on the wage and capital earnings of the middle- and lower-income receivers. Perhaps 75 percent of the adult population either pays income taxes directly or is a partner in a joint return. The income tax has become something it was never intended to be—a mass tax.

## The Breaking Point

When Joseph W. Barr, Secretary of the Treasury, pointed out in 1968 that a taxpayer's revolt was on the horizon, he was making reference to the injustices developing in the federal income tax. Now the revolt is a reality, and it is referred to as the "underground economy." Both the new role of the income tax along with the expanding payroll taxes and the increase in income tax progressivity due to failure to index as inflation continues combine to place a very heavy burden on the concept of income as a tax base.

Sometimes income tax reformers start campaigns of simplification. Congress attempted to make progress in this direction in 1966. Nevertheless, fourteen years later, form 1040 is more complex and has reached a degree of sophistication that the framers of the original income tax legislation could never imagine in their wildest dreams. The complications arise from efforts to define a basically undefinable concept. Tax expenditures as a method of extending favors to certain income receivers continue to grow, and in this growth the income tax gains in complexity, the base declines, and real rates increase on what is left after the deductions.

## Hobson's Choice

Nevertheless, with all its weakness and problems, the income tax remains popular in the liberal tradition of taxation as established in England over

100 years ago.[3] The income tax continues to be seen as taxation according to ability to pay. What is not brought into the tax-policy decision is that the income tax is over burdened. Examples are the retirement provision and the Employee Retirement Income Security Act of 1974, the head-of-family provision, minimum-tax provision, earned-income provision, pension-contribution tax reductions, and so on. The inability of the income tax to carry the burden placed on it can be handled in a number of ways. Expenditures of government from tax revenues can be reduced; a new tax relying on a transactions base rather than profits or an adjusted income can be introduced; or the burden can be scattered over the economic countryside through deficit spending. Whatever choice is made results in dissatisfaction and satisfactions, and a consensus does not readily take shape. Or, in Lester Thurow's words, ours is a *zero-sum-society*.

Perhaps the whole idea of developing a tax system that equated satisfactions and dissatisfactions at the margin was faulty. Myrdal, a 1974 Nobel Prize winner in economics, points out that value judgments must be concerned with total satisfactions.[4] If this point is accepted, as it must be if one stays within this framework of analysis, than the conceptual job of dealing with the problem is unresolved. This leaves us with the rough justice of the market system. The taxation of transactions at a flat rate becomes the preferred solution. Of course, the tax that does this best is VAT.

*Horizontal Equality*

To the average voter and taxpayer, the personal income tax is just because the amount paid corresponds with the individual's ability to pay. The meaning of this abstraction is that those with larger incomes, however measured or defined, can pay a bigger portion of these incomes in taxes without giving up expenditures for goods and services included within the good life and that this is the way it happens under the progressive personal income tax. It was not until 1968 that studies were publicized which demonstrated how many wealthy receivers of large incomes paid very little income taxes. In addition, as we all know, income finding uses in foreign countries and unrealized increases in capital values are not a part of the income base subject to the U.S. income tax. These untaxed incomes are, of course, largely controlled by the wealthy.

More than likely, the average voter will always give little consideration to the way the high and progressive rates goad "the capitalist into irrational and anti-social behavior in order to escape taxes."[5] The effect of taxes on society's well-being that arises from the uneconomic decisions stimulated by the progressive income tax is not yet a portion of the voter picture of the tax.

The social cost or impact on the efficiency of a basically market economy of high-income receivers acting in a tax-determined fashion is indeterminant. There may be a social benefit. As, for example, the apparent considerable expansionary impact on charitable and other gifts to private institutions because they are deductible in calculating taxable income.[6] There may also be a social benefit arising from the pressure toward home ownership arising from the exclusion from taxable income of imputed rent from occupancy of an owner-occupied home.

These social benefits, if they exist, must be weighed against a number of likely difficulties, for example, the locked-in effect high income taxes have on successful investments, the pressure high profit taxes develop to increase business consumption-type spending, and the impact high personal income tax rates have on the level of corporate profit distributions in countries which have not integrated the corporate profit and the personal income taxes.

The social benefit of some income-use shifts must be weighed against the horizontal inequality they also create. The inequality is created by the deductibility provisions allowed in arriving at taxable income.

*Expenditures*

Persons in the same economic position, but one renting and one owning his own heavily mortgaged home, have, as a result of the law, quite different tax liabilities. Also, one taxpayer married and another unmarried, with identical incomes, find themselves with quite different tax liabilities. None of the benefits provided by the wife are taxable income, while the purchase of these services by the unmarried taxpayer is not deductible. Also the head-of-household concept with progressive income tax rates causes confusion and injustice.

Out of habit, the labor movement and the liberal community continue to support the income tax despite the problems and the inefficiencies related to the use of the system. One can hope for the overcoming of habit and the adoption of sensible procedures to raise funds largely used for social purposes and defense of personal freedom. Perhaps France developed a portion of the answer when it introduced VAT back in 1954, and the Common Market countries adopted provisions requiring a very similar basic VAT of all member states. In the United States, Michigan continues to look with favor on VAT, and the single business tax is the second successful use of VAT.[7]

*Conclusion*

The highly touted progressive personal income tax has been a federal tax for over sixty-five years, and it has not brought about the more equal distribution of incomes it was to provide. In fact, the current trend is toward making the tax more and more a simple flat percentage of earnings of income (defined in some manner).[8] The relation of the income tax to ability to pay is being reduced.

If the personal income tax is unable to redistribute income, much of the justification for enduring all the administrative problems of the tax is also reduced. The shortcomings of the progressive personal income tax related to horizontal equality, tax-determined business decisions, and the incompleteness of any definition of taxable income are becoming more serious. In addition, the weakness of the nineteenth-century concept of minimum sacrifice measured as marginal-income receipts enjoys little scientific support. These shortcomings are too important to be swept under the proverbial rug or for one to optimistically assume that the next session of Congress will close down the tax shelters through limitation of artificial losses (LAL) legislation.[9]

## Where Is the Justice of the Income Tax?

To a degree, each taxpayer and each voter possess their own ideas of tax justice. This personal opinion of what is just may be overlaid with considerable self-interest, or it may be very selfless. Not to be left out, tax philosophers and general economists with a moralist stripe have, through the ages, tackled the hoary monster of tax justice with whatever weapons were at hand. The very uncertain outcomes of these efforts are frequently ladled out as well-established concepts in high school and college courses of economics and in publications of all descriptions. A leading British tax economist, Nicholas Kaldor by name, concludes income cannot be defined and thus certainly cannot be measured nor can a tax based on it be equitable. This is also the basic position of Myrdal.[10]

### Ability-to-Pay Taxation

In the current political economic climate, a tax is just to the ordinary voter if its liability varies closely with taxpayer capacity-to-pay taxes. John Stuart Mill's ideas, expressed in 1861 to the British Parliament's Select Committee on Income and Property Tax, remain basic to the hedonistic tax philosopher's concept of taxing so that the aggregate of personal sacrifices is minimized. In a general way, the voter's idea of capacity-to-pay taxes is associated with the political metaphysics of the concept of minimum aggregate sacrifice. It is perfectly obvious that both the comitment and the concept suffer from a built-in high level of vagueness. Nevertheless, the result has been a firm conviction that the taxation of income and application of progressive rates are the road to tax justice. The acceptance of the accuracy of the belief that income taxes are just because the rates increase with the size of the taxable income has been reduced by the findings of tax expenditure (loophole) studies.

What constitutes tax justice and equity was acceptable because of a strong disposition to avoid examination of what makes up a *taxable* income to be included in the income classes to which the various tax rates are to be applied. Or, put differently, the taxation of income at progressive rates is a procedure of taxation on which the tax philosopher and the ordinary voter can agree as long as income is not defined and a particular degree of rate progressivity is not justified.

This armchair approach was eminently acceptable in 1913 when the voters, through their representatives, democratically decided to use the individual income tax as a new source of federal revenues. After all, the impact of the new tax would not be great. The total of collections from application of the individual income tax in fiscal 1915 was $41 million, and only 367,598 persons filed returns. Actually, the adoption of ability as a general criterion for the distribution of all tax payments means little more than that a political decision has been made not to distribute taxes on the basis of individual benefit from government spending.[11] The justice of this must be doubted, but its practicality must be admired. It was aimed squarely at getting the money where it was at.

*Income Tax Rates*

In fiscal 1980, federal collections from the application of the individual income tax are estimated at $239 billion from 70 million returns.[12] The armchair approach of 1913 or even of 1939 and 1966 is no longer appropriate. The justice of the tax under these conditions, or the degree to which it really meets an informed voter's general concept of capacity-to-pay taxes, must rest where this huge amount is actually collected and the impact. For these relationships to exist, the capacity-to-pay tax must be defined sufficiently accurately to make it usable as the base for determining tax-paying capacity.

The schedule of rates that has actually existed in the United States since 1966 (that is, prior to inflation-related adjustments), which provided a rate of 14 percent on the first $500 of taxable income and a 70 percent rate on income above $100,000, perhaps roughly corresponded to what the voter considers to be capacity-to-pay taxes at various income levels.[13] However, it is also true that both the voter and Congress add a few percentage points to the published tax rates applicable to lower income and quite a few percentage points to the rate applicable to high incomes to compensate for tax avoidance and evasion. So it may be that the traditional 10 percent biblical tithing is considered by the voter to be about right for the low-income receivers and 50 percent to be about right for the highest income receivers. However, if this is what might be called a voter's consensus, it is undoubtedly based on a number of considerations other than the voter's general opinion of capacity-to-pay taxes. What might be true is that the average voter is something like Neville Chamberlain who, when as Chancellor of the Exchequer, was asked why he introduced a corporate income tax, answered, "I went to where the money was." The year was 1937, and the tax was known as the national defense contribution.

*Wartime Justice*

The United States federal individual income tax rate schedule through the years shows the impact of war and attitude that men should not become rich, or maybe that everyone should make an additional sacrifice when the boys are fighting overseas. Also, of course, the higher rates introduced during a war represent the additional revenue needs of the federal government and the tendency for war to overheat the economy. For example, as late as 1939, taxable income in the $4,000 to $6,000 bracket was taxed at an 8 percent rate, but the rate rose to 29 percent in 1944-1945, and then fell to 22.9 percent in 1948-1949, to rise to 29 percent again during the Korean War. The rate for this bracket income in 1966 after 60 percent inflation was 22 percent, and ten years later, after an additional 80 percent of inflation, the tax rate for income at this level for joint returns was 19 percent. An estimate of the impact of various provisions changing the effective rates of the individual income tax concludes that within the $4,000 to $5,000 bracket (the highest bracket that did not have its income tax liability reduced by provision allowing income splitting for married couples) the rate changes are perhaps as representative of the political consensus of the proper rate to be paid by the younger income earner and the subprofessional and wage-earner groups as any. The schedule-rate and the effective-rate increase from 1939 to 1966 was substantial. Since 1966 only the effective rate has gone up. Today the income tax rate on $5,000 of income in 1939 dollars is 36 percent on a joint return.[14]

Can one also conclude that it is the consensus that tax-payment capacity of the $5,000 (1939 dollars) income-bracket group has increased by the amount represented by the effective-rate increase? When it is kept in mind that during the 1939-1966 period the purchasing power of the dollar decreased by 60 percent and since 1966 by another 80 percent, it becomes apparent that inflation has caused a considerable shift in the political consensus of the capacity of receivers of $4,000 to $5,000 of income in 1939 dollars to pay income taxes. The substantial increase in legislated and effective rates at this current-dollar income level, which approximates income brackets up to $14,000, seems to represent a use of the individual income tax to substantially reduce consumption levels of earners with what is usually classified as minimum adequate budgets.

### Economic Reform

This is not the type of tax Joseph Pulitzer was fighting for in the *World* when he dedicated it "to the cause of the people rather than that of purse proud potentates" back in the 1880s, or that the "pupulists' ferment" caused to be placed in state Democratic platforms in the 1890s.

### Income Tax Avoidance

It is impossible to construct a distribution of individual income taxpayers by total individual income and actual taxes paid. The theoretical worldwide concept of income, that is, income wherever credited to the taxpayer must be subject to the U.S. individual income tax, is really unenforceable without a much closer internation cooperative arrangement than now exists. The individual income escaping U.S. taxation because it is credited to a bank account in Switzerland, for example, must be concentrated in the incomes of upper-income receivers. Also, non-realized capital gains, which must also be enjoyed largely by the upper income receivers, are not a part of taxable individual income. Finally, income taxes paid to foreign governments can be deducted from taxes due the United States.

Despite these shortcomings, and many others,[16] attempts to relate the rate of actual tax to total income classes, and comparing this with the statute or nominal rate, are helpful in understanding how the U.S. individual income tax works. An early effort concluded that reductions of total reported income due to personal exemptions, deductions, capital-gains provisions, and income splitting caused the actual tax (effective rate) on income over $1 million to be 29.8 percent when the nominal rate was 87 percent and the actual tax on income of between $50,000 and $100,000 to be 30.1 percent. A more recent study using a somewhat different set of assumptions concludes the effective individual income tax rate is 12.4 percent on incomes above $1 million and 13.4 percent on incomes between $50,000 and $100,000.[17]

The general conclusion of quantitative studies of this type, plus reasonable modifications, point to an actual U.S. income tax that is very imperfectly related to individual capacity-to-pay taxes as represented by income received. The actual federal income taxes paid tend to decline as a percentage of income. There is hardly any indication of progressivity. Yet, individual tax payments that are progressive in relation to income are the generally accepted good purpose of all government enforcement efforts involving individual record keeping and the services of countless laywers, accountants, and unwashed "tax experts" required by the U.S. individual income tax. No effort, of course, is made to make the income tax relate to ability to pay as represented by the net worth of the taxpayer.[18]

The record-keeping detail and tax consideration points required under the U.S. individual income tax in money-making, spending, or giving decisions of the taxpayer, anxious to meet the tax-liability requirements of the law, but only those, and desirous of utilizing beneficial actions encouraged by the law, have grown steadily through the years. There are many reasons for the development of the situation, and this entire area of tax legislation has provided a heyday for all kinds of pressure groups. A basic underlying cause of the situation is perhaps no more obtuse than that the tax base, that is, individual income, is just difficult to define. A clear idea of what should be a tax base for a progressive individual income tax does not exist.

*Definition of Tax Base*

Of the principal taxes used in the United States, the property tax, and particularly the portion resting on land, possesses the clearest definable base. The base of the sales tax is somewhat less clear. The taxes with basis most difficult to define are the individual income tax and the corporate profits tax.

Despite the vagueness of the concept of income, the base of the income tax is subject to much the greatest variation of rates and must also be subject to the highest rates. The result of this combination frequently makes the income tax liability vary substantially between persons in basically similar spending-power positions.

The accepted economic definition of income is the "net accretion of economic power between two points in time." Here we have accrued gains or unrealized losses treated like cash receipts and cash costs. This concept of income is the one which is genuinely consistent with the idea of ability-to-pay taxes or capacity-to-pay taxes that consider only income. It is, however, a basically unworkable concept for use as a practical income tax base.

It is quite impossible each year to determine changes in the value of assets or the accumulation or disposition of income rights by individuals. Kaldor has called the search for the increment of economic power as a "chase of a will-o'-the-wisp."[19] A central bank policy reducing the availability of central bank credit would tend to increase interest rates and thereby decrease the value of all fixed-income assets while increasing the income received by those controlling a fixed quantity of liquid assets. Also, in order to make some progress in limiting the meaning of an increment in economic power, the ongoing economic power arising from the control over durable consumer goods, including housing, is ignored. Expansion of economic power through the ownership of previously produced units, as, for example, when housing or automobiles are rationed as in a war, is substantial, but, of course, not considered as taxable income.

### Problems of Income Definition

In the late 1930s Paul H. Wueller wrote three articles, published in the *Political Science Quarterly*, dealing with the problem of defining income and particularly of defining income for taxation purposes.[20] In the first article, which considers German efforts, he concludes very little progress to have been made because the approach was not basically analytical. The Germans got caught up in such difficulties as, Does a beggar earn income? Is there any difference between a tip to a waiter and an allowance for children? (This is the recipient interpretation of income.) They also held very closely to the position that the return of capital or of income required to maintain capital, even human capital, could not be considered income (the preservation-of-source criterion). When applied to human capital, the effect is to largely eliminate income as a base for taxing families in the United States with incomes within the great $15,000 to $20,000 band. Generally speaking, German writers, in their efforts to equate a concept of income with that of ability, came up with a suggested definition of taxable income which did not provide a broad base to which tax rates could be applied. Some German writers, for example, F.W. Gartner, believed in a productivity concept which excluded from income and placed in the capital-gains category all income "without antecedent application of labor power."

Italian public-finance philosophers were among the first to consider taxation in relation to economic growth rates, as well as individual tax-paying ability or capacity. For them, therefore, the proper definition of income for the application of an income tax must exclude savings from the base, for they equated savings growth with capital growth and capital growth with economic growth. This approach caused Italian tax writers to find considerable value in the income-disposition approach to the definition of taxable income. The desire to encourage savings leads them toward an income tax that might be defined as an expenditures tax. However, they see a difference in types of individual expenditures. Battistella, who was a strong believer in the net-accretion criterion for defining taxable income, advocated an interesting personal-exemption formula. He would exempt from individual taxable income the "minimum expense necessary to develop each child into a productive factor, such productive factor to be of the same value as the head of the family." Apparently Battistella saw this procedure, which would generally give greater personal exemptions per child to the high-income receivers, to be consistent with income taxes distributed among income recipients, according to the least-sacrifice principle. It is really a form of reducing the individual income tax burden on the basis of cost of replacement of the existing human capital. To some extent, this is done by the U.S. income tax and its exemption of an amount of income rather than providing a tax deduction for each child. At least this is the case if those with the most expensive educations are also in the higher tax brackets.

## Expenditures as Income

The income disposition expenditure approach to income was a favorite topic of Yale economist Irving Fisher of the 1920s.[21] At about the same time, the greatest name in U.S. public finance, E.R.A. Seligman, was developing the separation doctrine of taxable income.[22] These two ideas are related in that in neither case is current accrual of purchasing power considered to be income. For Fisher, actual enjoyment of satisfactions from spending was necessary to have income; and for Seligman, money payments had to be received to have income. The concepts of income of both Fisher and Seligman are considerably narrower than that developed by German writers, and also by fellow U.S. economists of somewhat less influence at the time (for example, R.M. Haig, C.C. Plehn, W.W. Hewett, and H.C. Simons).

## Conclusion

The theoretical business of defining income and the justice of income tax rates on different income levels is not finished. Each year the definition of taxable income is changed by court decisions, Treasury rulings, and legislation.[23] The question that needs answering is this: Since the income tax has become a very substantial tax on mass income, and not only a tax on the rich, is a new approach to raising the needed revenue required? For example, should the needed revenues be raised with two basic taxes, one on wealth and one on expenditures?[24]

## Expenditure and Negative Income Taxes

The VAT of the subtractive type is a major tax reform aimed primarily in placing a charge on each business transaction. The aim is to collect a portion of the costs of government on the basis of value added, that is, GNP, sourced in each level of business operation. The VAT of the additive type is a major tax reform aimed at placing an equal tax rate on gross income arising from all sources with the tax not affected by who receives the income or how much income is received. The transfers of purchasing power to the government affects all incomes from all sources similarly. The tax base of VAT is approximately the same under the additive or the subtractive procedure.

The expenditure tax (ET) is a major tax reform aimed at developing tax payments based on personal expenditures with progressive rates. It is a tax of transactions with a collection system based on ability to pay.

The negative income tax (NIT) is a major tax reform that expands the personal-income-tax system to include provision for payments to low-income receivers as well as collections from modest- and high-income receivers. The aim is to bring all incomes up to the official poverty level.

The basic concepts and approach to taxation of both the additive and subtractive types of VAT are considered throughout this discussion.[25] This section is dedicated to considering ET and NIT and relating these major tax reforms somewhat to VAT.

### Goals of NIT and ET

Both the NIT and ET approaches are very much concerned with changing the distribution of economic satisfactions away from those established in the market. The NIT and ET are tied to a personal concept of ability to pay, as is true of the individual income tax. The ability to pay to be met by the tax is personal and not societal. For example, the manner of collecting taxes could sharply reduce productivity and at the same time increase the equality of wealth and income distribution. The result would be more equal portions of a constantly decreasing pie. Under these circumstances, the ability to pay of society is being reduced while the tax payments, by being pushed to the higher-income receivers and wealth holders, are being collected more and more according to individual ability to pay.

When the society was suffering from an excess of savings, highly progressive taxes, generally speaking, helped to expand economic activity because the excess of savings above investment use was reduced. Today high interest rates indicate a shortage of investment funds or/and undesirable federal government deficits. Also the data of personal savings as a percentage of personal income demonstrate a shortage of savings. Under these conditions, a reduction of savings, which progressive income tax rates and corporate profit taxes cause, becomes an undesirable characteristic for a tax to possess.

*Treasury's Blueprints for Tax Reform*

In 1977, the U.S. Treasury, after a year-long study aimed at a practical and just major reform of the U.S. tax system came up with a consumption tax base to which progressive rates were to be assessed. The proposal is for a consumption tax base with a progressive rate schedule to replace the income tax.

The central feature of the reform recommended is to use the consumption-expenditure base without at the same time establishing an expensive bureaucracy to monitor all consumption-type spending. The nub of the procedure is the establishment of what are called *qualified accounts* to hold both the savings and loan accounts of a worker, for example, as well as the financial assets of a millionaire. When qualified account balances are not changed, comprehensive income is equal to consumption. A single-family unit would have to keep a number of qualified accounts. The concept works out rather well when one works through organized institutions such as stockbrokers and bankers. This administrative approach is not so readily available when the savings are in the form of ownership of real estate or a family business. To avoid this basic difficulty in taking account of wealth changes, the proposal permits purchase and sale of assets without passing through a qualified account. When this is done, capital gains would be tax-free and capital losses would not decrease tax liability.

Because, for all practical purposes, the consumption-expenditure or cash-flow approach exempts wealth changes, the reform is subject to ability-to-pay type of criticism. The holders of substantial investments at the time the reform is initiated who keep all earnings in qualified accounts and sell assets to support expenditures would be basically enjoying a tax-free level of consumption.

*Kaldor's Approach*

The Advisory Commission on Intergovernmental Relations (ACIR), in its 1974 study of an expenditure or consumption tax, utilized the analyses developed by Nicholas Kaldor in 1955.[26] The tax has not been adopted, except for a period and then only partially in India. This is explained by administrative difficulties foreseen and the injustice apparent when large emergency expenditures are required and the rates of the expenditure tax are progressive. To avoid these basic difficulties, it has been suggested that the tax be limited to the very high-income and wealthy taxpayers.[27]

A broad expenditure tax along the Kaldor lines can avoid requiring a tax return listing all expenditures only if the taxpayer each year reports the value of all assets owned less indebtedness.[28] The value of the capital account can decrease, of course, because of undesirable market conditions as well as expenditures in excess of earning, but the ET provisions would have to assume that any decrease in the value of an asset was caused by expenditures in excess of income. Of course, this assumption would not be workable. Therefore, elaborate and loophole-prone procedures would have to be introduced.

## Negative Income Tax

The negative income tax is not, strictly speaking, an expenditure tax. Rather it is a procedure for using the personal-income-tax system to make payments as well as to collect taxes. If the procedure were introduced without at the same time cutting other transfer and welfare expenditures by an amount equal to the NIT payments, the federal budgetary position would deteriorate.

The rational for the negative income tax, that is, transfer by taxation, rather than the public-welfare approach, is basically that the coverage is much broader and in-kind payments, (that is, school lunch programs) are eliminated. The negative income tax finds its basic operational justice in that income is taken from individuals with incomes above a certain size, therefore why should payments not be made to those who are poor to bring their incomes up toward the poverty level or up close to the point where income tax liability starts?

The negative income tax goes one step further than the personal income tax in making the income tax a procedure to reduce economic inequality. The ability-to-pay fundamental justification of personal income taxes with progressive rates is also, in a sense, a justification for transfer by taxation of funds to those living below the level at which personal income taxes take hold. A symmetrical approach is viewed with favor by those who advocate the negative income tax.

A negative income tax might provide for a minimum family income of, say, $6,000. The income earned or received from investments up to this level would be free of the personal income tax, and income above would be subject to a 50 percent tax. A large portion of the collections from the relatively high personal income tax rate would go to the financing of transfer payments to bring all family incomes closer to the $6,000 level. The negative tax rate at the 50 percent level would provide for a transfer payment of 50 percent of the difference between income received and the minimum income required to reach the poverty level.[29] It is assumed under the NIT approach, also in the granting of personal exemptions in the regular personal income tax, that the cost of providing the basic necessities of life should not form a portion of the tax base. The NIT concept goes further than the personal exemption idea; NIT provides financing for making grants in some proportion of the income shortage to the family unable to reach the poverty level, that is, unable to achieve a "clear income."

A personal income tax system with rates that do not stop with zero has gone a long way toward removing the stigma of being subsidized when supplements are received to maintain a family's required consumption level. A number of economists in Canada, the United States, and the United Kingdom have advocated "social dividend taxation." Just as the negative income tax exceeds the commitment of personal deductions, so "social dividend taxation" goes beyond the negative income tax and guarantees a minimum income to all financed out of the income tax. The essence of negative income taxation is to fill only a portion of the poverty income gap. A 50 percent flat NIT rate is the usual percentage decided on.

An advantage of the negative income tax seldom mentioned is related to the reduction of positive income tax rates currently taking place. The negative income tax would permit the poor nonincome taxpayers to benefit from the tax-reduction action. This would happen if provision were made to increase the negative tax rates, that is, an income supplement, as the positive tax rates were being reduced.[30]

## Conclusion

This discussion is limited to basic tax reforms other than VAT. None of them have become a portion of the federal or state tax codes. Two of the new approaches are somewhat similar to VAT in that they encourage investment spending. The negative income tax, on the other hand, encourages consumption. This sharp difference of aims has made the tax code continuously more complicated as tax reform after tax reform stimulates amendments to the basic individual and corporate income taxes.

The shortcomings of a nearly complete reliance on income defined in some complicated and often irrational way becomes more obvious as the need for tax revenues increases. A reform more fundamental than treating some income sources differently is needed. Patchwork reform by exempting this and taxing that makes matters worse.[31]

## Relation of Price Adjustment to Type of Tax

Consideration of the price, investment, savings, and consumption impacts of taxes is evidenced in the discussion of tax incidence and shifting. The literature of economics includes these analyses in price theory and what has come to be known as fiscal theory. (The use of the term *fiscal policy* to refer to budget deficits and surpluses is considered to be monetary-type fiscal effects. Consideration of the difference in the impacts of taxes and public expenditures of an equal quantitative total is fiscal policy with monetary considerations removed.) In most cases, the relationships described are not fully supported by economic data arising from current conditions. The analyses rest largely on logic and some theories as to the way in which prices of goods sold and payments to the factors (land, labor, and capital) are determined.

## Tax Payment

The payment of taxes is the transfer of income or savings (capital) from individual and business control to government control. Although the funds, if left under the control of individuals and businesses, would have been used in some manner and the funds placed under the control of government through the payment of taxes will also be used, and more than likely in some different manner, it is generally agreed that consideration of the incidence (economic burden) of taxation is best carried out if expenditure considerations are excluded.

Incidence is decided through the process of tax *shifting*, that is, ability or lack of ability of the taxpayers to recover taxes paid. Shifting is the process of distributing the economic burden of the original *impact* of the tax payment.

Neither incidence nor shifting is properly understood if they are considered to be simple concepts. The economic impact of taxes (incidence) and the placing of this incidence (shifting) take place through changes in the way in which the myriad parts of the economic system interact.

## Tax Wedge

When the personal income tax is used, people working and owning resources have the income from these activities reduced after they receive the money or in the payment process. The income effect of property and wealth taxes generally, and also of corporate income taxes, is to reduce what is received by those owning or having claims against property. The income tax is a wedge between contracted income and income enjoyed. Sales taxes of all kinds drive a wedge between the price that is paid and the income received by the factors of production. Under both income and sales taxes, the economic power enjoyed by the people who made and sold the good or service is less than the total price at which the product or the personal services were sold. The reduction is the amount of the tax collected—the tax wedge.

Our national-income accounts are worked out in such a fashion that the aggregate of sales taxes or the indirect tax wedge is very clear. These accounts are less satisfactory in pointing out the wedge which the income tax drives between contract income and income enjoyed.

## National-Income Accounts

Gross national product is the aggregate of the market prices of all goods sold and purchased by government, individuals, and organizations during the data-gathering period. National income is the return to all the factors of production used in producing the goods (before direct taxes). National income is less than GNP, largely by the depreciation allowances taken by business firms and the sales (indirect) taxes collected by governments. Sometimes the similarity of the economic effect of sales taxes and income taxes is shown by setting up a period sequence table such as table 2-1.

## Tax Payments and Economic Power

This may be the place to relax for a moment the prohibition against consideration of government expenditures. In the period I situation of table 2-1, the wedge concept referred to previously could also be considered a tie-in purchase. The tie-in purchase was the package of government services which the government made available by spending the income it diverted to its use through the collection of indirect taxes. In period II, when the income tax is used, the payment for the package of goods provided by the government is not associated with private goods purchased. The financing takes place by reducing the income available to spend below the income bargained for. The quantity of private goods and services that can be purchased or enjoyed is reduced. Both indirect and direct taxes reduce purchases from the private sector. They follow a different procedure, but the effect is basically the same.

**Table 2-1**
**Income Effect of Excise and Income Taxes**

|                                  | Period I | Period II |
|----------------------------------|----------|-----------|
| GNP                              | 1,000    | 1,000     |
| Sales tax collections            | 200      | 0         |
| National income plus depreciation | 800     | 1,000     |
| Income tax collections           | 0        | 200       |
| Disposable income                | 800      | 800       |

To the businessman, the important difference between the two tax approaches (direct and indirect, or income and sales) used by governments to dip their fingers into the production of the private sector is that indirect taxes, by avoiding double taxation of savings (that is, once when the portion of income saved is received and again when earnings from these savings are received), stimulates savings and investment. Direct taxes, particularly when the rates are progressive, reduce savings and increase the before-tax investment return required by those able to finance investment.

## Tax Burdens and Economic Decisions

The use of the income tax does not exclude from the tax base the income that might be used for investment. Instead, this tax is apt to reduce the income destined for investment more sharply than gross receipts taxes or excise taxes.[32] It does this through application of higher rates on the income of the large-income receivers. These are the income receivers using a large portion of income received for investment spending. An additional impact is the manner in which the income tax affects the type and location of the investments. Losses arising from tax-induced investment decisions cannot be estimated with a useful degree of accuracy. Perhaps there is an efficiency loss of 5 percent, or about $20 billion in 1980.

If beer is taxed and wine is not, the price of beer becomes relatively higher than that of wine. This means that less beer will be purchased than would be the case if beer had remained untaxed. As a result, the resources going into beer decrease. If we assume for the moment that wine is a close substitute for beer, the resources going into wine increase. When this takes place, the prices of some of the resources used to produce wine will increase. The price of beer, before tax, is lowered somewhat, and the price of wine is raised a bit. This jockeying back and forth of prices and costs take place until a new equilibrium has worked itself out between the wine industry and the beer industry.

The price of beer before taxes becomes somewhat lower than previously, and the price of wine is up a bit. If the components as well as the final products were taxed as under a turnover or value-added tax, the productive process itself would be affected, including the relative use of labor and machines. The final impact on price under these circumstances becomes most uncertain, and the obvious is no longer acceptable.

Spending habits affect the location of the economic burden of sumptuary taxes and the sources of income in relation to income tax rates. A person living in the Unites States who enjoys hiking and not driving a car and does not smoke or drink alcoholic beverages has had her or his relative welfare increased in the postwar period. The person who concentrates spending on these items has had his or her relative welfare worsened.

The tax system has worked to decrease the relative economic well-being of the salary earner. This was caused by inflation and progressive income tax rates. Also, higher payroll tax rates and a higher taxable wage base have acted to decrease real take-home wages. On the other hand, the farmer who produces a portion of what he consumes and does his saving through the rising value of his land and investment aimed at increasing the productivity of the farm has improved his relative economic position—at least as it is affected by taxes.[33] The renter of housing, by not benefiting from rising real estate values and deductibility of housing costs, including property taxes, has also experienced a deteriorating economic position.

Tax payments reduce willingness to invest and take risks. Through the collection of taxes at various spots in the economic process the government can grasp the transaction, wealth, or income handle. These decisions affect the attractiveness of consumption and willingness to work, invest, and save.[34] The failure of monetary-influenced economists to consider the difference in the impact of raising the same quantity of funds through use of different taxes has retarded the development of fiscal policy.

In the past, the businessman as well as the ordinary citizen has tended to become impatient with the uncertainty of tax incidence. He has found the complicated ways in which incidence analysis has been carried out as just too much, and he has frequently taken the easy way out. Typically the businessman has become a believer in a crude form of the *diffusion theory* of taxation.[35] The diffusion theory, as usually understood, teaches that it does not make any difference where taxes are collected, because the incidences become diffused throughout the economy in the same manner. The public frequently gives up on the question of incidence and concludes that incidence is just where the name of the tax says it is, that is, an income tax rests on income and a sales tax on prices. Neither approach is useful if the community wishes to play a role in seeing that tax policy permits the private-enterprise system to exercise its full potential.

The ordinary citizen is now becoming aware that ability-to-pay taxation is not provided by the income tax. At the same time, he has not been able to decide on a complete or even a partial replacement.

## Incidence of the Corporate Income Tax

The corporation income tax (CIT), a major tax paid by business to the federal government, is also used by some forty-two of the fifty states. The collections of this tax at the federal level amount to 4 percent of GNP. At the state level, collections are about 0.5 percent of GNP. During the past ten years, the federal CIT collections as a percentage of GNP have declined by 12 percent, and state collections have increased by about 100 percent.[36]

In considering the incidence of this tax, the major point of emphasis is what the tax has done to profits as a percentage of national income, as a rate of return on investment, or as a percentage of business sales. Recently considerable attention also has been given to the effect of corporate income taxes on prices. The data support the general conclusion that when the rate of return on capital is used as the basis for the analysis, the corporate income tax does not reduce profits because the historic rate of return on equity has not fallen as corporate profits taxes have increased, but neither have after-tax profits generally increased enough to keep abreast with the rate of inflation.

*Profit Trends*

When profits are considered as a portion of national income and sales, the data demonstrate them to be a decreasing portion of the total. One must conclude from these data that profits have been decreased by the increased rates of the corporate profits tax.[37] This decline also demonstrates that profits have not been able to keep up with the inflation rate as reflected in the national income data.

Economic theory has always differed considerably relative to the incidence and therefore the shifting of the CIT that take place in the long run. A fundamental reason for the uncertainty has been the difference of opinion as to how the CIT has affected the quantity of capital in the long run, that is, the existing quantity of investment. Economists have differed much less on the incidence of the CIT in the short run, because the short run has been defined to mean the quantity of capital does not change. The effect on the level of business investment in the long run of a tax on profits is quite another matter.[38]

*Price Setting and Profit Maximization*

Traditional marginal economic analysis teaches that if firms are maximizing their profits before a tax measured by corporate profits is imposed or are attempting to do so, the new tax gives them no reason to change their prices. The price and output that will yield maximum profits before the tax is levied or removed will yield maximum profits after the tax situation is changed. Any change in prices by a firm operating at its optimum level will reduce profits before taxes and will leave it with smaller after-tax profits than it would earn at the old price.

Certain qualifications of the incidence conclusion of this type of analysis have usually been conceded. One is that the self-restrained monopolist or oligopolist will find in the tax increase an excuse for exercising full market power and might raise prices when the tax is increased.

For one to believe that in the short run the corporate income tax is shifted to prices so the incidence does not fall on profits, one must believe that pricing in the U.S. economy is dominated in the short run by the decisions of restrained oligopolists or by the view that price theory and its emphasis on profit maximization are irrelevant to the understanding of price behavior in the market.

*Conclusion*

It is recognized that the one who pays taxes may not ultimately bear the economic burden of the tax. This is also true of prices. The uniformity of treatment under tax legislation or a wide distribution of a cost change increases the likelihood of the shift being reflected in prices. In general, prices can rise with higher taxes only if monetary supplies are expanded. Taxes on a portion of the economy can cause relative prices to change. More than likely, in the short run, higher indirect taxes will cause a greater price increase than direct taxes. In the long run, higher direct taxes will cause a greater price increase than indirect taxes. In addition, indirect taxes enjoy important administrative and international usage advantages.

**Use of the Corporate Income Tax**

The corporate income tax finds its support in classical economics that treats profits as surplus arising largely from monopoly control rather than the legitimate return to those providing equity capital. [To call the tax an income tax is misleading. A better choice would be corporate profits tax. The use of the word *income* gives the incorrect impression that the base being taxed is the same as that used in the individual (personal) income tax.] This attitute legitimizes a high tax rate on profits and even double taxation, once at the level of the firm and again at the stockholder level if distributed as dividends.

Efforts of businesses to avoid the full impact of the CIT have resulted in government counteractions. The end result is very complicated legislation and regulations. Such a wealth of special deals and pitfalls have been created that the oracles of the Internal Revenue Code must be consulted at each business decision and personal investment choice.[39]

The selection of the particular accounting concept as the base to which a high tax rate is applied has resulted in continued pleas to Congress for places to locate earnings so that they will not be counted in taxable income. The high CIT rates make efforts to reduce taxable corporate profits eminently worthwhile. Possible savings justify allocation of the very best corporate brain power to this activity.[40]

*Countercyclical Impacts*

In 1968, CIT accounted for about one-half the revenues of the individual income tax. The sharp reduction of profits in 1970, plus some impacts of the tax legislation of 1969, pushed CIT collections in 1970 and 1971 down to about one-third of individual income tax collections, where they continued to be in 1979 and are expected to decline to 31 percent in 1980.[41]

At the very time when a downturn in the economy points to more active government spending as appropriate economic policy to absorb idle capacity, CIT collections decline sharply, causing an expanding deficit. The growing deficit makes expansion of government spending more difficult.

At the 1973-1975 juncture in our fiscal life, the old "new economics" was revived. The cyclically balanced-budget idea of the 1930s was renewed under the name *full-employment balanced budget*. The full-employment balanced budget was introduced to make the $23 billion back-to-back budget deficits of fiscal years (FY) 1971-1973 politically acceptable. The policy generated a huge $66 billion federal deficit in 1976. We know now with a federal debt of over $870 billion that the full-employment balanced budget was a disastrous gimmick.

*Tax Burden on Income and Profits*

The individual income tax and the CIT provide about 85 percent of total federal tax revenues (excluding the social security payroll tax). (See tables 2-2 and 2-3.) The very heavy concentration on taxes based on income and profits means that very little use is made of other tax bases. The federal government does not use a wealth tax as state and local governments do in

**Table 2-2**
**Taxes on Corporate Income as a Percentage of Total Revenue of Central Government**

|               | 1968  | 1971  | 1972  | 1977 |
|---------------|-------|-------|-------|------|
| Canada        | 12.81 | 10.36 | 10.85 | 15.2 |
| France        | 4.62  | 5.90  | 5.94  | 6.1  |
| Germany       | 6.90  | 4.46  | 4.67  | 4.5  |
| Japan         | 18.97 | 18.78 | 18.24 | —    |
| Sweden        | 4.95  | 3.63  | 3.94  | 2.4  |
| United States | 13.73 | 10.37 | 11.19 | 14.8 |

Source: International Monetary Fund, *Government Finance Statistics Yearbook* (Washington, D.C., 1979), p. 15.

**Table 2-3**

**Taxes on Income and Profits as a Percentage of Total Revenue of Central Government**

|  | *1974* | *1976* | *1977* |
|---|---|---|---|
| Canada | 54.0 | 54.5 | 52.0 |
| France | 19.4 | 18.2 | 18.6 |
| Germany | 21.2 | 19.6 | 21.2 |
| Japan | — | — | — |
| Sweden | 20.8 | 24.6 | 22.9 |
| United States | 56.5 | 55.6 | 56.9 |

Source: International Monetary Fund, *Government Statistics Yearbook* (Washington, D.C., 1979), p. 24.

their application of the property tax. Neither does the federal government employ a general transaction or production tax.

The federal tax approach is appropriate if the aim is to tax only what one puts into the economy. It neglects the taxation of what a citizen withdraws from the economy. This approach is popularized Keynes. Consumption is stimulated and savings are discouraged. Corporate profits and personal income were the taxes that corresponded most closely with the 1913 concept of ability to pay. In addition, these taxes, while meeting the huge costs of a major war, did not fall on consumer purchasing power.

In the United States, the Depression developed a deep popular resentment of the control of the economic process by business firms. This attitude was exceptionally strong in the United States because the Depression was more severe and longer here than in Western Europe. What we did was develop the world's harshest corporate profits and capital-gains tax. This antibusiness investment-and-savings revenue system persevered through World War II and all the cold and hot wars since. (Also, the collections from CIT increase so rapidly as prosperity is approached that full prosperity is not reached. The shortfall of the economic expansion arises from the combined effects of the draining off of savings through CIT payments and the high earnings level required for new investments when the real CIT rates are high.)

The growth of the labor union movement and the conservation and consumerism legislation have changed the production environment from that existing in the 1930s. Also, the terrible citizen disappointment over business's failure to continue to provide two chickens in every pot when it was calling the tune in the 1920s is now forgotten. Today it is the promises of government that are going unfulfilled and causing citizen disappointment. These changes have not been fully recognized in tax legislation. As they are felt, the U.S. love affair with CIT and the graduated income tax can be expected to cool.

### Need for Savings

Excess savings may again become a problem, but this is not the current expectation. The rebuilding of many cities and the investment needs for preservation of the environment and urban transportation are a few among the many expected savings absorbers.[42] This year, and down the road as many next years as can be seen, it looks as if all the potential savings will be needed that can be generated in a society bombarded continuously by consumption appeals and enjoying continued improvement in its protection from loss of income and poverty through sickness or old age. One development decreases the ability to save, and the other decreases the need to save, a one-two punch that could quite effectively keep savings in short supply.

Another shortcoming of CIT is arising from the favors it gives to business debt financing relative to the use of equity. The individual income tax is applied to corporate profits distributed as dividends at the same rate as corporate payments of interest. Often these same dividends, as corporate profits, already have been taxed at the high CIT tax rate of 46 percent. Interest payments, on the other hand, are deductible from corporate profits before the CIT rate is applied. The effect is to encourage financing with debt capital and to discourage the use of equity capital. As a result, businesses must maintain stable cash flows, a situation unsuited to aggressive entrepreneurship and an economy possessing substantial discretionary purchasing power that shifts rather quickly between various offered products and services.

### Integration of CIT

In order to raise the high revenues needed while the profit and income base is used nearly exclusively, the U.S. corporate income tax cannot be integrated with the individual income tax, that is, treated as withheld individual income taxes on dividends.[43] It is also true that the U.S. approach requires a hard-nosed definition of capital gains and the application of relatively high rates. Capital gains are not taxed in Germany. Capital gains as a tax base have been declining in Western industrial nations. This same very heavy U.S. reliance on taxes using profits and income as the base has prevented income tax indexing and generous tax allowances to businesses which invest in identified desirable areas, for example, in pollution-control facilities and in high-unemployment areas.

Finally, the U.S love affair with CIT makes it very difficult to encourage the return to the United States of foreign-earned profits of U.S. corporations. In order to protect its tax base, the Treasury exerts pressures from one administration to the next to make certain these profits are taxed by at least as high a rate as domestic profits. Usually this requires the payment of substantial profit taxes when earnings are returned home. The homecoming welcome is not exactly encouraging.[44]

Tables 2-2 and 2-3 present some summary data of the relative intensity of the use of CIT and income and profit taxes by the United States. In France, Germany, and Sweden, CIT provides less than one-third of the percentage of total taxes that comes from this source in the United States. In Canada and Japan, the role of the CIT is comparable with that existing in the United States. All income and profit taxes provide over 50 percent of all federal government revenue in the United States. In Western Europe, the percentage is less than half this high.

The high domestic tax rates that provide these relatively large CIT and income and profit tax collections in the United States encourage investment abroad of U.S.-sourced savings and the retention abroad of earning from foreign operations. The effect is a reduced multiplier impact from the investment of U.S. savings and greater difficulties in keeping a high level of employment and a strong U.S. balance of international payments.

## Modern Role for CIT

The fact that CIT is proving to have serious shortcomings does not require that it be abandoned. One commentator very familiar with U.S. business practices envisages the value-added tax (VAT) collections becoming sufficient to reduce the U.S. CIT rate to around 35 percent.[45]

The British study of VAT, completed by their National Economic Development Office in 1969, does not envisage elimination of CIT. After going over the pros and cons of VAT replacing CIT, the report concludes: "Whatever the balance of this debate, in practical terms it seems likely that only a very small cut in corporation tax (or perhaps only the avoidance of some small future increase) would be possible in the immediate future."[46]

## CIT and Foreign Trade

Occasionally, U.S. observers have recommended that GATT treat the CIT as it does VAT relative to internationally traded goods. If this were done, the U.S. position would be strengthened, but would remain inferior. Even if CIT marginal rates were equal in all industrial nations and CIT, relative to internationally traded goods, were treated like VAT, U.S. producers would benefit less than their competitors. The reason is that studies show European exporters are the high-profit industries of Europe and Japan while U.S. exporters tend to be low-profit firms. Of course, the tax refund of CIT as a portion of export price would, under these conditions, be greater for European and Japanese exporters than for people in the United States.

United States exports tend to be made by U.S. firms that find the domestic market to be unsatisfactory and from agricultural sources that have not been large payers of CIT. Also, U.S. exporters tend not to be firms largely established to exploit foreign opportunities. On the other hand, the small domestic markets of European nations force even the most efficient firms producing a basic commodity to consider exports as an important portion of operations. The less efficient European firm is the one forced to stay in its local market. Even without these considerations, the proposal to treat CIT like VAT is not really practical because the calculation of the profit rate applicable to a particular export or import is very nearly an impossible task.

*Conclusion*

The CIT was developed in the United States as a method of taxing businesses on the basis of ability to pay. However, as the tax has evolved and as market control by large firms has increased and savings shortages have developed, CIT has lost many of its attributed original strengths. In addition, the need for international tax harmonization, more jobs and economic growth, and, of course, very large tax revenues all point to the use of a major VAT by the United States and reduced use of the CIT.[47]

**Notes**

1. Roy G. Blakey and Gladys C. Blakey, *The Federal Income Tax* (New York: Longmans, Green, 1940), p. 1.

2. Richard Goode, *The Individual Income Tax* (Washington: Brookings Institution, 1965), p. 2.

3. Nicholas Kaldor, *An Expenditure Tax*, 4th ed. (London: George Allen and Unwin, 1965), p. 24.

4. Gunner Myrdal, *The Political Element in the Development of Economic Theory* (London: Routlege and Kegan, 1953), p. 185; George M. Von Furstenberg, "Individual Income Taxation and Inflation," *National Tax Journal* 28, no. 1 (March 1975):117-125. The real estate, agriculture, and minimum-tax loopholes have turned out to be substantial and very dif-

ficult to close. In 1975 proposed legislation by the Ways and Means Committee aimed at limitation of artificial losses (LAL) to close down tax shelters largely failed. *Taxation with Representation Newsletter* 4, no. 8 (1975):4.

5. Kaldor, *An Expenditure Tax*, p. 171.

6. Michael Taussig at M.I.T. ["Economic Aspects of the Personal Income Tax Treatment of Charitable Contributions," *National Tax Journal* 20, no. 1 (March 1967):1-19] is trying to isolate "the net effect of the taxpayer's marginal tax rate on the amount of charitable giving." He has not found the answer yet, but he is not working alone in this field. It has become a favorite research area for public-finance economists of privately supported education institutions. For example, see Martin Feldstein, "The Income Tax and Charitable Contributions: Part II—The Impact on Religious, Educational and Other Organizations," *National Tax Journal* 28, no. 2 (June 1975):209-226. Feldstein concludes that deductibility from taxable income is more important to educational than to religious organizations.

7. Impacts as theorized and observed in the EC are given in considerable detail in *Tax Policy and Investment in the European Community* (Brussels: Commission of the European Community 1975).

8. Senator Russell B. Long, "Tax Simplification," *Proceedings of 58th Annual Conference of the National Tax Association* (Harrisburg, Pa.: National Tax Association, 1965):637-643. Also see Benjamin A. Okner, "Effective Individual Income Tax Rates," *National Tax Journal* 32, no. 3 (September 1979):368-378.

9. Malcolm Gammie and Carole Lucas, "Income Tax: Some International Comparisons," *British Tax Review*, no. 5 (1979):274-293.

10. When Gunnar Myrdal briefly considers taxable income in his chapter "The Theory of Public Finance," *Political Element in the Development of Economic Theory* (London: Routledge & Kegan, 1953), he says: "The word means what we want it to mean. By changing the definition of taxable income, we can always change the concrete political meaning of the principles which lay down rules about the relation of income and tax."

11. *Ibid.*, p. 163

12. See Internal Revenue Service (IRS), *Statistics of Income, 1976: Individual Income Tax Returns* US GPO (1979), p. 9, for details.

13. Richard Goode, *The Individual Income Tax* (Washington: Brookings Institution, 1964), 326.

14. In 1973 the below $15,000 Adjusted Gross Income taxable-income groups contributed 34.1 percent of income tax collections after credits (IRS, *Statistics of Income, 1973*, p. 6). Also see the discussion in George F. Break and Joseph A. Pechman *Federal Tax Reform* (Washington: Brookings Institution, 1975), pp. 36-41.

15. Herman P. Miller, *Rich Man, Poor Man* (New York: Thomas Y. Crowell, 1964), p. 82.

16. For example, distribution of income among members of the family to avoid high rates, exclusion of income of closely held corporations to avoid individual income tax, and exclusion of inheritances from taxable income.

17. Goode, *Individual Income Tax*, p. 326, and Joseph A. Pechman and Benjamin A. Okner, *Who Bears the Tax Burden?* (Washington: Brookings Institution, 1974), p. 45.

18. It is becoming more acceptable to consider net resources as "a measure that quite accurately indicates a person's ability-to-pay." Harold M. Somers, *The Sales Tax* (Sacramento: California Assembly, 1964), p. 41.

19. Nicholas Kaldor, *An Expenditure Tax*, (London: Unwin University Books, 1955), p. 45.

20. Paul H. Mueller, "Concepts of Taxable Income," *Political Science Quarterly* 53 (1938):83-110, 557-583.

21. I. Fisher, "Income in Theory and Income Taxation in Practice," *Econometrica*, January 1937, p. 1.

22. E.R.A. Seligman, "Are Stock Dividends Income?" in *Studies in Public Finance* (New York: Macmillan Co., 1925), pp. 98-123. The analysis originated as a statement relative to the famous basic Supreme Court case of *Eisner v. Macomber*, 252 U.S. 298 (1919). The position stated was accepted by the Court.

23. Jerome R. Hallerstein, *Taxes, Loopholes and Morals* (New York: McGraw-Hill, 1963), pp. 125-129.

24. A. Blinder, "Can Income Tax Increases Be Inflationary? An Expository Note," *National Tax Journal* 26, no. 2 (June 1973):295-301

25. U.S. Department of the Treasury, *Blueprints for Basic Tax Reform* (Washington: GPO, 1977), pp. 113-144.

26. Advisory Commission on Intergovernmental Relations, *The Expenditure Tax* (Washington: GPO, 1974), pp. 34-47.

27. Richard E. Slitor, "Administrative Aspects of Expenditures Taxation," in *Broad-Based Taxes—New Options and Sources*, ed. Richard A. Musgrave (Baltimore, Md.: Johns Hopkins Press, 1973), pp. 227-263.

28. Nicholas Kaldor, *An Expenditure Tax* (London: Unwin University Books, 1955), pp. 22-53.

29. Christopher Green, *Negative Taxes and the Poverty Problem* (Washington: Brookings Institution, 1967), pp. 52-61.

30. David Hsieh, *Fiscal Measures for Poverty Alleviation in the United States* (Geneva, Switzerland: International Labour Office, 1979), pp. 135-148.

31. A.F. Ehrbar, "Manifesto for a Tax Revolution," *Fortune*, April 1977, pp. 90-114; Meade Committee, *The Structure and Reform of Direct Taxation* (London: Allen and Unwin, 1978).

32. Armco Steel Corp., in a letter from William Verity, President, to

the House Ways and Means Committee, pointed out a proposed 10 percent CIT increase would force them to raise prices substantially or sharply cut back on the investment program. *Wall Street Journal*, August 25, 1967, p. 2.

33. Efforts to determine tax incidence in the United States during the 1951-1964 period are most closely associated with the name R.A. Musgrave. For example, see R.A. Musgrave, "Estimating the Distribution of the Tax Burden," in *Income and Wealth Series 10*, eds. Colin Clark and Geer Stuvel (London: Bowes and Bowes, 1962), pp. 186-219.

34. M. Chatter, "A Note on Progressive Taxes and the Supply of Labour," *Journal of Public Economics* 12, no. 2 (October 1979):215-220.

35. Robin Barlow, Harvey E. Brazer, and James N. Morgan, in *Economic Behavior of the Affluent* (Washington: Brookings Institution, 1968), seem to conclude these impacts are not very important.

36. *Economic Report of the President, 1976* and *Advisory Commission on Intergovernmental Relations, Federal-State-Local Finances: Significant Features of Fiscal Federalism* (Washington: GPO, 1974).

37. Joint Economic Committee *The Federal Tax System: Facts and Problems, 1964* (Washington: GPO, 1964), p. 48.

38. Marian Krzyzaniak and Richard A. Musgrave, *The Shifting of the Corporation Tax—An Empirical Study of Its Short-run Effect on the Rate of Return* (Baltimore, Md.: Johns Hopkins Press, 1963).

39. *Income Tax Regulations, "Final" and "Proposed" under Internal Revenue Code* (Chicago: Commerce Clearing House), annual editions, four volumes.

40. *Tax Reform* (Administration and Public Witnesses), Public hearings before the Committee on Ways and Means, 94th Cong., 1st Sess., five parts, July, 8-31, 1975.

41.

| Fiscal Year | Federal Corporate Profits Taxes (billions of dollars) |
|---|---|
| 1967 | 34.0 |
| 1968 | 28.7 |
| 1969 | 36.7 |
| 1970 | 33.3 |
| 1971 | 26.8 |
| 1972 | 32.2 |
| 1973 | 26.1 |
| 1974 | 38.6 |
| 1975 | 40.6 |
| 1976 | 41.4 |
| 1977 | 54.9 |
| 1978 | 60.0 |
| 1979 | 70.0 |
| 1980* | 71.0 |

*Estimated

42. The brief U.S. experience with the undistributed corporate profits tax indicated it could be used to reduce corporate savings. George Lent, *The Impact of the Redistribution of Profits Tax* (New York: Columbia University Press, 1948), p. 195.

43. George F. Break and Joseph A. Peck, in *Federal Tax Reform* (Washington: Brookings Institution, 1975), have spent much of their space recommending integration of corporate profit taxes (pp. 44-104). Two other approaches for the treatment of corporate profits not paid out as dividends are often mentioned. One associated with Henry Simons, *Personal Income Tax* (Chicago: University of Chicago Press, 1938), would tax corporate capital gains as though it were regular income. The other is associated with William Vickrey, *Agenda for Progressive Taxation* (New York: Ronald Press, 1947), pp. 156-161. He advocates an annual income tax on deemed interest on accumulated corporate earnings.

44. An analysis made by the Treasury and reported in 1962 was concerned with the outflow of capital. The Treasury analysis fails to determine the quantity of net-capital export which the U.S. overall international and domestic economic position permits. Some mention is made of the stimulation of the domestic economy of switching investments made abroad to the United States, but the case is not developed much beyond the statement that "A dollar invested in this country in new plant and equipment is normally thought to create a continuing stream of 40 cents worth of current output, if demand keeps up with capacity." The data presented supported a figure of 10 cents for each dollar of capital investment abroad (*Revenue Act of 1962, Hearings of Senate Finance Committee*, pt. I, p. 192). Large outflows of capital from the United States in mid-1974 were undoubtedly reflected in the weakness of the U.S. economy. Despite U.S. savings shortages, U.S. capital continued to be reinvested abroad, from 1975 to 1980, in excess of capital imports.

45. Organization for Economic Cooperation and Development, *Company Tax Systems in OECD Countries* (Paris: OECD Publications, 1973). H.R. 7015 reduces the maximum rate to 36 percent.

46. National Economic Development Office, *VAT* (London: Her Majesty's Stationery Office, 1969), p. 57.

47. Richard W. Lindholm, "Value Added Tax vs. Corporate Income Tax," *Business Economics* 5 (January 1970):62-65.

# 3 Tax Payments and Economic Decisions

## Overview

A major change in the direction of the U.S. approach to taxation is certain to be a slow process. It is, however, a requirement if the U.S. tax system is to meet evolving international and domestic needs.

General rebatable excise (GRE) Taxes under the General Agreement on Tariffs and Trade (GATT), rather than taxes on income, wealth, and property (IWP), have found favor under today's high total tax collections, supply shortages, and sharp international competition (see the second section). The support for GRE taxes rests on belief that they stimulate savings and investments while improving international competitiveness, the rate of economic growth, and employment opportunities. By far the leading expanding GRE tax is VAT.

Support for GRE taxes is always modified by the political need for a tax system that meets the voters's test of being equitable. The new tax development supports the concept that taxes which reduce economic growth also reduce the possibility of justice based on a rising standard of living for all. Under the GRE approach, the poor have their living standards directly improved through tax-financed expenditures aimed at increasing productivity and financing social expenditures, and not through the use of progressive taxes to redistribute income and manmade wealth. Data available do not show that nations emphasizing GRE taxes have higher prices than nations with IWP taxes; but when military expenditures are excluded, they are somewhat bigger spenders.

In the third section, H.R.7015, the Tax Restructuring Act of 1980, is applied in a very general way to give an idea of the shape in which it might be enacted and the revenues to be expected. Payroll, individual income, and corporate income taxes could be reduced 24, 12, and 49 percent, respectively. This reduction of major taxes would stimulate employment and investment and increase the strength of the U.S. international economy and permit the reduction of poverty.

In the fourth section, we consider the characteristics of a retail sales tax (RST) and a VAT. The discussion is limited to an analysis of the administrative and economic qualities of RST and VAT if used as substantial national taxes. A major strength of VAT is that it sharply reduces the tax-collection pressures placed on the retailer. A 10 percent retail sales tax makes purchase at "wholesale" worthwhile. Under VAT, on the other hand, failure to purchase retail saves the buyer only the tax on the retail-mark up portion of the price. In most instances, this would be in the 2 to 4 percent tax-rate range.

By including fixtures, some raw materials, and fuel in its base, RST causes taxes on these items to become a portion of the final tax base. A subtractive VAT, by providing for the deduction of VAT paid from VAT due on sales, avoids this tax-on-tax situation. The additive VAT as used in Michigan also avoids this basic weakness. The RST is applied only at the final end use sale, while the VAT is paid along the production and marketing process. As a result, the exemption of RST does not stimulate export development. By being zero-rated on exports, as is true in Europe and recommended in both H.R. 7015 and 5665, VAT provides a refund of all the VAT paid as the goods move toward export. This is a very useful plus of VAT over RST and, of course, also over income and payroll taxes which under GATT understandings may not be refunded without being considered a subsidy, making the refund unacceptable.

The brief discussion included in the fifth section emphasizes that the price paid must cover costs of investment and government that are not directly a portion of the labor and materials included in the product or service. If investment is substantial and government services are first-class, the price of marketable goods and services will be relatively high until the investment and government spending pay off in reduced labor and materials costs.

In the sixth section, we spend a little more time considering regressivity that was previously defined for tax purposes. The RST is considered income-regressive because those having incomes not subject to RST, because they save some of their income, are generally recipients of higher incomes. The VAT is levied on all production including capital goods, because capital goods are purchased with savings. The VAT is not income-regressive in the sense that the RST is.

In the seventh section, we take another look at tax incidence and prices and along the way at the conditions appropriate for the introduction of a major national VAT. *A country is demonstrating a need for VAT if the electorate is desirous of a level of government plus income and payroll tax reductions that make large and continuous government deficits unavoidable.*

There is no need to fear that VAT will cause additional inflation if it is introduced. The belief is unfounded that because VAT is levied on prices it is more inflationary than a tax on income. In none of the Western European countries which introduced VAT has the inflation rate become a worse problem than before. In fact, available evidence points to VAT as the "cause of a reduction of the inflation rates." Stable revenues of government and reduced deficits reduce inflationary pressures. Also one must not forget that VAT could be shifted backward in reduced land prices, rents, and so on, rather than be shifted forward in higher prices. Apparently something along this line took place in Europe.

In the eighth section, we look at our national-income accounts (NIAs) and the manner in which taxes are treated by the accounts. In addition, an effort is made to interpret the manner in which the treatment of the government sector of NIA affects attitudes toward government productivity and the effect of taxes on the earnings of the factors of production and the final resting place of tax burdens. This is a big task that deserves more attention than it receives here or is generally given by fiscal economists.

The NIAs recognize that the sale of a product to someone not recognized as being engaged in a commercial transaction ends the use of a tax paid to reduce a tax due. This is true for property and income taxes as well as transaction taxes.

One of the wonders of NIAs is its preservation of the direct and indirect tax dichotomy. Undoubtedly this fact affects the thinking of people interested in turning around the U.S. tax system. They must be influenced by the fact that national income does not include indirect business taxes, does include profit-tax liability, but makes no provision for the reduction of wages and salaries by income tax liability. Of course, later on NIA develops a disposable-income total which is an after-tax total.

No place is provided to integrate tax collections and government services. Also, the large government investment, consumer goods, and services sectors are not reported separately.

The NIAs are useful in the demonstration they provide that all taxes, income as well as sales, are included in the price paid for goods and services. The NIA procedure does not differentiate between different types of taxes. They are all basically a cost that reduces the income available to income receivers to spend and save while providing financing for government expenditures.

## Shift from Income to Transaction-Based Taxes

Few would deny that to assist in making international adjustments is an important plus for any domestic tax system and that if a general tax measured by value of product does this better than a general tax measured by income, then product taxation possesses an advantage justifying consideration of adoption. Support stops here if the acquisition of international strengths requires the surrender of important attributes which the domestic tax system must possess. Domestic tax effectiveness cannot be surrendered to gain international advantages. The tail cannot be permitted to wag the dog.

The first basic objection to use of a general national tax based on the value of product rather than on incomes arising from sale of products is the difference in the effect on prices of collecting the same revenues in these two allegedly different ways. The second basic objection is that taxes based on the value of goods cannot be related to ability to pay, as can income taxes, and are therefore less just than income taxes. A third basic objection is that taxes based on value, except retail sales taxes, are hidden taxes, and therefore taxpayers are not aware of the tax cost of government activities. This is believed to prevent citizens from equating benefits of government service with tax cost, and therefore it results in uneconomic use of resources. A fourth basic objection is that tax collections, based on production and sales, lose a large portion of the built-in cyclical flexibility enjoyed when collections arise largely from corporate and individual income taxes. The fifth, and perhaps by far the most important, objection is that an economy making heavy use of income as the tax base must make substantial and painful adjustments if the use of income as a tax base is to be sharply reduced and replaced with tax or taxes using product as the tax base. These five basic objections to a general revenue tax measured by value of product are discussed in the order in which they are given.

*Prices*

Whether a movement toward general rebatable (rebatable on exports under rules of GATT) excise (GRE) taxes and away from income, net wealth, and property (IWP) (nonrebatable on exports under rules of GATT) taxes, with no change in aggregate tax collections, would increase prices has been considered by many theorists, and the findings are inconclusive. (The analysis of the effect on prices of substituting a tax of equal yield for an existing tax is sometimes called *differential incidence analysis*.) Nevertheless, the fear of price increases more than likely constitutes a major undesirable domestic impact expected from greater emphasis on GRE taxes in countries now placing a relatively heavy emphasis on IWP taxes. The state of the art of fiscal theory and analysis being what it is, their fears can be neither justified nor removed.

The changeover of the tax system of a major industrial nation has never taken place in the real world. In the United States, corporations operating in states making use of the corporate income tax and in states relying on corporate taxes measured by value of capital stock or value added (Michigan) actively and effectively carry on price competition. However, the rates of the taxes are relatively low, and in production areas where the type of tax does affect ability to compete, firms have been free to locate in the low-tax areas. When the location change is between countries with different tax systems rather than states with different tax systems, this freedom of choice is considerably restricted. The effect is to create pressures for protection from foreign competition in areas where domestic costs are high.

The relative prices of goods and services produced in different nations entering into international trade are determined by the international exchange rates existing for each currency. An equilibrium group of exchange rates would include as a part of the determination of each exchange rate whatever effect the different tax systems, the level of taxes, and the efficiency of government expenditure of tax collections had on prices of internationally traded goods and services. If in one nation the method of collecting taxes, the quantity of taxes raised, or the efficiency of government expenditure is changed so that the export price of goods and services is decreased, then the exchange rate of that nation becomes a disequilibrium rate. Equilibrium is restored as the exchange rate of the nation's monetary unit drifts upward and gains value relative to the currencies of most other countries. Adjustment also could be made if all other countries reduced their export prices by similar fiscal action or through general deflation or increased efficiency not reflected in income payments to production factors. Adaptation to new conditions through similar fiscal action would be the most appropriate course.

It seems impossible to measure a variation in domestic prices of internationally traded goods and services that arises from a difference in the portion of total taxes arising from GRE and IWP sources. In addition, the difference that has historically existed has been included in current international exchange rates. If the effect on export prices of a shift of a nation from GRE to IWP tax sources or IWP to GRE taxes is substantial, then the nations of the world must either keep the basic characteristics of their tax systems pretty largely as they are or be willing to make the types of adjustments identified above. Thus GRE tax improvement of international competitiveness is only measurable as the change permits additional tax rebates on exports and additional compensatory taxes on imports and the relation of this to domestic prices of goods entering international commerce.

## Ability to Pay

The control of governments by popular majorities is tied to taxation based on ability to pay. It is the popular aim of taxation based on ability to pay to collect as taxes a larger portion of the incomes and maybe wealth of the middle-income groups and the rich than that of the poor. Because in all societies, until the modern affluent societies, the number of poor has been much larger than the middle-income groups or the rich, popular support for ability-to-pay taxation has been dominant. Personal income taxes with progressive tax rates possess the apparent ability to collect taxes according to ability to pay, while this is not an obvious characteristic of taxes based on product.

If a measure of degree of democracy could be applied to industrial nations, the large users of IWP taxes would get a higher rating than the large users of GRE taxes. Therefore it might be argued that a strong reliance on IWP taxes is both a cause and a result of democracy operating in the tax field. The position that IWP tax emphasis and democracy go together possesses a strong historical basis for acceptance; however, the support is historical and does not seem to be a relationship found today between the major industrial nations. With their relatively high collections from the rich, IWP taxes had redistribution of income as an important goal. It was a democratic goal aimed at increasing the well-being of the poor, by reducing the well-being of the middle class and of the rich. Income redistribution has proved to be unobtainable. Also, productivity has reached such a level in the major industrial nations that it is possible to eliminate real poverty without basically changing the distribution of income.

In the United States, and especially since the 1930s, the income-redistribution goal has been pushed more actively than in most other countries. But despite the world's highest top individual income tax rates and the inclusion of capital gains in taxable income, plus what must be the best income tax enforcement organization, the progress made in the United States toward the goal of more equal income distribution through tax collections has been disappointing.[1] In recognition of the shortcoming of progressive income tax rates in redistributing income, their use has been nearly abandoned in Germany.[2]

The democratic method to help the poor is rapidly shifting from taxing policy to spending policy.[3] The size of the economic pie has increased rapidly and continuously since World War II. This new economic stability and expanding productivity point toward democratic governments spending to maintain the income their citizens throughout life and spending to increase citizen education and productivity. *Under the circumstances of the present and the visible future, the role of taxation in a democracy will be to provide stable revenues while encouraging economic growth and investment within a framework of close international interaction.* This type of tax goal does not require democratic governments to continue their historical tax attitudes, they no longer need favor use of only those taxes that are aimed at a redistribution of incomes, so that the after-tax incomes of the low-income receivers become relatively higher than had resulted from the operation of market and other economic forces.

*Fiscal Decision Making*

The voter, by his decision to have governments spend for this and that, determines the ultimate size of tax collections. The decision to spend as a consumer is intimately associated with a money payment. In the case of a decision to have government spend, the spending and the money payment are not as closely associated. This is perhaps undesirable.

The already weak link between government spending and paying is worsened when payment is included (hidden) in the price paid for consumer purchases. Where this is done, the decision to spend where price and benefit are closely connected (marketplace spending) is affected by costs of government spending that are added to marketplace prices. The result is to weaken the ability of income receivers to weigh benefits with costs in making marketplace spending decisions and to realize the relation to costs of public-sector spending decisions.

This highly tenuous but logically appealing set of speculations does not appear to have caused differences in aggregate public-sector spending or to have been important elements in selecting things government money buys in high-GRE-tax countries compared with high-IWP-tax countries. Also the private sectors of high-GRE-tax countries do not appear to have become less efficient in resource use or in satisfying income earners' desires than those of high-IWP-tax nations. These generalizations of real-world influence of emphasis on GRE taxes are less tenuous than logical speculations.

The expenditure of tax collections other than social security taxes varies considerable from nation to nation. The United States, for example, spends a larger portion of tax collections for armaments and armament development than the other capitalist industrial nations.

Differences in the allocation of tax collections surely affect costs of producing and selling. However, the difference is not reflected in treatment permitted under GATT in granting subsidies to exporters or in allowing collection of surcharges on imports. A producer in a country that spends a large portion of its tax receipts on armaments, leaving the producer with badly educated workers and inadequate government services, does not become eligible for more liberal subsidy benefits or border tax protection than that enjoyed by a producer in a country where tax funds are carefully spent to increase production efficiency.

Efficiency or business orientation of public expenditures does not seem to bear any close relation to type of tax base or measure used. There is no indication that France and Germany, large-GRE-tax users, spend their tax receipts any less efficiently than the United States. Emphasis on general excise taxes does not seem to have pushed tax collections to higher levels than an emphasis on income taxes. For example, the low level of Japanese government expenditures seems to be largely explained by very low armament costs, arising directly out of World War II, and a low level of highway and social expenditures directly related to the Japanese way of life, and not to a rather heavy reliance on IWP taxes.

The post-World War II experience indicates that high GRE tax rates are consistent with a sound domestic economy. The countries with high GRE tax rates generally enjoy rapid growth rates and high, stable levels of employment. Some of the major nations with relatively low GRE tax rates have experienced a somewhat slower growth rate and less stability.[4]

*Built-in Flexibility*

The loss most frequently identified by fiscal economists from reduced use of IWP taxes is the weakening of a domestic tax system's built-in flexibility. The built-in flexibility of the U.S. tax system traditionally has been considered to be very helpful in maintaining economic stability.[5] The record indicates the CIT is by far the most cyclically sensitive major revenue source.[6] Although desirable flexibility of this type would diminish under a tax system dominated by a VAT, as an example, it would not disappear. The tax base of VAT is income, directly or indirectly, and consists to a considerable extent of wages and profits.[7] On the other hand, the U.S. problem of tax collections rising so rapidly that business growth is cut off before full employment is reached is avoided when tax rates, particularly those applicable to corporate profits, are reduced.

The relative desirability of enjoying economic stability through government-expenditure stability and some built-in expenditure flexibility (for example, unemployment-benefit payments) seems to have suffered too great a decline since the fiscal and monetary policy discussions of the 1930s. Built-in flexibility of tax collections makes government-expenditure maintenance or expansion more difficult during periods of economic decline. The large budgetary deficit required for an appropriate expenditure program creates international monetary problems and frightens away middle-of-the-road and conservative political support.[8] Therefore, a government-expenditure program to use up uncommitted resources during a recession is retarded by built-in tax flexibility. Also, the decreased tax collections arise largely from reduced capital gains and business profits and do not directly stimulate private spending. Basically, built-in tax flexibility as an economic stabilizer is a monetary approach to the problem. The concept rests on a budget deficit and surplus, and the resulting demand for savings and the relation of this to the money supply. It is doubtful if it is desirable to rest an appropriate money-supply policy on fiscal determinants. If this is done, monetary policy loses a degree of its independence. When this happens, the central bank is no longer able to make independent judgments of appropriate policy.

The loss of some built-in tax flexibility may not be so bad after all. In fact, it may be desirable.

## Adjustments

Perhaps change is always painful. We are told this is true even when the change is from impure river water to clean, piped-in water. Some of the social hardship of the new water system can be avoided if the piped water is made available at first only in central places near the old water-drawing spots. In this way, some of the traditional meetings at water-drawing time can be preserved. Introductory techniques along this line are appropriate when a tax system is changed.

A major hurdle to be overcome by a tax that would largely replace use of the income tax is the many tax specialists who would experience a sharp reduction in the market value of their specialized knowledge and skills. Because these people are strategically placed in all areas where tax decisions are made and their advice is looked to by nonspecialists, their influence is very great. They will have to be unusual specialists to generally rise above individual self-interest. Government tax administrators have a built-in hesitancy to change the rules, causing them in a general way to echo the sentiments of the tax specialists.

Related to this adjustment hurdle is the problem that would arise because GRE taxes more than likely would require tax payments from business firms that are unprofitable according to conventional accounting practice. It is argued that these firms to not have a tax-paying ability and to require a tax payment would drive them to bankruptcy. Clearly this argument would be inapplicable if the tax caused a general price increase. It is also possible to argue that inevitable, isolated business hardship cases will cause bankruptcies that could spark a general loss of business confidence and the development of recession conditions.

The fear of an undesirable or desirable (depending on the point of view) impact of GRE taxes on small and unprofitable firms seems to be unjustified. France, the traditional nation of small business, is a very intensive user of GRE taxes.

It may be that the encouragement to profit from withholdings of high IWP tax rates has dried up small-business capital sources in the United States and that high income tax rates relative to capital-gain tax rates have encouraged the sale of small corporations to large corporations. Also, as mentioned, a reduction of IWP tax rates increases after-tax wage income, and this increase could become somewhat of a substitute for wage increases, which would leave the unprofitable business firm's costs largely unchanged. Finally, there is the basic traditional economic approach. It concludes that the pressure exerted on the unprofitable business would cause resources to flow into the hands of those who could use them more effectively. This would be labeled "good," because it would result in an increase of general efficiency and productivity. The result here would be a more rapid rate of economic growth and a higher level of economic well-being.

The domestic fears of a switch to greater use of GRE taxes by heavy-IWP-tax nations may be nothing but shadows, shadows that are larger than real life. No effort has been made in this discussion to catalog the many problems, both domestic and international, that arise with the use of relatively high IWP tax rates. However, these are not shadows, but big, real-life shortcomings.[9]

## Conclusion

Tax change is certain to affect the size of the check that taxpayers send to the U.S. Treasury. It is also certain that a larger check will develop greater voter response than a reduced check. Nevertheless, a reduction in the size of the tax check affects voter attitudes favorably. Therefore, a large number of taxpayers enjoying reduced tax payments create a politically desirable impact. If this situation were accompanied by efficiency stimulants and an increased level of investments and exports, the tax change would combine a good degree of both political and economic acceptability. This would be the basic result of a VAT that zero-rated exports and exempted small businessmen who are labor-intensive.[10]

## A Brief Look at VAT as a Major Federal Tax

A VAT system introduced as a replacement for a considerable portion of the federal payroll, individual, and corporate income taxes, plus federal excise taxes other than those on alcoholic beverages, gasoline, and tobacco, has the potential to stimulate the domestic economy and balance international payments, while increasing state and local government tax bases. Revenue estimates and the general procedure for the introduction of this type of a tax system, as well as how the change would affect the economy and the balance of payments, are considered in the following subsections.

### Gradual Introduction

The rate of a United States VAT should be at least 10 percent, and the base should be very broad to permit international harmonization with the existing VAT legislation of Western Europe and to make possible a major revision of the federal government's revenue system. By the federal government's initiating a VAT system now, the transformation can be made gradually to a tax system suited to current international and domestic business and economic conditions. This is very important.

The relationship of gradual to abrupt introduction on tax incidence and tax effects is not susceptible to careful useful analysis. The most that can be said is that gradual introduction provides more time than an abrupt change for working out new arrangements to replace those based on the former tax situation. Whether the kind of arrangements made changes because of less or more time is uncertain. Taxpayers losing from the change have their losses spread over a number of years, and those who gain enjoy a lengthened period of stimulation.[11] This causes losses and gains to appear less like windfalls and more normal, which may cause reactions to the changes to be more complete.

*Revenue Potential*

If VAT were adopted at a rate of 10 percent to be applied to value arising in the areas identified in H.R. 7015, the tax, when fully effective, say in 1982, could provide about $135 billion in revenues. These revenues would be sufficient to permit the elimination of excise taxes other than those in the alcohol, tobacco, and gasoline group and a considerable reduction of individual payroll and corporate income tax collections. In order to harmonize with European practice, the corporate income tax should be integrated with the individual income tax. When this is done, the corporate income tax becomes largely a tax on undistributed profits. The expanded VAT collections would make unnecessary a sharp increase in payroll taxes to finance expanded social security and medical benefits.[12]

If VAT were introduced at 3 percent and raised by 3 percentage points in the second year and by 4 percentage points in the third year, the added revenues from VAT would be about as summarized in table 3-1.

*Revenue Distribution*

Revenues from VAT would permit tax reductions and expenditure expansion, as summarized in table 3-2.

**Table 3-1**
**Estimated Revenue Potential of the Value-Added Tax**

| Calendar Year | VAT Collections (Billions of Dollars) | VAT Rate (Percent) |
|---|---|---|
| 1980 | 35 | 3 |
| 1981 | 80 | 6 |
| 1982 | 135 | 10 |

**Table 3-2**
**Distribution of Revenue Potential of Value-Added Tax**
*(billions of dollars)*

| Calendar Year | VAT Collections | Payroll Tax Reduction | Annual Individual Income Tax Revenue Reduction | Annual Corporate Tax Revenue Reduction |
|---|---|---|---|---|
| 1980 | 35 | 10 | 12 | 13 |
| 1981 | 80 | 30 | 25 | 25 |
| 1982 | 135 | 50 | 50 | 35 |

*Impact of Gradual Introduction of VAT*

The gradual introduction of VAT would directly cause employee take-home pay to increase at a rate somewhat above 2 percent a year for the three-year period. The take-home pay increase would be available to all workers, those belonging to strong or weak unions or no union at all, those working for state and local governments and the "ma and pa" store. It would be available to those working on their own or those living off returns from investment. The economic justification of labor-union bargaining for dollar wage increases would be reduced and with it some of the upward price pressure that may arise from the cost push of additional aggregate tax payments by business firms under VAT. The portion of VAT paid on value added represented by profits, interest, and rent would be compensated for largely by reduced corporate income taxes and lower personal income tax rates. Generally, as this gradual switch in tax payment took place, it would cause all property and business income (whether profits, interest, or rent and also whether it arose from a firm organized as a cooperative, a corporation, a partnership, or an individual proprietorship) to be taxed similarly. The effect would be more rational financial and administrative business decisions. The three-year period of adjustment would permit orderly realignment to meet shifted tax liabilities.

Another advantage of a fundamental tax shift to take place over a three-year period is that the future regarding an important portion of the federal tax picture would be known. This permits business firms to plan and capitalize future expectations with greater confidence; one major element of uncertainly has been eliminated.

*Relation of VAT to Balance of Payments*

If the VAT rate as introduced is immediately offered as a rebate on production exported and a border tax on imports, the international competitive position of production carried on in the United States will be improved each year for the three-year period. If VAT is not immediately utilized in this way, because a strong U.S. international economic position makes it inappropriate, the United States still has a new effective weapon to defend the international value of the dollar as needed. The usefulness of VAT as a balancer of international payment fluctuations would be improved if the legislation provided for administrative flexibility in the portion of the full VAT rate utilized as rebate on exports and as a border tax on imports. This procedure or variations providing even greater flexibility are used by the European Common Market countries and Sweden.

With exchange-rate, tariff, and interest-rate changes becoming less available as international economic adjusters, the role of VAT in this area is very likely to expand. The United States without VAT has encountered difficulties in utilizing its major international competitive potential. The emerging use of VAT as an international adjuster by Western nations bears some similarity to the European use of the central-bank rediscount rate at the end of the nineteenth century and France's use of VAT in the 1950s.[13]

*General Economic Impact of VAT*

The U.S. economy would be indirectly and directly stimulated by a number of the impacts from the introduction and use of VAT as has been described.[14] These economic stimulants are identified below in summary fashion:

1. The VAT would reduce costs by causing better economic resource allocation through sharply reducing the inducement to make business expenditures and business decisions because of the tax angle, that is, by reducing the advantage of capital-gains treatment, delaying income receipt, earning income from foreign sources, dividing income among a number of receivers, and purchasing capital goods with certain life expectancies.

2. Business tax compliance costs can be reduced through greatly simplified regulations relating to the corporate and individual income taxes.

3. United States investment in manufacturing will be stimulated by increasing international competitiveness of domestic-based production.

4. The sharp reduction of the tax rate applied to the corporate-profits base will encourage efficient business firms and increase availability of capital for the profitable, rapidly growing firm.

5. Through reduction of payroll and income tax rates, the spendable income of many low- and middle-income receivers would be immediately increased and would be raised each year for three years.

6. Under an integrated corporate and personal income tax, corporations with little need for capital from internal sources would be induced to distribute earnings to reduce the corporate tax liability on undistributed profits. This would increase the availability of investment funds for small

business and would work toward keeping investment of U.S. savings at home, that is, permitting the domestic economy to enjoy their multiplier effect.

7. The competitive U.S. income tax rates would induce U.S. citizens to bring foreign earnings home, helping the U.S. balance of payments.

8. The increased corporate and personal income base that would be made available as a base for state and local government taxation would permit orderly growth of this sector of the U.S. economy.

9. A U.S. tax system similar to that of Western Europe will encourage foreign long-term investment in the United States, helping to balance U.S. international payments and stimulate employment and growth of the U.S. domestic economy.

10. Reduced payroll taxes will make profitable the use of more labor in the production mix.

*Conclusion*

A balanced federal tax system would include a tax similar to a substantive VAT. The use and adoption of VAT at this time can help rectify a number of bothersome economic problems. Used as outlined, VAT increases employment and investment. It also increases the competitiveness of U.S.-made goods in the international markets.

**Retail Sales Tax Compared with VAT**

On occasion one hears (usually from economists) that if you want to replace certain income and payroll tax liabilities, you should do this with a retail sales tax (RST) instead of a VAT. Actually, there is a rather considerable and persuasive list of reasons for preferring VAT over a national RST. Briefly, and somewhat incompletely, the advantages of VAT over a RST are as follows.

1. The retail sales tax provides no revenues if the tax is not collected or turned in at the retail level. On the other hand, VAT is collected as the good or service passes through the production process, and the retailer is responsible for only the VAT due on retailing costs reflected in selling price. Only the VAT due on the retail markup can be evaded or avoided by the retailer.

2. Purchases made at wholesale or some other level other than retail are not liable for the RST. The RST rates being used by states and cities already have reached a level where buying it "wholesale" becomes worthwhile. A retail sales tax that goes above 5 percent encounters serious administrative problems. A 10 percent national RST added to state and local

RSTs would result, in some cases, in a tax of 15 percent. Evasion would become a major problem. The burden of collecting a 15 percent tax would be just too great for the retailer to bear. The VAT included as a portion of the cost of acquiring goods or services to be paid directly or indirectly through an added cost is like any other expense.

3. The RST is not adaptable to purchases of services, as demonstrated by the fact that it is nearly entirely a tax on goods. The breadth of coverage is somewhat of a problem for VAT, but much worse for an RST. The VAT can readily exempt small businesses or high-labor-content firms. This is done in Michigan and Europe where VAT is used (see point 6).

4. The base taxed by an RST frequently includes office machines, fixtures, raw materials, fuel, supplies, and so on used by companies, and therefore these are producer goods, not end products. RST collections from this base amount to 20 to 25 percent of revenues. The VAT avoids this problem because the VAT paid on purchase is deductible from the VAT due down through the production process until the end use is reached. In this way, VAT avoids being cascaded down through the production process. The RST is only about 75 to 80 percent effective in this respect.

5. The VAT is treated under GATT as an accepted refund to exporters. It is also available as a border tax to be levied on imports selected for taxation. The RST cannot provide these benefits to exports and therefore does not provide the stimulant to export businesses that VAT provides. A manufacturing firm which markets its goods domestically through a jobber, a wholesaler, and another fabricator and then to a marketing specialist firm and finally to a retailer is not directly affected by the RST and whether it is or is not paid somewhere down the line of domestic marketing and production.

This same manufacturer is very directly induced to export when he receives a refund of VAT included in invoices of purchases related to his export operations, but he does not receive this tax refund on his domestic operations. Also, the VAT refund makes it easier for the manufacturer to compete with production arising from the VAT-using nations of the world.

The RST is not collected as goods are imported. Of course, imports, just like other goods, are subject to RST when they are finally sold at the retail outlet. The fact that VAT is due at the time of import increases costs of purchasing and holding imports. This retards imports and preserves jobs for U.S. workers. It is also only fair that imports into the United States bear a border tax; U.S. exports are likely to be subject to an immediate 15, 20, or 25 percent border tax when sales are made to buyers of VAT-using nations.

Sweden, because of the international-trade advantages of VAT, abandoned the RST. (Sweden also encountered administrative problems.) Also, most of the nations of Western Europe abandoned their gross-turnover taxes, and in the case of the United Kingdom, a wholesale purchase tax for VAT. This was done largely to enjoy the international competitive advantages of VAT.

6. Under VAT, small businesses can be made exempt of the tax without loss of all the revenues.[15] A small business exempt of VAT on its sales gains a competitive advantage because the difference between its selling price and the purchases made from suppliers subject to VAT escapes the tax. Under RST, the exemption of a small business means loss of the entire tax. For this reason and because of administrative problems that arise when a substantial tax difference exists, the RST has not been typically written to benefit small businesses.

7. The retail sales tax has been judged regressive because high-income people save a larger portion of their income than do receivers of low incomes. Actually, because income saved is spent on capital goods that become a portion of the retail selling price, savings are a portion of the retail tax base. The retail price includes all costs. The same situation exists in relation to VAT.

The total of real income (end-use goods and services) is taxed at a flat rate. What the subtractive-consumption type of VAT does, by allowing the purchaser of capital goods to deduct the VAT on these invoices from VAT due on sales, is to avoid double taxation of capital. Double taxation takes place when the cost of capital in the final selling price is taxed and the VAT on a capital purchase is not deducted from the VAT due on sales. Savings are used to finance capital goods; therefore, as capital is taxed as a portion of the end-use selling price, savings are included in the VAT base. In the case of the RST, most capital as purchased by businesses is not taxed; thus the deduction of RST paid on capital has not been legislated (see point 4.)

8. The share of disposable personal income spent for consumer goods and services is taxed as spent under both VAT and RST. The share of income saved under RST pays no tax until the final sale. In the case of VAT, savings are taxed when the capital goods financed with the savings are sold. This tax payment is used by the purchaser of the capital good to reduce his tax liability on sales subject to VAT. The cost of the capital good becomes a portion of the selling price of all end-use goods and services, and this sales price is subject to VAT. Here savings are again part of the tax base of VAT and are, of course, included in the RST base.

9. Like the RST, VAT discourages consumption and encourages savings and investment. This is done by eliminating the double taxation on savings that exists when business profits are taxed as business income and again as personal income when paid out as dividends. Also the taxation of interest on savings that were already taxed as income earned can be avoided. Again, double taxation is prevented. By encouraging the allocation of more income to savings, VAT and RST reduce consumption because the return from this type of economic action has been increased.

10. Under VAT, the tax is paid as added value is marketed.[16] This VAT that is paid is deductible from the VAT due from the purchaser when he becomes liable for VAT on his sales. The paperwork which is required when VAT is paid and later refunded through the reduction of VAT due as sales subject to VAT are made, does not mean VAT is not paid to the government treasurer as goods and services are produced and marketed. The VAT is being paid just as labor, interest, and raw materials are being purchased as the process moves toward end use. Also, just as each sale goes to cover the cost of purchases from other firms and the remainder is value-added, so also each sale includes the VAT previously paid plus VAT due on the value added at the marketing and production step under consideration.


*Conclusion*


The price received for the end product must be high enough to cover all labor, raw materials, capital costs, and the like, plus the VAT. In the case of VAT, just as in the case of labor, it is a cost required to bring a product or service to end use. *Also in the case of VAT, just as in the case of labor, payments are made along the production and marketing process, but they all are finally included in the price of the end product or service.*

The reduction of VAT due through deducting the amount given on the invoice as being previously paid is not a meaningless shuffling of papers. Neither does the deduction mean that the jobber, say, has not paid VAT. He has paid it just as he met his payroll. Also, just as the amount paid for payroll by the jobber plus the cost of other labor included in the goods or service comes back to the jobber when the sale is made by the jobber, so also the VAT included in invoices of purchases plus the VAT on value produced is returned as sales are made. If sale prices do not cover costs, for example, VAT and wages, then the burden of the costs is carried in lower prices to the factors of production. When this happens, the economic burden is said to have been shifted backward. A new relationship among the items making up costs and therefore receiving income is formed.

Under the RST, the purchaser of products does not acquire a tax credit for RST included in the cost of goods and services subject to the RST upon sale. The RST due is not affected by differences in the total cost consisting of RST and the portion comprising labor. When VAT is used, a cost consisting of VAT is a tax credit, while a cost consisting of wages or RST makes up a portion of the costs included in the tax base to which a VAT rate will be applied upon sale. The amount arrived at in applying the VAT rate to aggregate sales is reduced by the VAT credit. A similar situation, of course, does not exist when the RST is used. The size of the RST payment is determined entirely by the rate and the size of the retail sales base. The VAT payment, on the other hand, is determined by the rate times the sales base less the VAT credit—very major and important difference.

### Composition of Price Paid and Inflation

The payment of a price and the receipt of money arising from a sale are the two most common economic acts. At the same time, the function of price and what is paid for out of the price received are badly understood. This is the case at the level of the professional economist because of his tendency to overemphasize the influence of discretionary central-bank monetary policy. All observers of the national economic scene are put on a false scent by the manner in which the national-income accounts are reported. The amounts spent by government and the amounts spent for investment and for the net balance of international sales are added with consumption and reported as GNP. No reference is made to the fact that consumation expenditures alone include investment and government costs as a portion of the price paid for an end-use item.

The price charged is the only source of income to meet investment and government spending as well as the wages of workers and the royalties received by resource owners. Of course, this means that, *ceteris paribus*, additional investment means higher prices. And it is also true that every item sold transfers purchasing power equal to the price collected. However, the historical record of the relationship between price levels and investment does not completely follow what this relationship between prices and investment would forecast.

For example, the 1870s was a period of rapid investment expansion, but it was also a period of falling prices. The two existed alongside each other because investment expansion was possible out of substantial voluntary savings from current income and the investment was largely to reduce the cost of providing food. This was apparently a possibility again in the 1930s, but investment opportunities were not realized.

### Prices and Income

If we return to prices and look at them in terms of the income they provide, and not as the income they absorb, then it becomes obvious that incomes must increase as government expenditures and investment increase. The expansion of income provides more purchasing power to bid for consumer goods and services, unless the use of this income has been restrained in some fashion.

The reduction of expenditures by government and the reduction of investment expenditures push down the income received from prices charged to the level of the incomes of those producing consumer goods and services. The way to prevent prices from rising is to eliminate government and investment spending. This approach also means the creation of a stagnant private economy and the loss of the satisfaction of government services.

If government services are to be enjoyed and investment is to take place without continuously rising prices, incomes received from prices must be reduced by the amount spent for government and investment activities of the society. Savings and taxes must cover costs. If this is not done, the payment for government and investment is made through a reduction of the purchasing power of those holding savings in the form of deposits or bonds and by those unable to maintain the relative level of the price for the product or service providing them with their income.

*Conclusion*

When taxes become a portion of the bargaining for wages, government costs will be increasing prices, and any expansion of the level of government services in that sense will become inflationary. Also, when voluntary savings out of current income are not available, any increase in investment is inflationary.

**Regressivity Considered**

On occasion, the enactment of a broad-based, substantial VAT is opposed because it is "income-regressive." This statement gives the impression that VAT taxes low incomes at a higher rate than large incomes. This is true of the social security tax and perhaps in the application of the individual and corporate income taxes of the middle-income brackets, but not of VAT. A VAT covering the value of all end-use goods and services can be proportional only if one rate is used on domestic sales.

The idea that the major purpose of a tax system is to redistribute income, usually from the wealthy and large-income earners to the poor and the aged, and not to provide stable revenues to support government programs, has gained a strong hold on the U.S. public. The adoption of VAT by the federal government with a broad coverage and a minimum of different rates would be a badly needed switch in emphasis.

*Revenue Base of VAT*

In neither the United States or other industrial nations have studies been able to establish that highly progressive income and estate tax rates caused a redistribution of income and wealth down to the poor. To the extent that the condition of the poor has been improved through fiscal action, government expenditure programs have done the job.

A tax system that provides a base of stable, substantial revenues and, in addition, levies a substantial rate on large windfalls, economic rents, and monopoly profits must be the goal of responsible fiscal policy. The use of a basic stable revenue source such as VAT is recognition that general government services, from defense to home care for the elderly, are important. In addition, these services must be financed year after year. Potentially, and actually, everyone benefits when a basic tax is available to do this.

The VAT is a tax that ideally includes in its base the cost of producing and marketing all end-use goods and services. The use of VAT amounts to the government's collecting from all members of the economy a portion of the costs, based on the amount each uses, of the nation's production of goods and services. Other portions of these costs are met in other ways. Ten to fifteen percent, during recent years, have been met through an increased money supply. The result is inflation, often called the cruelest of taxes.

The VAT is an income-proportional tax if its coverage is complete and only one rate is used. The VAT base could be calculated in the additive manner by requiring each firm to pay a flat-rate tax based on total profits, wages, net interest, and rents. In practice, this base was used in applying the Michigan business activity tax (BAT), a type of VAT, and the legislated procedure of calculating the Michigan single business tax (SBT) now in effect.


*Conclusion*

Undoubtedly, we are going to continue to think of tax justice in terms of some calculation of ability-to-pay. This is as it should be. In addition, now that we can no longer meet government costs by taking the frosting off the cake and we must cut into the cake itself, procedures to do this without destroying the cake are needed. The "Tax Restructuring Acts of 1979-1980" (H.R. 5665 and 7015) are this type of legislation. The progressive income tax is not. It increases tax burdens at a faster rate than inflation.


**Inflation if the United States Made Use of a Major VAT**

The portion of the current inflation consisting of impacts arising from taxes collected, failure to collect taxes high enough to cover government expenditures, and the types of expenditures covered with taxes being collected must remain uncertain. This discussion is aimed at considering whether the inflationary problem and the general soundness of the U.S. economy could be improved if a major national VAT were introduced.

To a considerable extent, an analysis of this type makes sense only if it is true that (1) social security taxes of over 12 percent on salaries, without any deductions, of $25,900 cannot go much higher, personal income taxes cannot be raised very much, and this also goes for corporate profits taxes and gasoline taxes; (2) government borrowing has reached its limit; (3) continued reliance on existing taxes will injure our society, and a new approach is badly needed; (4) government will continue to provide revenue sharing and social services, and a real possibility exists of a further expansion of government expenditures in these areas and defense.

The VAT has become the greatest revenue raiser in Western Europe. It has provided stable revenues and must be given a major share of the credit for the generally balanced budgets of all the member states of the EEC except Italy, where only now is VAT being really utilized. However, this sound, balanced-budget fiscal position has not resulted in an inflation-proof EEC. Nevertheless, Germany has continued as the major industrial nation experiencing a low rate of inflation, and Germany continues to make substantial use of its VAT (Mehrwertsteuer).

Much of the inflation of Western Europe arises from price-linkage impacts and from costs of imports directly consumed or included as a portion of the cost of a product or service. The dependence of Western Europe on imported oil, other raw materials, and food is much greater than that of the United States. This should have resulted in prices moving up much more rapidly than those in the United States. The fact that this has not generally taken place provides some support for the position that the adoption of a major VAT by the United States would have a price-stabilizing influence.

The first portion of this section identifies in a general way some of the pros and cons of a VAT for the United States when it is considered largely on the basis of its stabilizing impact on prices. The second portion details some price-movement experience related to the introduction of VAT. The third portion outlines some tax incidence theories with some detail related to the incidence of the corporate income tax.

## Costs of Movement

Although government expenditures directly enter into costs and therefore prices, it is also true that government expenditures, highways in the United States, for example, can be the cause of falling prices. As a cost of doing business that cannot be reduced by bargaining activity VAT may result in lower prices for other services and products used in the industrial process.

By being completely set at a given level VAT can force down the price of other components possessing a degree of price elasticity. The result could be no change in the total production costs after the introduction of VAT.

If price increases equal to the VAT collection rate cause a decline in sales, the demand for the components of the product or service will fall. Again, this may cause an adjustment that removes much of the upward price movement arising from a new VAT cost. If monetary expansion does not provide for high general prices as VAT is introduced, then goods and services possessing the greater price elasticity will absorb the VAT cost through a decline in sales and later prices. The firms remaining in this price-elastic industry will be those best able to adjust to the new conditions.

The adjustments required because of the introduction of VAT have many characteristics similar to business adjustment to any tax. The one difference is that the costs of all elements in the production process bear the same additional tax burden. This means the lowest-cost combination of production factors before VAT continues. In the case of the introduction or increase of payroll taxes or profit taxes, the lowest-cost combination of labor and capital is changed and the efficiency of the market allocation is partially lost. The use of VAT does not alter the optimal decision from that existing before the tax. This relationship is the basic reason why VAT is said to be neutral.

The use of payroll taxes discourages the use of labor. The use of personal property taxes levies the heaviest tax burden on high-technology industries. The VAT applies equally to all.

*Advantages of a Less General Tax*

The use of an excise tax on one product, for example, tobacco, that is very price-inelastic reduces the purchasing power available to buy other goods. The impact of this is likely to be lower prices for all other consumer goods, along with the higher price for tobacco. A general price increase is less likely when a special excise tax is used rather than when a broadly based tax such as VAT is assessed. However, the tobacco consumer has been forced to bear an additional fiscal burden not required under VAT. But maybe Napoleon's tax wisdom is applicable here. He is reported to have said, "Tax the vices, they have broad shoulders."

Also it is often true that any tax (but particularly if the tax is on a particular type of expenditure) may lead to greater efficiency. For example, the cost of labor is up because of a higher payroll tax. As a result, the manager is stimulated to make better use of his labor resources.

## Prices Experience with VAT Introduction

Over ten years ago when Holland and Germany were introducing their VAT, the price impacts were quite different, despite the fact that the strengths of the two currencies were about equal, as demonstrated by their relative values during the past ten years. The introduction of VAT in Holland pushed prices up, but in Germany there was little price effect.

The price shifts related to introductions of VAT are related to preparations made and the economic conditions existing at the time of introduction. The experience in Europe points to lower price impact if the introduction is made when the economy is weak and if price controls are introduced and then gradually removed. The same effect as gradually removed price controls would be provided if VAT were introduced gradually. This procedure is recommended for the United States when a VAT is introduced.

After VAT is once enacted, the tax appears to have a price-stabilizing effect. This can be expected because VAT ensures a stronger revenue system and reduced likelihood of inflationary borrowing. France, for example, started introducing its VAT in 1949. The tax was in place, except for the retail sales level in 1954.[17] A few years ago, when all EEC member states were required to use a VAT through the retail level, France moved her VAT to include retail sales. The general impact of this gradual introduction of the French VAT must be rated as being deflationary.

The German's *Mehrwertsteuer* went into effect on January 1, 1968. At the same time, a lower revenue-producing turnover tax was removed. During the same period, the United States raised its CIT rates. The prices in Germany after the introduction of VAT declined.[18] The prices in the United States after the introduction of higher CIT rates increased.[19] Of course, many elements other than these tax shifts were affecting prices in both nations.[20]

A well-known German newspaper, the *Neue Westfalische Zietung* of Bielefeld, West Germany, (January 8, 1969) reported that VAT had not increased German prices. *The New York Times* estimated that the impact on the international value of the German mark of the introduction of the German VAT equaled that of a 4 to 5 percent devaluation of the mark.[21] The official U.S. trade negotiation group estimated the impact to be the equivalent of a devaluation of 2 to 3 percent.[22] In addition to these immediate competitive trade advantages, the VAT produces stable substantial revenues year after year. A devaluation arising from an inflated money supply provides direct revenues only once.

It is always difficult to pinpoint what has caused an international strengthening of a national currency. For example, strengths may be entirely relative and due to policies of other nations. However, it is a matter of record that economics Minister Karl Schiller identified the "stormy" growth of German exports in 1968 as causing an economic growth rate of 7 percent rather than the forecasted 4 percent.[23]

The VAT is a type of general indirect tax. Therefore, the traditional incidence conclusion is that VAT is not shifted forward and does not cause an increase in the general after-tax price level. The U.S. experience with VAT seems to support this position. The Michigan BAT was officially a subtracted VAT, but calculation by the additive method was accepted. It is of interest that it was declared to be a direct tax by the Michigan Supreme Court.[24] Here we have another example of the slippery nature of the concepts of direct and indirect taxes.

*Reflections on the Taxation Burden*

A general theory of incidence was developed by the physiocrats, a French group of economic analysts of the mid-eighteenth century. They saw the incidence of all taxes resting on the landowner, that is, controller or owner of natural resources, for he was the only person producing a *surplus*. Because natural-resource owners received surpluses, their incomes could be reduced without decreasing the level of productivity.

A general or broad-based tax such as VAT is sometimes considered to be a tax without burden, or without incidence. This is the result if it is assumed that all incomes or prices remain in the same relation to each other after the tax as before. The tax has not placed a burden on anyone because no one is relatively worse off. Under these conditions, the incidence arises entirely from the types of expenditures financed. The individuals or groups benefiting least from expenditures of the tax collections bear the incidence of the tax—an interesting idea: burdenless tax but burdensome expenditure distributions.[25] Actually, it fits in well with the role assigned to VAT by EEC member states.

The aim of tax collection is to make economic resources available to the government that had been earned and/or received by a member of the private sector. One way to bring about this transfer other than through tax collections is for government to increase the money supply or absorb savings and use these funds to purchase the resources required for its purposes.[26] If the production of the private sector is to be allocated to the public sector, it is a forced exaction unless fees and prices are used. When the public sector uses prices to acquire resources, the importance of locating the incidence of the allocation is sharply reduced.

It is the basic difference in the way governments gain control over resources that causes the concept of incidence, that is, tax burden, to be so fundamental. Another intriguing aspect of the effect of taxes on prices is the concept of transparency. It seems that the greater the buyer's actual knowledge of the tax (that is, the greater its "transparency"), the more likely the tax will be passed forward in high prices.[27] For example, the RST is generally agreed to be easier to pass forward than the VAT.

The least transparent of taxes are those included in the price of raw materials used to produce a product or service to be sold on the market. The name *taxe occulte* is sometimes given to this tax cost. All taxes paid, down to the end use, belong in this category. The individual income tax and VAT are *taxe occulte*. The tax is included in the price paid for supplies, capital, and labor.

A tax with very high rates, such as the personal income tax at the high-tax income brackets, generates avoidance procedures. Frequently these loopholes are so readily available that the tax at a high rate level provides very little revenue for the government. It is also quite possible that the waste of resources stimulated by tax-avoidance activities reduces economic efficiency and therefore the total economic base available to bear taxes and meet private-sector needs.

The CIT is the major U.S. business tax, and has been used both here and around the world for many years. Despite this experience with CIT, the incidence and shifting of the burden of the tax are unclear.

*Conclusion*

A major VAT in the United States through stimulation of savings and investment may decrease and not increase prices.[28] In addition, a major VAT at the federal-government level would decrease public sector inefficiency by ensuring stable government revenues. The result would be a decrease in the cost of government and an increase in private-sector supplies. The impact of this development would push down prices.

The burden of taxation in the most fundamental sense is measured by the impact of tax collection on the quantity of goods and services enjoyed by the people of a nation. The VAT has many useful characteristics that can be expected to be helpful in maximizing this level of satisfaction.

**GNP Accounts and Types of Taxes**

It is generally agreed the treatment of incomes, taxes, receipts, payments, investment, consumption, exports, and imports in arriving at national-income account (NIA) conceptual aggregates provides a fundamental insight into the functioning of our economy. Such agreement does not exist as to the contribution NIAs make in providing an understanding of the location of the burden of taxes and the impact of taxes levied on NIA components.

The value-added tax is often said, and assumed, to be a tax on the consumer. Frequently it is concluded from this attitude that VAT is also just an RST that has been made unnecessarily complicated. If it is important to know whether a tax rests on consumption or on savings, then an acceptable procedure to make this calculation is also needed.

The difference in the location of the economic burden affects the allocation of economic effort. If consumption bears a low tax burden, effort devoted to increasing human satisfactions in the future is expanded.

The base of VAT is limited to the money value of sales adjusted as the legislative bodies of the countries using the tax have decreed. The inclusion of all sales in the VAT base means that a distinction is not made between sale of goods and services conventionally identified as consumer or investment sales. However, as a firm makes its VAT payment, it can deduct the VAT previously paid as shown on the invoice. The final user, usually a consumer, does not develop a VAT liability from a future sale; therefore, the VAT included as a portion of the costs cannot be used later to reduce a VAT liability. But, because VAT is a portion of costs to be covered by sales prices, it becomes an element in wage and price settlements.

The relationship existing when a VAT liability is not developed from which VAT paid can be deducted, also exists when the purchase price, excluding the VAT portion, cannot be used to decrease taxable income or as a tax credit. There is a reduction in degree under the second situation, but the "buck stops here" concept is the same: taxes paid can be deducted from taxes due only when the law so provides or when a tax liability arises from a commercial transaction. The sale of a product to someone not recognized as being engaged in a commercial transaction ends the use of a tax paid to reduce a tax due. This is true of a property tax, an income tax, and a transaction tax. This commonalty of taxes related to human effort that is so often denied, is accepted and demonstrated in the NIA.

The NIA was introduced in 1934 but included data back to 1929. It was seen as a method of measuring a defined concept of economic activity and indirectly economic well-being.[30] Now and again, the concept measured has been modified and refined; but basically the structure remains as developed just before and during the Depression. The data developed were widely utilized in the 1940s to demonstrate the Keynesian theoretical economic structure.

*Public-Sector Size*

Back some fifty years, government activities and particularly federal government spending and tax collecting were not considered to be important elements in providing goods and services to households and in employing production factors. The federal government's receipts from all sources were $3.9 billion in 1929, and total state and local government revenues were about $7.5 billion for a total of $11.4 billion. The GNP for the same year is estimated to have been $103 billion. The federal government had a surplus of $734 million, and state and local governments enjoyed about a $100 million surplus.[31] Government collecting and spending was about 10 percent of GNP, and budget surpluses existed. Therefore, government, through its financing and spending, was making a contribution to the funds available for investment and was not crowding out private borrowers from the money market in order to cover its deficits.

*Taxation Concepts*

It was under these circumstances that the manner of treating taxes in the national economic accounts was established. The selection did not possess a high priority, and nobody with power apparently wished to tie government economic activities closely to private-sector buying, selling, producing, investing, and trading abroad. At hand for use as a working tool was the division of taxes between direct and indirect that had developed in nineteenth-century economic literature and had proved useful to the writers of the U.S. Constitution when they were looking for ways to restrict the taxation powers of the new national government. The direct and indirect tax concepts became the dichotomy around which the national-economic-accounts treatment of taxation was built. Also, the textbook definition of incomes of the factors of production was used to establish a national income total distinct from gross national product.

The summary of the national income and product accounts for 1978 (table 3-3) is in sufficient detail to demonstrate to some extent the direct-indirect tax dichotomy and the failure of the accounts to relate taxes to government purchases of goods and services and to generally integrate the public sector with the private sector.

Line 21 includes indirect business taxes, and line 12 includes profits tax liability. No mention is made of taxes being paid out of wages or out of incomes from other sources. On the product side of the accounts, line 40 shows government purchasing $435.6 billion of goods and services. However, the total of the two tax lines on the income side is only $262.6 billion. Obviously the national account in the summary form presented does not provide a useful understanding of how taxes affect prices, incomes, and wealth or, for that matter, the relation between taxes and government income and spending. The source of funds of the public sector is not clear, nor is it clear how the public sector is integrated with the private sector.

**Table 3-3**
**Summary of National Income and Product Accounts, 1978**
*(billions of dollars)*

| Line | | |
|------|---|---:|
| 1 | Compensation of employees | 1,304.5 |
| 2 | Wages and salaries | 1,103.5 |
| 3 | Disbursements (2-7) | 1,103.3 |
| 4 | Wage accruals less disbursements $(3-11)+(5-4)$ | 0.2 |
| 5 | Supplements to wages and salaries | 201.0 |
| 6 | Employer contributions for social insurance $(3-10)$ | 94.6 |
| 7 | Other labor income $(2-8)$ | 106.5 |
| 8 | Proprietors' income with inventory valuation and capital-consumption adjustments $(2-9)$ | 116.8 |
| 9 | Rental income of persons with capital-consumption adjustment $(2-10)$ | 25.9 |
| 10 | Corporate profits with inventory valuation and capital consumption adjustments | 167.7 |
| 11 | Profits before tax | 206.0 |
| 12 | Profits tax liability $(3-16)$ | 84.5 |
| 13 | Profits after tax | 121.5 |
| 14 | Dividends $(2-11)$ | 47.2 |
| 15 | Undistributed profits $(5-6)$ | 74.3 |
| 16 | Inventory-valuation adjustment $(5-7)$ | $-25.2$ |
| 17 | Capital-consumption adjustment $(5-8)$ | $-13.1$ |
| 18 | Net Interest $(2-13)$ | 100.5 |
| 19 | *National Income* | 1,724.3 |
| 20 | Business transfer payments $(2-18)$ | 9.2 |
| 21 | Indirect business tax and nontax liability $(3-17)$ | 178.1 |
| 22 | *Less*: Subsidies *less* current surplus of government enterprises $(3-10)$ | 4.2 |
| 23 | Statistical discrepancy $(5-12)$ | 3.3 |
| 24 | *Charges against Net National Product* | 1,910.7 |
| 25 | Capital-consumption allllowances with capital-consumption adjustment $(5-9)$ | 216.9 |
| | *Charges against Gross National Product* | 2,127.6 |
| 26 | Personal-consumption expenditures $(2-3)$ | 1,350.8 |
| 27 | Durable goods | 200.3 |
| 28 | Nondurable goods | 530.6 |
| 29 | Services | 619.8 |
| 30 | Gross private domestic investment $(5-1)$ | 351.5 |
| 31 | Fixed investment | 329.1 |
| 32 | Nonresidential | 221.1 |
| 33 | Structures | 76.5 |
| 34 | Producers' durable equipment | 144.6 |
| 35 | Residential | 108.0 |
| 36 | Change in business inventories | 22.3 |
| 37 | Net exports of goods and services | $-10.3$ |
| 38 | Exports $(4-1)$ | 207.2 |

**Table 3-3** *(continued)*

| Line | | |
|---|---|---|
| 39 | Imports (4 − 3) | 217.5 |
| 40 | Government purchases of goods and services (3 − 1) | 435.6 |
| 41 | Federal | 152.6 |
| 42 | National defense | 99.0 |
| 43 | Nondefense | 53.6 |
| 44 | State and local | 283.0 |
| | *Gross National Product* | 2,127.6 |

Source: *Survey of Current Business*, July 1979, p. 24.
Numbers in parenthesis indicate accounts and items of counterentry in the accounts.

## Circular Flow of Taxes and Government Spending

Another way in which the national accounts are presented is as a circular flow of income between households and the factors of production. A simplified diagram illustrating this approach is shown in figure 3-1. The arrows out of the household circle show personal income taxes taking away household income to the left and the subtraction of excise and sales taxes doing the same to the right. Both types of taxes directly reduce the resources under control of the households by the full amount of the taxes collected.

The other reduction of private control over resources in order to finance government activities is taken from the income of the factors of production, land, labor, and capital. These are called business taxes. Although in the presentation the deduction is made from factor income, the arrows connecting H and F demonstrate that any reduction in H is going to reduce F and any reduction of F is going to reduce H.

## Business Taxes

Actually "business taxes" is a very fuzzy concept.[32] In figure 3-1, they would include corporate profit taxes, social security taxes, and customs duties. This is not the definition used in the aggregate "Indirect Business Tax and Nontax Liability" given on line 21. Neither is this a definition of business taxes that would be very meaningful to either ordinary taxpayers or economists. For example, social security taxes are certainly divided between business and workers. Over 50 percent of social security taxes are paid by business, and they do not show up as a deduction from the worker's paycheck. The remainder is a deduction from wages just like the personal income tax, and the negotiated wage is reduced by this amount.

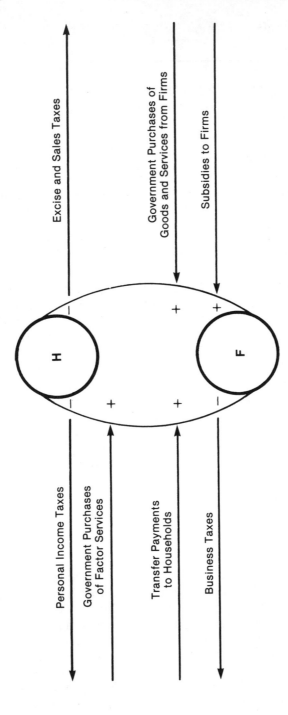

**Figure 3-1.** Household and Factors of Production

Source: Richard G. Lipsey and Peter O. Steiner, *Economics* (New York: Harper & Row, 1966), p. 536. Copyright © 1966 by Richard G. Lipsey and Peter O. Steiner. Reprinted by permission of Harper & Row, Publishers, Inc.

*Preservation of the Factor-Income Concept*

The gross national income (GNI) and product accounts are frequently given as a circle of incomes and products with the beginning and ending points being GNP/GNI; that is, the value of all products sold is equal to the value of all incomes received. The first step in breaking down the aggregates is the reduction of GNI to national income. This is done basically by subtracting indirect business taxes and depreciation from GNI.

The national economic accounts use the term *indirect* partially in the way it was defined by the nineteenth-century economists.[33] The taxes included in this grouping are all sales, excise, gross receipts, and customs duties, plus property taxes paid by businesses. The grouping also corresponds to some extent to that of indirect taxes as provided in the U.S. Constitution.

The grouping of taxes in the national income accounts that are deducted before national income is calculated has helped to perpetuate the idea that some taxes increase prices and other do not. The group of taxes placed in the category of indirect business taxes is treated like depreciation. The justification for doing this is apparently that they both bring about an increase in price prior to the price's becoming an income of the factors of production. They are a cost, but not an income of the factors of production and therefore not a part of national income.

Depreciation is not first received as dividends by the owners and then paid back to the firm to cover depreciation costs. Also indirect taxes are not first received by wage earners and then paid back to the firm so that the business can cover its indirect tax liabilities. This is obviously true. However, it is also true that both depreciation and indirect taxes are costs just as wages and a normal return on equity are. So why the special treatment?[34] Apparently it is the tradition regarding separation between indirect and direct taxes, some economic theory, and the definition of national income that limit it to *payments* to the factors of production; and that is about it.

National income equals the income of the factors of production, that is, profits, wages, rents, interest, and so on. They are all treated in the accounts as though tax liabilities did not go along with the payment. Later adjustments are made for the various tax payments. The treatment of taxes seems to imply that the real income is the income before taxes and the real price is the price after indirect taxes. This unequal treatment of taxes, whether they are a part of price or of income, in the national income accounts does not appear to have an economic justification. Profits are higher because corporate profits taxes must be paid; wages are higher because social security and income taxes must be paid; and prices are higher because these taxes and "indirect business taxes" must be covered by prices charged buyers.

*Corporate Profits Tax*

Table 3-3 reports profits tax liability on line 12. The adjustment is made quickly, and "Profit before Tax" is the title of line 11. So that no confusion will exist as to what the profits really are, line 13 reports profits after taxes. The "summary" does not report a similar after-tax figure for wages, business and professional income, rent, interest, and so on. However, there is a widely used national-accounts concept called *disposable income*. This is the after-tax total of income available to individuals and unincorporated businesses. This adjusted total of income is available to pay for consumer goods and services that are placed on the market. Also some of it is saved. These savings finance investments of unincorporated businesses and become deposits of savings institutions, payments on mortgages, and the like.

   In many respects, disposable income is the bottom line of the national accounts, but not quite; the real honest-to-goodness bottom line is personal-consumption expenditures, which is reported in the NIAs, plus spending to pay for the construction of housing, which is not reported.

   At this point, the bottom of the income-product circle, the products to match the income appear. These are divided into four large groupings: personal-consumption expenditures (excluding residential structures), gross private domestic investment (including residential structures), net exports of goods and services and government purchases of goods and services.

*End-Use and Intermediary Goods*

The prices paid for consumer goods is the payment for end use. All the investments in both the private and public sectors have been made to put these end-use goods on the market and to provide facilities that are taken and used from the public sector. Although gross private domestic investment is one of the four sectors of GNP, it is, of course, an intermediary good and not an end-use good. And government includes large investment, consumer goods, and service components that are not separately reported.

   Investment, both private and public, has value only because it is useful in producing an end-use consumer good.[35] The value of capital goods arises because the investment is required to produce the consumer good and service or because the consumer satisfaction can be produced more cheaply through use of machines. The accounts can make investment a separate sector because along the way they have subtracted depreciation and savings from gross incomes. These gross incomes, in turn, arose from the sale of goods and services at prices high enough to cover the cost of capital as well as wages, energy, raw materials, and so forth. Also these prices were high enough to permit payment of taxes by the sellers. The taxes were deducted along the way as the gross income from sales worked its way down to the bottom line, as is demonstrated below with national income account data.

*Taxes as Prices*

If taxes were increased to provide more free consumer goods, in other words, if taxes were used to pay the price for a larger portion of consumer goods, for example, medical services, then the prices of market-provided goods and services would go up to permit this resource transfer. However, consumers would have more money to cover these higher prices because medical services would now be free. Prices would be up, but inflation would not have taken place. The higher prices would, however, bring about a reallocation of consumer satisfaction. Those not using medical services would have a reduced scale of living. The large users of medical services would have their scale of living expanded.

The concepts of national income and taxation incidence as included in the national income and product accounts were satisfactory in 1929, but they no longer meet the test of helpfulness in the 1980s.[36] Taxes at nearly one-third of incomes bring about too great an adjustment of factor incomes to allow continuation of reporting the before-tax income figure and the after-tax price figure. Wages and profits and other factor incomes must be reported as the after-tax figure. Indirect business taxes plus depreciation must be treated as other taxes and business production costs. National income must be moved up to gross national income.

Taxes are prices. Every consumer purchase includes a tie-in purchase of government spending. Also, every consumer purchase includes a tie-in purchase of capital goods. The present special treatment of indirect business taxes and depreciation as a deduction separate from the regular adjustments of factor incomes is confusing. In addition, this treatment perpetuates the idea that depreciation costs and indirect business taxes affect prices more directly than other costs. The more appropriate stance at this point in our understanding of the economic process is that of neutrality, which means the abandonment of the national income total, and instead working down from only a gross figure, as is done on the product side.[37]

*Price Includes All Taxes*

The national income accounts given in table 3-4 demonstrates that GNP, the price of all goods and services, includes within its total all taxes paid. Although the procedure utilized deducts "indirect business tax" before national income, these taxes, dollar for dollar, have the same impact on GNP, that is, the aggregate price of sales of goods and services, as the contributions for social insurance. In the case of corporate profits taxes, about the same effect is realized by subtracting corporate profits and adding back dividend payments, with corporate savings included along with the taxes. Table 3-4 leaves no doubt but that all the taxes paid within the economy are included in the final money value of GNP. Also, all taxes directly add, dollar for dollar, to price what they provide in government revenues.

These tax effects on prices must be considered in assessing the international competitive position of U.S.-produced products. Because all taxes, with the possible exception of natural-resource taxes, are included in price, countervailing U.S. duties are needed to harmonize the prices of U.S.-produced goods with those of nations using VAT.

Disposable income and GNP are the two major national-income aggregates, one being the gross base available to support economic activity and the other being total end-use income, (that is, personal saving and consumption). The size of each is not affected directly by the type of taxes used. The same amount of taxes is included in the GNP aggregate whether income or transaction taxes are used, and the same is true of the deductions in arriving at disposable income.[40]

The concept of a stable public-revenue source resting evenly on all GNP and not related to income redistribution or monopoly returns is attractive. It is generally realized that all economic activity benefits from public-sector services that are best financed as an even portion of GNP rather than by collecting a price or by attempting to reach surpluses of one type of another. The VAT is a tax that functions in this general manner.

In addition to the deduction of business contributions to social security and the addition of dividends paid, national income is reduced by net interest of business and increased by transfer payments, personal interest income, net interest which is received from government less interest paid government, and so on. The resulting personal-income figure is reduced by taxes as shown in table 3-5. The resulting disposable income is available to individuals to save or spend; as pointed out in table 3-5, it is the bottom line of the national income accounts and all that has gone before consists of intermediary goods (public and private investment), government provision of consumer goods and services, and net exports.

The disposable income is smaller because business taxes were deducted in arriving at national income and personal income just as truly as it is smaller because personal taxes in the form of income and social security taxes are deducted from personal income before the disposable-income total is arrived at. The location of the deduction does not affect the final result. It is also perhaps true, as has been mentioned by theorists of national income accounts, that taxes and government spending should be more closely integrated into the accounts.[38]

# Table 3-4
# From GNP to Personal Income, 1975-1978
*(billions of dollars)*

| | 1975 | 1976 | 1977 | 1978 | 1975 IV | 1976 I | 1976 II | 1976 III | 1976 IV | 1977 I | 1977 II | 1977 III | 1977 IV | 1978 I | 1978 II | 1978 III | 1978 IV |
|---|---|---|---|---|---|---|---|---|---|---|---|---|---|---|---|---|---|
| | *Millions of Dollars* | | | | *Billions of Dollars, Seasonally Adjusted at Annual Rates* | | | | | | | | | | | | |
| Gross national product | 1,528,833 | 1,702,156 | 1,899,508 | 2,127,560 | 1,598.0 | 1,653.7 | 1,683.1 | 1,715.8 | 1,756.1 | 1,820.2 | 1,876.0 | 1,930.5 | 1,971.3 | 2,011.3 | 2,104.2 | 2,159.6 | 2,235.2 |
| *Less:* Capital-consumption allowances with capital-consumption adjustment | 161,954 | 177,769 | 195,445 | 216,888 | 169.5 | 173.6 | 176.4 | 178.8 | 182.2 | 186.9 | 191.9 | 198.7 | 204.3 | 209.1 | 214.4 | 219.6 | 224.6 |
| Capital-consumption allowances without capital-consumption adjustment | 130,433 | 141,170 | 157,446 | 172,019 | 134.1 | 136.7 | 139.2 | 142.3 | 146.5 | 150.6 | 155.4 | 160.8 | 163.0 | 167.5 | 170.9 | 173.2 | 176.5 |
| *Less:* Capital-consumption adjustment | -31,521 | -36,599 | -37,999 | -44,869 | -35.4 | -36.9 | -37.2 | -36.6 | -35.7 | -36.3 | -36.5 | -37.9 | -41.3 | -41.6 | -43.5 | -46.4 | -48.0 |
| *Equals:* Net national product | 1,366,879 | 1,524,387 | 1,704,063 | 1,910,672 | 1,428.5 | 1,480.1 | 1,506.7 | 1,536.9 | 1,573.9 | 1,633.3 | 1,684.1 | 1,731.8 | 1,767.0 | 1,802.2 | 1,889.8 | 1,946.0 | 2,010.6 |
| *Less:* Indirect business tax and nontax liability | 139,246 | 154,400 | 165,009 | 178,065 | 145.3 | 146.6 | 149.8 | 153.0 | 156.2 | 160.1 | 162.7 | 166.9 | 170.6 | 173.6 | 179.3 | 177.2 | 182.1 |
| Business transfer payments | 7,599 | 8,024 | 8,748 | 9,158 | 8.1 | 8.0 | 8.0 | 8.0 | 8.0 | 8.6 | 8.7 | 8.9 | 8.9 | 8.9 | 9.0 | 9.2 | 9.5 |
| Statistical discrepancy | 7,371 | 6,118 | 7,515 | 3,315 | 6.4 | 3.3 | 4.5 | 7.4 | 9.3 | 9.1 | 8.6 | 7.7 | 4.6 | 3.0 | 2.3 | 3.9 | 4.1 |
| *Plus:* Subsidies less current surplus of government enterprises | 2,339 | 964 | 3,079 | 4,197 | 3.1 | 1.0 | .6 | 1.1 | 1.2 | 1.5 | 1.2 | 2.8 | 6.8 | 4.3 | 4.6 | 2.8 | 5.1 |
| *Equals:* National income | 1,215,002 | 1,359,809 | 1,525,780 | 1,724,331 | 1,271.8 | 1,323.1 | 1,344.9 | 1,369.6 | 1,401.6 | 1,456.9 | 1,505.3 | 1,554.1 | 1,589.8 | 1,621.0 | 1,703.9 | 1,752.5 | 1,820.0 |
| *Less:* Corporate profits with inventory valuation and capital-consumption adjustments | 95,902 | 126,844 | 149,956 | 167,673 | 110.3 | 130.1 | 125.6 | 126.9 | 124.6 | 137.1 | 148.0 | 160.8 | 153.0 | 141.2 | 169.4 | 175.2 | 184.8 |
| Net interest | 78,615 | 83,772 | 93,990 | 109,455 | 80.0 | 80.6 | 82.1 | 85.2 | 87.2 | 89.3 | 92.7 | 95.8 | 98.2 | 101.5 | 106.8 | 111.9 | 117.6 |
| Contributions for social insurance | 110,579 | 125,989 | 142,457 | 164,117 | 114.1 | 122.3 | 124.7 | 127.1 | 129.9 | 137.7 | 140.7 | 143.8 | 147.6 | 158.3 | 162.6 | 165.7 | 170.0 |
| Wage accruals less disbursements | 0 | 0 | 0 | 221 | 0 | 0 | 0 | 0 | 0 | 0 | 0 | 0 | 0 | 0 | 0 | .5 | .4 |
| *Plus:* Government transfer payments to persons | 170,567 | 185,817 | 199,624 | 214,935 | 178.1 | 182.1 | 181.3 | 188.3 | 191.6 | 194.5 | 195.6 | 202.4 | 206.0 | 208.5 | 209.8 | 219.1 | 222.3 |
| Personal interest income | 115,529 | 127,048 | 141,722 | 163,277 | 119.3 | 122.1 | 124.9 | 128.7 | 132.5 | 135.6 | 140.2 | 143.9 | 147.2 | 152.2 | 159.4 | 167.2 | 174.3 |
| Net interest | 78,615 | 83,772 | 93,900 | 109,455 | 80.0 | 80.6 | 82.1 | 85.2 | 87.2 | 89.3 | 92.7 | 95.8 | 98.2 | 101.5 | 106.8 | 111.9 | 117.6 |
| Interest paid by government to persons and business | 33,547 | 40,053 | 43,803 | 49,771 | 36.4 | 38.4 | 39.6 | 40.4 | 41.8 | 42.6 | 43.4 | 44.1 | 45.1 | 47.1 | 48.9 | 51.2 | 52.1 |
| *Less:* Interest received by government | 19,665 | 21,917 | 26,347 | 30,701 | 20.7 | 21.0 | 21.5 | 22.4 | 22.7 | 23.7 | 24.6 | 25.9 | 27.2 | 28.7 | 30.3 | 31.4 | 32.4 |
| Interest paid by consumers to business | 23,032 | 25,140 | 29,276 | 34,752 | 23.5 | 24.1 | 24.7 | 25.5 | 26.3 | 27.5 | 28.7 | 20.8 | 31.1 | 32.4 | 34.0 | 35.6 | 37.1 |
| Dividends | 31,885 | 37,484 | 42,108 | 47,164 | 32.6 | 34.6 | 36.9 | 38.4 | 40.0 | 40.8 | 41.5 | 42.7 | 43.4 | 45.1 | 46.0 | 47.8 | 49.7 |
| Business transfer payments | 7,599 | 8,024 | 8,748 | 9,158 | 8.1 | 8.0 | 8.0 | 8.0 | 8.0 | 8.6 | 8.7 | 8.9 | 8.9 | 8.9 | 9.0 | 9.2 | 9.5 |
| *Equals:* Personal income | 1,255,486 | 1,381,610 | 1,534,576 | 1,717,309 | 1,305.4 | 1,336.9 | 1,363.7 | 1,393.9 | 1,432.0 | 1,472.5 | 1,509.0 | 1,548.5 | 1,596.4 | 1,634.8 | 1,689.3 | 1,742.5 | 1,803.1 |

Source: *Survey of Current Business,* July 1979, p. 29.

**Table 3-5**
**From Personal Income to Disposable Income, 1975-1978**
*(billions of dollars)*

| | 1975 | 1976 | 1977 | 1978 | 1975 IV | 1976 I | 1976 II | 1976 III | 1976 IV | 1977 I | 1977 II | 1977 III | 1977 IV | 1978 I | 1978 II | 1978 III | 1978 IV |
|---|---|---|---|---|---|---|---|---|---|---|---|---|---|---|---|---|---|
| | Millions of Dollars | | | | Billions of Dollars, Seasonally Adjusted at Annual Rates | | | | | | | | | | | | |
| Personal income | 1,255,486 | 1,381,610 | 1,531,576 | 1,717,399 | 1,365.4 | 1,336.9 | 1,363.7 | 1,393.9 | 1,432.0 | 1,472.5 | 1,509.0 | 1,548.5 | 1,596.4 | 1,634.8 | 1,699.3 | 1,742.5 | 1,803.1 |
| Wage and salary disbursements | 805,872 | 889,977 | 983,991 | 1,103,273 | 836.1 | 860.7 | 880.5 | 898.0 | 920.7 | 945.8 | 971.8 | 995.0 | 1,023.4 | 1,052.0 | 1,090.0 | 1,116.8 | 1,154.3 |
| Commodity-producing industries | 274,976 | 307,186 | 343,141 | 387,378 | 285.2 | 297.4 | 304.3 | 309.9 | 317.1 | 327.9 | 340.5 | 348.1 | 356.1 | 363.9 | 383.4 | 393.7 | 408.6 |
| Manufacturing | 211,045 | 237,423 | 265,956 | 298,292 | 230.1 | 229.4 | 235.1 | 239.8 | 245.4 | 254.8 | 263.3 | 269.4 | 276.4 | 285.6 | 294.1 | 300.8 | 312.7 |
| Distributive industries | 195,317 | 216,300 | 239,087 | 269,421 | 202.1 | 208.6 | 214.1 | 218.7 | 223.8 | 230.0 | 236.0 | 241.8 | 248.5 | 257.6 | 265.5 | 272.5 | 281.6 |
| Service industries | 160,138 | 178,495 | 200,458 | 228,703 | 166.5 | 170.9 | 175.8 | 180.7 | 186.6 | 192.2 | 196.8 | 202.9 | 210.0 | 218.2 | 225.4 | 231.9 | 239.4 |
| Government and government enterprises | 175,441 | 187,996 | 201,310 | 217,771 | 181.3 | 183.9 | 186.4 | 186.6 | 193.2 | 195.7 | 198.5 | 202.2 | 208.8 | 212.3 | 215.3 | 218.7 | 224.7 |
| Other labor income | 65,128 | 77,418 | 91,759 | 100,459 | 69.5 | 72.6 | 75.8 | 79.0 | 82.3 | 86.2 | 89.7 | 93.7 | 97.4 | 101.1 | 104.7 | 108.2 | 111.9 |
| Proprietors' income with inventory valuation and capital-consumption adjustments | 86,980 | 89,348 | 100,155 | 116,789 | 91.2 | 89.0 | 89.8 | 87.6 | 91.1 | 96.9 | 97.6 | 98.6 | 107.6 | 109.1 | 115.0 | 117.4 | 125.7 |
| Farm | 23,471 | 18,320 | 19,637 | 27,698 | 25.1 | 20.9 | 19.6 | 16.5 | 16.3 | 19.2 | 17.9 | 16.8 | 24.7 | 25.7 | 27.7 | 26.1 | 31.3 |
| Nonfarm | 63,509 | 71,028 | 80,518 | 89,091 | 66.1 | 68.0 | 70.2 | 71.0 | 74.8 | 77.7 | 79.8 | 81.7 | 82.9 | 83.4 | 87.3 | 91.3 | 94.4 |
| Rental income of persons with capital-consumption adjustment | 22,426 | 22,074 | 24,747 | 25,899 | 22.5 | 22.0 | 21.6 | 21.9 | 22.8 | 23.6 | 24.6 | 25.2 | 25.5 | 25.2 | 24.4 | 26.8 | 27.1 |
| Dividends | 31,885 | 37,484 | 42,108 | 47,164 | 32.6 | 34.6 | 36.9 | 38.4 | 40.0 | 40.8 | 41.5 | 42.7 | 43.4 | 45.1 | 46.0 | 47.8 | 49.7 |
| Personal interest income | 115,529 | 127,048 | 141,722 | 163,277 | 119.3 | 122.1 | 124.9 | 128.7 | 132.5 | 135.6 | 140.2 | 143.9 | 147.2 | 152.2 | 159.4 | 167.2 | 174.3 |
| Transfer payments | 178,166 | 193,841 | 208,369 | 224,093 | 186.2 | 190.1 | 189.3 | 196.4 | 199.6 | 203.1 | 204.2 | 211.3 | 214.8 | 217.4 | 218.8 | 228.3 | 231.8 |
| Old-age, survivors', disability, and health insurance benefits | 81,426 | 92,807 | 104,944 | 116,280 | 86.1 | 88.1 | 89.3 | 95.8 | 98.3 | 99.6 | 101.7 | 108.4 | 110.0 | 111.4 | 112.4 | 119.8 | 121.5 |
| Government unemployment-insurance benefits | 17,387 | 15,454 | 12,468 | 9,233 | 18.0 | 17.0 | 14.8 | 15.2 | 14.8 | 14.7 | 12.6 | 11.4 | 11.2 | 10.5 | 9.2 | 9.0 | 8.2 |
| Veterans' benefits | 14,471 | 14,367 | 13,810 | 13,883 | 15.1 | 15.8 | 14.4 | 13.5 | 13.8 | 14.3 | 13.9 | 13.4 | 13.7 | 14.0 | 13.7 | 13.7 | 14.1 |
| Government employees' retirement benefits | 22,680 | 25,906 | 29,229 | 32,899 | 24.0 | 24.6 | 25.8 | 26.4 | 26.9 | 27.6 | 28.9 | 29.6 | 30.8 | 31.4 | 32.5 | 33.1 | 34.6 |
| Aid to families with dependent children | 9,234 | 10,058 | 10,579 | 10,700 | 9.7 | 9.8 | 10.0 | 10.2 | 10.3 | 10.4 | 10.6 | 10.7 | 10.7 | 10.7 | 10.8 | 10.7 | 10.7 |
| Other | 32,968 | 35,189 | 37,339 | 41,098 | 33.3 | 34.9 | 34.9 | 35.3 | 35.6 | 36.4 | 36.7 | 37.8 | 38.5 | 39.5 | 40.3 | 42.0 | 42.6 |
| Less: Personal contributions for social insurance | 50,500 | 55,580 | 61,275 | 69,555 | 51.9 | 54.2 | 55.1 | 56.0 | 57.0 | 59.5 | 60.8 | 61.8 | 63.0 | 67.3 | 69.0 | 70.2 | 71.8 |
| Less: Personal tax and nontax payments | 168,828 | 197,098 | 226,443 | 259,011 | 179.6 | 184.8 | 193.5 | 200.8 | 209.4 | 222.4 | 223.0 | 225.3 | 235.2 | 239.8 | 252.1 | 266.0 | 278.2 |
| Equals: Disposable personal income | 1,086,658 | 1,184,512 | 1,305,133 | 1,458,388 | 1,125.8 | 1,152.2 | 1,170.2 | 1,193.1 | 1,222.6 | 1,250.1 | 1,286.0 | 1,323.2 | 1,361.2 | 1,395.0 | 1,437.3 | 1,476.5 | 1,524.8 |
| Less: Personal outlays | 1,003,010 | 1,115,924 | 1,240,168 | 1,386,362 | 1,046.0 | 1,078.4 | 1,099.3 | 1,126.8 | 1,159.2 | 1,197.6 | 1,220.2 | 1,251.3 | 1,291.7 | 1,320.4 | 1,366.1 | 1,405.6 | 1,453.4 |
| Personal-consumption expenditures | 970,070 | 1,089,867 | 1,209,968 | 1,350,762 | 1,021.6 | 1,053.3 | 1,073.7 | 1,100.5 | 1,132.0 | 1,169.1 | 1,190.5 | 1,220.6 | 1,259.7 | 1,287.2 | 1,331.2 | 1,369.3 | 1,415.4 |
| Interest paid by consumers to business | 23,032 | 25,140 | 29,276 | 34,752 | 23.5 | 24.1 | 24.7 | 25.5 | 26.3 | 27.5 | 28.7 | 29.8 | 31.1 | 32.4 | 34.0 | 35.6 | 37.1 |
| Personal transfer payments to foreigners (net) | 908 | 917 | 924 | 848 | .9 | 1.0 | .9 | .9 | .9 | 1.0 | 1.0 | .9 | .9 | .8 | .9 | .7 | .9 |
| Equals: Personal saving | 83,648 | 68,588 | 64,965 | 72,026 | 79.8 | 73.8 | 70.9 | 66.3 | 63.4 | 52.5 | 65.9 | 71.9 | 69.5 | 74.6 | 71.2 | 70.9 | 71.5 |
| Addenda: Disposable personal income: Total, billions of 1972 dollars | 859.7 | 891.8 | 929.5 | 972.6 | 871.7 | 883.1 | 887.7 | 893.4 | 903.3 | 908.0 | 921.5 | 936.3 | 951.8 | 956.6 | 966.1 | 976.2 | 981.5 |
| Per capita Current dollars | 5,088 | 5,504 | 6,017 | 6,672 | 5,255 | 5,369 | 5,444 | 5,540 | 5,665 | 5,782 | 5,937 | 6,096 | 6,257 | 6,402 | 6,584 | 6,749 | 6,955 |
| 1972 dollars | 4,025 | 4,144 | 4,285 | 4,449 | 4,069 | 4,115 | 4,130 | 4,148 | 4,185 | 4,200 | 4,255 | 4,313 | 4,375 | 4,390 | 4,426 | 4,462 | 4,522 |
| Population (millions) | 213.6 | 215.2 | 216.9 | 218.6 | 214.3 | 214.6 | 214.9 | 215.4 | 215.8 | 216.2 | 216.6 | 217.1 | 217.5 | 217.9 | 218.3 | 218.8 | 219.3 |
| Personal saving as percentage of disposable personal income | 7.7 | 5.8 | 5.0 | 4.9 | 7.1 | 6.4 | 6.1 | 5.6 | 5.2 | 4.2 | 5.1 | 5.4 | 5.1 | 5.3 | 5.0 | 4.8 | 4.7 |

Source: Taken from *Survey of Current Business*, July 1979, p. 35.

*Conclusion*

The proper treatment of taxes in the national-income accounts has been the subject of considerable difference of opinion through the years. One problem continued to bother the developers of the accounts: the theory taught that indirect and direct taxes had quite different incidences, but the system of the accounts resulted in all taxes being in the same pot—prices. Also, the difference between business taxes and personal taxes which lay behind the whole concept that democracies possess only the ability to tax according to the ability to pay disappeared when the collections from both direct and indirect taxes had the same effect on disposable income, as treated in the national-income accounts. Both direct and indirect tax payments acted to reduce disposable income and became basically the same kind of tax when it was looked at in terms of aggregate spending power for end-use goods and services,[39] the production of which is the whole purpose of the economic process.

**Notes**

1. *Hearings before the Committee on Finance, U.S. Senate*, Revenue Act of 1963, table 1, p. 378. H.R. 7015 decreases the top income tax rate to 50 percent.

2. "Germany has practically given up the progressive [income] tax and has initiated methods of attaining the social effects of progression in other ways, with fewer of its disadvantages." Frederick G. Reuss, *Fiscal Policy for Growth without Inflation* (Baltimore, Md.: John Hopkins Press, 1963), p. 82.

3. At the same time as the Swedish government was presenting plans for adoption of a value-added tax and some reduction of income taxes, it was providing for large increases in children's allowances. Karl-Olof Faxen, "A Programme for Tax Policy, 1966-1970," *Skandinaviska Banken Quarterly Review*, 1964, pp. 3, 77.

4. Member states of the EEC are large users of GRE taxes, and their gross reserve of gold and convertible currencies rose from a 1958 level of $10,135 million to an end-of-1964 level of $19,776 million. French reserves rose most spectacularly, increasing from $1,050 million in 1958 to $5,172 million in January 1965. During this period, the U.S. gross reserve of gold and convertible currencies fell from $20,582 million to $15,903 million, and the United Kingdom level fell from $3,069 million to $2,316 million. *Journal of Commerce*, March 11, 1965, p. 23. The United Kingdom did not have a VAT yet.

5. This characteristic, at least for the personal income tax, is perhaps less important than assumed. "A flat-rate tax of 23 percent on all taxable

income would have produced virtually the same degree of built-in flexibility as was experienced in the years 1954-1960." Richard Goode, *The Individual Income Tax* (Washington: Brookings Institution, 1965), pp. 291-292.

6. Nancy Teeters, "Federal Tax on Corporate Profits," Federal Reserve Board Memorandum, December 5, 1963, (mimeographed), p. 3.

7. "Its [Michigan business activity tax] collections vary considerably with changes in the level of business activity but more than likely not as violently as the corporate income tax liabilities." Richard W. Lindholm, "Business Activity Tax," *Michigan Tax Studies*, (Lansing: Michigan Legislature, 1958).

8. Wilfred Lewis, *Federal Fiscal Policy in the Post-war Recessions* (Washington: Brookings Institution, 1962), pp. 195-196.

9. George S. Tolley and C. Eugene Steuerle, "The Effect of Excises on Taxation and Measurement of Income," in *1978 Compendium of Tax Research* (U.S. Treasury, 1979), pp. 67-83.

10. J.F. Wood, "Business Problems under Sales and Use Taxes," in *State and Local Taxes on Business* (Princeton, N.J.: Tax Institute of America, 1965), pp. 26-27.

11. John S. Nolan, "How VAT Should Operate in the United States," *Tax Policy* (Princeton, N.J.: Tax Institute of America, 1972), pp. 20-26.

12. Committee on Ways and Means, "Explanation of the 'Tax Restructuring Act of 1980'" (H.R. 7015) (Washington: GPO, 1980), pp. 15-21.

13. National Economic Development Office, *VAT* (London: Her Majesty's Stationery Office, 1969), appendix, summary of replies to the industrial questionnaire, pp. 79-98.

14. Cambridge Research Institute, *The Value Added Tax in the United States, Its Implications for Retailers* (Cambridge, Mass.: CRI, 1970), pp. 170-181.

15. William I. Stoddard. "Effect of a VAT on Service Industries," in *Tax Policy* (Princeton, N.J.: Tax Institute of America, 1972), pp. 59-65.

16. Douglas H. Eldridge, "Equity, Administration and Compliance, and Intergovernmental Fiscal Aspects," in *The Role of Direct and Indirect Taxes in the Federal Revenue Systems* (Washington: Brookings Institution, 1964), pp. 141-177.

17. Conversations with Professor Carl S. Shoup, (Columbia University, New York) January 1965.

18. *General Statistical Bulletin*, no. 12, table 65 (Brussels, Belgium: Statistical Office of the European Communities).

19. *Economic Report of the President*, January 1969, table B-48, p. 282; and *Survey of Current Business*, June 1969, table S-8.

20. A.C. Harberger, "A Federal Tax on Value Added," in *The Taxpayer Stake in Tax Reform* (Washington: U.S. Chamber of Commerce, 1968), pp. 21-32.

21. *The New York Times*, December 1, 1969, "Mark Revaluation Lifts Prices of U.S. Imports" p. 73.

22. Executive Office of the President, Office of the Special Representative for Trade Negotiations, *Press Release* no. 120, December 3, 1968, p. 3.

23. *Die Zeit*, January 7, 1969, p. 13.

24. *Armco Steel Corporation v. Department of Revenue* (359 Mich. 430, 1960).

25. James M. Buchanan, *Fiscal Theory and Political Economy* (Chapel Hill: University of North Carolina Press, 1960), p. 139.

26. E.A. Rolph, *The Theory of Fiscal Economics* (Berkeley: University of California Press, 1954), chapters 6 and 7.

27. Organization of Economic Cooperation and Development, *Report on Tax Adjustments Applied to Exports and Imports in OECD Member Countries* (Paris: OECD Publications, 1968), p. 79.

28. "Inflation and the Redistribution of Income: The Norwegian Experience," *The OECD Observer*, Paris, France February 1973, pp. 38-39.

29. Albert T. Sommers, "Inflation and Economic Policy (in the Light of American Social Realities." *Conference Board Record* 11 (October 1974):2-6.

30. "Sources and Methods of National Income Estimation," pt. III, *National Income* (a supplement to the *Survey of Current Business*) (Washington, D.C.: USGPO, 1954), pp. 61-152; also, "Data Sources and Procedures," *U.S. Income and Output* (a supplement to the *Survey of Current Business*) (Washington, D.C.: USGPO, 1958), pp. 70-105, chapters 7, 8.

31. *Economic Report of the President, 1972*, pp. 195, 269, 279.

32. Ansel M. Sharp and Bernard F. Sliger, in *Public Finance* (Homewood, Ill.: Dorsey Press, 1964), do not include *business tax* in their index. Herbert E. Newman, in *Introduction to Public Finance* (New York: John Wiley & Sons, 1968), starts his discussion of a group of taxes levied on businesses with this question: "First, what is meant by a business tax?" Then he proceeds to quote experts and analyze possible answers (pp. 509-515).

33. U.S. Steel Corporation, *"Legal and Economic Brief,"* September 17, 1975), pp. 50-56.

34. Of course, depreciation does not represent a cash outlay; rather, it is an accounting item and is to this extent different from other costs making up selling price. "While investment may be a final product in terms of national income identities, in economic terms it is really an intermediary good." Ann F. Friedlaender, "Incidence and Price Effects of Value-Added Taxes," *Proceedings of National Tax Association* 1971, p. 278.

35. David L. Grove, in *Survey of Current Business* 51, no. 7, (July 1971):91-92, pt. II, pointed out need for refinement of government purchases.

36. Carl S. Shoup, *Principles of National Income Analyses* (Boston: Houghton Mifflin, 1947), pp. 155, 231-288.

37. National Bureau of Economic Research, *The National Economic Accounts of the United States*, General Series 64(1958):12-13, 75-84, favors a reclassification and integration of national economic accounts. Appendix A demonstrates the approach. The taxes are all included in a single account titled "tax and income payments by producing units to government". No separation is made between what is called "commodity and transaction taxes" and the "corporate profits tax." "Tax payments by individuals" includes income and social security taxes.

38. Discussion included in footnote 37 plus Milton Gilber, "Objective of National Income Measurement: A Reply to Professor Kuznets," *Review of Economics and Statistics* 30 (August 1948), pp. 151-195.

39. Earl R. Rolph, "The Concept of Transfers in National Income Estimates," *Quarterly Journal of Economics*, May 1948, pp. 327-361.

40. J.C. Holland, in "Taxing a Fallacy," *The Accountant*, March 18, 1976, pp. 322-323, argues that all VAT collected before end use is completely unproductive.

# 4 Financing Social Security and Federalism

## Overview

All the subsequent sections in this chapter are concerned with the financing of social security. The next section is concerned with the broad general concerns of social security financing, for example, the degree to which social security financing must consist of the transfer of income between income levels and between generations. Another general social security financing consideration is the degree to which benefit payments are dependent on current contributions and the earnings from accumulated reserves.

Through its treatment of indirect taxes and its rules relative to the refund of social security contributions as a subsidy, GATT has encouraged the indirect use of VAT to meet social security need for support from general revenues. The discussion here takes the position that any increase in VAT collections results in VAT being used indirectly to finance social security. If this position is accepted, all users of VAT who deduct VAT from export prices are subsidizing their exports.

The third section looks at the general growth and the expected size of all social-welfare spending. In addition, an examination is made of the relative desirability of using the payroll tax or VAT to meet the expected demand for funds. The payroll tax's direct increase of labor costs and VAT's broader base plus its international trade advantage make VAT the preferred source if the employment level is a vital policy consideration.

A mature social-welfare expenditure program probably will absorb 16 to 18 percent of GNP. Currently the U.S. level of expenditure is about one-half of the level that can be expected as the average age of the population increases and stabilizes, and approximate birth-to-death support in the eight basic categories is provided.

The payroll tax has the same political advantage in maintaining breadth of coverage as is possessed by the additive-type VAT. The advantage is that wages or income arising from an industry producing necessities can be taxed at the same level as wages or income paid to producers of luxury goods without causing a cry of tax regressivity or of taxing necessities. Table 4-1 summarizes the levels of social expenditures of a number of the major industrial countries.

The fourth section continues the portion of the third section that examined the relative strengths of the payroll tax and a VAT. Calculations

**Table 4-1**

**Social Security and Welfare Expenditures as a Percentage of Total Expenditures of Central Government**

|  | 1974 | 1975 | 1976 | 1977 | 1978 |
|---|---|---|---|---|---|
| Austria | 39.12 | 39.56 | 38.74 | 39.26 | 39.59 |
| Canada | 38.84 | 35.23 | 35.36 | 34.67 | — |
| France | — | 40.98 | 41.70 | — | — |
| Germany | 45.61 | 49.52 | 49.41 | 50.58 | — |
| Italy | 41.10 | 33.48 | — | — | — |
| Japan | — | — | — | — | — |
| Luxembourg | 49.56 | 51.62 | 52.78 | 53.35 | — |
| Netherlands | 48.12 | 48.34 | 48.89 | 48.60 | — |
| Norway | 31.97 | 31.46 | 30.59 | 29.15 | — |
| Sweden | 44.84 | 44.30 | 45.06 | 46.34 | — |
| United Kingdom | 22.33 | 21.29 | 22.74 | — | — |
| United States | 33.91 | 36.56 | 36.09 | 34.17 | — |

Source: "Central Government: Expenditure by Function," in *Government Finance Statistics Yearbook,* vol. 3 (Washington: International Monetary Fund, 1979), p. 27.

based on the breadth implicit in H.R. 7015 conclude that a VAT rate of 11.5 percent would be needed to equal a combined payroll tax rate on the existing base of 12.26 percent. The payroll tax is a powerful revenue raiser.

The identification of the economic burden of both VAT and the payroll tax has proved difficult. General statements that approximated the relative economic strengths of the parties directly involved are not useful when the rates increase to meet the expanding need for revenues. However, it can be said with some confidence that the wage earner is somewhat worse off under the payroll-tax procedure existing today than he would be if VAT financing were used.

The fifth section considers the very serious difficulties existing today in financing the different governent units, particularly the cities, under our federal system of finance. Revenue sharing was the major new procedure developed in the 1960s to solve this problem. The high expectations developed at that time are not being realized today.

The portion of the financing of different levels of government that arises from business cycles can be reduced by moving away from unstable revenue sources. The so-called cyclically balancing revenue sources have provided greater rather than less economic instability. The use of VAT at the federal level along the lines of H.R. 7015 can be helpful here.

It would be appropriate to make a comprehensive VAT base available for use by state and local governments as well as by the federal government. Table 4-3 provides data on how a national VAT might be divided among the states as a genuine revenue-sharing tax operation. The distribution is made on the basis of the retail sales total arising in each state.

The last section takes another look at regressivity as it applies to VAT and why economic fine-tuning and its emphasis on the level of demand and lack of emphasis on supply have produced serious shortcomings. Supply is the result of productivity, and it is the payment for production that provides noninflationary purchasing power. Taxes, as they have become about one-third of GNP in the United States and around 50 percent of GNP in some other capitalistic industrial nations, have become a vital policy area. How this large portion of our resources is collected is important. The VAT is a procedure to help meet the revenue-need expansion without destroying willingness to invest at risk and to save from current income.

## General Consideration of Social
## Security Financing

When social security is being financed nearly entirely with payroll taxes, the program is being financed with direct taxes. Export prices, under GATT understandings, may not benefit from a refund of these taxes. However, indirect taxes, for example, of the VAT type, may be refunded on exports if they go into the general revenue fund. This tax refund on exports is available to VAT and other indirect taxes even though the direct taxes required to meet general revenue needs can be reduced because of the additional indirect taxes. This means that VAT taxpayers benefit from a refund of the taxes allocated to their exports, but this same benefit is not available to the payers of payroll taxes.

If the general revenues of a nation are expanded through VAT collections and, as a result, additional social security payments can be made without higher income or payroll taxes, this does not affect VAT-payment treatment. As an indirect general tax not assigned to the financing of social security VAT can continue to be refunded on exports and collected as a border tax on imports.[1]

When VAT is added to a nation's general revenues, the government's ability to use taxes to adjust international impacts of a given public-sector program increases.[2] With transfer payments of governments expanding at different rates and with the division between the public and private sector's financial responsibility for social services varying all over the lot, failure to utilize VAT's capability is short-sighted.[3]

The Tax Restructuring Act of 1980 (H.R. 7015) provides directly for the reduction of social security taxes with revenues to allow this provided by a federal VAT that would raise $115 billion of new funds during calendar year 1981. (The United States and other countries engage in exchange-rate rigging activities. The float remains a dirty float.) The direct assignment of VAT collections to subsidize wage income, by reducing the contributions which wage earners and employers make to cover costs of the program, encounters some international difficulties.[4] However, several Western European nations are also moving toward doing directly what has always been done indirectly.

This change in GATT's attitude toward what constitutes a subsidy of wages increases the desirability of having a substantial VAT in a nation's bag of taxes.[5] The new international treatment of VAT from that available to a payroll or income tax is, of course, increasing the advantage of financing social security with VAT rather than with payroll or income taxes. If H.R. 7015 were adopted, it would allocate $43 billion of revenues to the financing of social security. This amount could be refunded to exporters and added to imports as a border tax. If VAT were not available to finance social security, the expansion in revenues required to keep the U.S. program viable would increase costs of U.S. exports and prevent an increase of the prices of imported goods and services to compensate for the higher U.S. prices due to tax-collection expansion to meet social security's higher costs.[6]

Under H.R. 7015, both the employer and the employee payroll tax rate would be reduced by 1.8 percentage points from the scheduled 1981 rate. The legislated rate for both employees and employers will be 6.65 percent in 1981. The 1.8 percentage-point reduction of VAT, as established in H.R. 7015, amounts to a 27 percent reduction of the 1981 payroll tax level. The general economic effects of this shift should be favorable. The cost of employing a new worker is decreased, and the international competitiveness of U.S. firms in making both domestic and foreign sales is increased.

The Scandinavian countries traditionally have been big users of general revenues to support basic old-age, invalidity, and death benefits. When they adopted VAT in the late 1960s, they placed the new and higher tax collections into the general revenue fund. About 80 percent of the cost of the very substantial general social support programs of these Northern European nations are met out of general central-government revenues. This situation was not changed when the revenues of the general funds were expanded more with VAT collections than the sales and other taxes repealed and cut when VAT was introduced.

## Conclusion

The administration and generally Congress have failed to associate social security financing with employment levels, international trade, and limits on tax rates placed on wage and property income. Unless an economic understanding of this breadth is adopted, the future will be more uncertain than it need be, and problems of unemployment, international trade deficits, and inflationary federal-government borrowing will worsen.

**Financing Social-Welfare Spending**

The United States is entering a period of careful reconsideration of its social security, medical delivery, and welfare program expenditures. The expansion of the provision of these services to people through government financing seems to be in the cards. In moving in this direction we are not treading on untried paths. The European industrial nations of the Free World have had considerable experience. They appear to have decided that the best government-finance approach, if one takes into consideration the basic requirement that the private-enterprise system must prosper, is to make extensive use of the VAT along with payroll taxes to meet basic welfare revenue requirements and to finance programs going beyond basic needs.

The discussions that follow analyze the desirability of adoption of the European approach. The analyses consider particularly carefully the comparative economic impacts of financing expanded social security, medical delivery, and welfare with the existing payroll tax approach and alternatively with the assistance of a general and substantial VAT.

When one considers tax policy in this area, it is well to keep in mind what President Couve de Murville, the former French Minister of Finance, did during the French economic crisis of 1968 (a crisis that resulted in a devaluation of the French franc and was triggered by student riots in the streets of Paris). He eliminated the payroll tax paid by French employers. This was a 4.25 percent tax on total payrolls. The revenue lost, and a bit more, was made up by increasing the rates on the French VAT.

The switch was carried out in order to reduce labor costs and make French goods more competitive. The French measure essentially boiled down to eliminating the wages tax and taking an equivalent amount of revenue through a rise in the VAT rates. We have here a procedure for swallowing up taxes that under GATT understandings do not provide for refunds on exports and border taxes on imports because they are direct taxes. The result is an expansion of tax-related border adjustments on internationally traded goods and services without a corresponding impact on domestic prices.

*Relation to Wage Bargain*

The base of the value-added tax, as must be true of all broadly based taxes, direct or indirect, consists largely of the input of labor. The wage earners of a modern society are the final users and buyers of production as well as the major income receivers. *When compared with the payroll tax, VAT is one step farther from labor compensation and one step closer to labor as a final user of production. This difference is of sufficient importance to warrant consideration in thinking about financing a comprehensive social security program with VAT.*

The prevailing institutional economic arrangement in the United States causes workers to have much more control over the wages they receive than over the prices they pay. For example, higher wage demands are frequent, but a labor strike for lower prices is nearly unheard of, and labor monitoring of price policies is nearly as rare. It is also true that neither prices nor wages are completely manageable, and the level of both continues to bear some of the mystery of the workings of Adam Smith's invisible hand.

The introduction of a VAT that provides the substantial additional revenues required to balance the intake and outflow of the portion of the public economy concerned with social security in the broadest sense removes this financing a greater distance from the wage bargain than exists under a system of payroll taxes. Under a payroll tax system, additional taxes are withheld from wages, and the employer is required to pay a wage-related tax increase each time social security reserves and/or benefits need more funds.

The relation of payroll tax rates and base to the wage bargain is apparent in negotiation efforts aimed at keeping and increasing the purchasing power of take-home pay. In the United States, the rapid increase in the withholding rates of social security with Medicare plus the increase in the maximum salary covered by social security taxes has triggered action to reduce employment and increase automation. Also, the U.S. tax climate developed by the push for the 10 percent federal income tax surcharge during the last half of 1967 and in 1968 contributed to the increased emphasis on the relationship between tax withholding and the level of take-home pay. When the level of take-home pay gained the position of central attention in wage bargaining, the level of tax withholding was added to price increases in setting wage scales.

The payroll tax is much more closely related to cost of labor than is an indirect tax like VAT. It is this relationship that appears to cause payroll taxes to have a greater deleterious effect on the level of employment than a VAT-type tax.

*Revenue Needs*

The VAT can make additional funds available to general government so that general revenues become available to finance a substantial portion of social-program expenditures. It is the use of VAT to provide substantial additional general revenues that must be a major portion of the social security financing aspect of VAT. The provision of these revenues also acts to ensure a current revenue base adequate to provide the purchasing power needed from the earnings-related portion of a national social spending program.

A tax-balanced budget from revenues collected in a manner that encourages business activity continues to bring in its full level of revenue receipts, year after year, while a debt-financed budget piles debt plus interest costs on top of each other, again, year after year. The German experience seems to be an example of the use of a broad-based VAT to provide general revenue levels that make use of deficits of 4 or 5 percent of GNP unnecessary to finance a national budget level which reasonably well meets total government economic responsibilities but relatively low defense spending.

### Cost of Mature Welfare Program

An estimate of the cost of a fully matured, efficiently managed social-expenditure program is 16 to 18 percent of GNP. Currently the U.S. effort is at about the 9 percent level, so expansion in this area can be expected to continue. The Swedes, who are now at the 18 percent level, were at the 9.2 percent level in 1962. Fiscal comparisons are always difficult and somewhat inaccurate, and this is also true of this one.[7] However, there is little doubt but that to meet the Western European level in the eight types of coverage identified as appropriate for a fully developed social-expenditure program, the United States will need to substantially expand tax revenues dedicated to this purpose.[8]

A study paper of the Joint Economic Committee of the U.S. Congress, released in September 1965, showed the United States to be spending for social security at a level considerably below that of the nations of Western Europe. This relative position has changed somewhat through the years, because U.S. social security payments appear to have expanded at a somewhat more rapid rate than those of Europe. This relatively more rapid expenditure growth can be expected to continue because the aged portion of the U.S. population is below that existing in Europe and is expected to reach the same level.[9]

### Payroll Tax Withholding Levels

Payroll taxes to raise 12 or 14 percent of the GNP of the United States would most likely have to include all wages and self-employed income in the base. Even when this broader wage and salary base were used, the total payroll tax rate (employee plus employer) would have to reach rates of 17 or

20 percent (assuming the wage and salary tax base was 70 percent of national income).

Rates at the current level for payroll taxes, when added to normal marginal federal income tax withholding rates of close to 20 percent plus a state income tax of 5 percent, cause the last dollar of individual take-home pay to be reduced by over one-third from the level of any labor-management wage bargain. The employer, because of pressure to keep the purchasing power of take-home pay rising through wage increases sufficient to cover the impact of progressive income taxes during inflation, while also meeting ever-higher employer payroll tax contributions, faces rising labor costs per unit of production. Labor to the employer becomes more expensive and therefore an item to be minimized in the production mix.

The situation that develops from the payroll tax method of financing social security is one that places the cost where it will have the greatest possible deterrent effect on business decisions to hire additional labor. Payroll taxes "are, in effect, a tax on employment. . . ."[10] On the other hand, the use of a broadly based VAT to meet basic government-financed social expenditures generalizes the cost. As a result, "there has been a tendency for the state's proportion of the total cost to increase in a number of countries, and for some schemes to be financed wholly by the state."[11]

*Income and Wage Tax Impacts*

High payroll taxes, when added to the U.S. tax system that already uses high personal-income taxes and high corporate profit taxes, produce very strong incentives to reduce domestic employment, income, and profits.[12] One important result of this pressure is an expansion of the portion of U.S.-controlled business activities carried out in foreign nations. Another result is to reduce domestic mobility of U.S. capital. This impact arises through efforts to keep total taxes down on corporate profits through minimization of earnings' payouts to stockholders. This policy causes stockholders to have less money to purchase new capital issues. Also, the tax-caused high cost of hiring additional labor and the high pretax earnings required from domestic-invested capital reduce the number of attractive new domestic business undertakings.[13]

The theory of the general transaction tax teaches that the tax does not affect business decisions or consumer decisions.[14] The requirements of a general business tax are violated when rates become different depending on business organization and items sold. The basic nature of the cascade turnover tax (lower taxes for integrated industries) was a prime cause of the breakdown of generality and uniformity in the turnover tax system of Germany. By eliminating a variation in tax liability depending on number of turnovers, VAT has added considerably to the generality and uniformity of the transaction-tax system of Germany and Western Europe. The VAT is also a tax possessing a proclivity toward increasing generality of coverage.[15]

The "antisocial" taint of being a tax as high on goods purchased by the poor as by the rich is carried by transaction taxes generally and is not removed by using VAT rather than a gross-turnover or a retail sales tax. The use of a value-added tax instead of retail sales or turnover taxes does, however, avoid tax-liability differences based on different procedures of bringing identical goods to market. Also, the ability of business firms engaged in any line of production to pass VAT forward in price depends largely on the elasticity of supply and the relative inelasticity of the final user demand for the product sold.[16] (A payroll tax will not develop a tax that is refunded on exports and a new tax on imports as does VAT.)

It is also true the CIT and even the individual income tax, *ceteris paribus*, are more likely to be shifted forward in higher prices if the amount sold does not sharply decrease when prices are raised and supply falls rapidly with lower offer prices. *In fact, from this particular point of view, the transaction-based tax, by violating the theoretically desirable tax feature of complete generality and using its unique ability to grant exemptions for particular products, has a distinct advantage over taxes using the profits, wage or income base, which cannot, or at least do not, exempt profits and incomes earned by producers of a necessity consumed in relatively large amounts by the poor.*[16]

There can be little doubt but that general EEC interest in moving rapidly toward a common VAT was stimulated by the 1954 French development of a value-added tax. The favored position of French industry as seen by other EEC member states, under the high French VAT and the application of the destination principle, is as follows:

[the] country of destination principle as presently applied to the turnover tax gives a distinct advantage to France. While the rate of the "taxe sur la valeur ajoutee" (TVA) is very high, the burden of direct taxes imposed on French enterprises is correspondingly lighter. Since the detaxing equalization removes the whole TVA from French exports at the frontier, France gives greater tax relief to its efforts than its neighbors . . . through the operation of the equalization machinery, French goods enjoy a virtual customers' protection. . . .[17]

## Social and Welfare Spending Trends

Nearly without exception, the portion of national-government revenues used to finance social security and welfare has been increasing. The percentage of national-government revenues dedicated to social expenditures is affected by the allocation of responsibilities in this field to provincial and local governments. A highly centralized fiscal system such as in France absorbs more of the expenditures for purposes other than social and military. Therefore, a high percentage of national government expenditures going for social and welfare purposes in France indicates greater activity than the same percentage in a more decentralized nation such as Canada or the United States.

In Germany where over 50 percent of national-government expenditures are for social and welfare purposes, the provincial and local governments' revenue-raising and expenditure activities are of considerable importance, somewhat on the level existing in the United States. Germany's total central-government revenues in 1977 totaled M 326 billion, provincial governments M 123 billion, and local governments M 77 billion., In the United States, central-government revenues totaled $371 billion in 1977 with state revenues equaling $133 billion and local government $104 billion.[18]

The relatively larger U.S. expenditures for defense accounts for the ability of Germany to spend a large portion of its total national-government expenditures for social and welfare purposes. In 1977 German defense expenditures totaled M 34 billion, or about 10 percent of total national tax revenues. The United States, on the other hand, spent $91 billion, or about 23 percent of national-government revenues, on national defense.

During the period from 1974 through 1977, the portion of U.S. central-government expenditures for social and welfare purposes increased by about 10 percent in 1975-1976 and then declined to about the 1974 level in 1977. The incomplete data comparisons appear to show that if the United States is going to continue its current level of defense expenditures, and not fall behind in its general level of social and welfare expenditures, it will have to develop a new stable, basic revenue source dedicated largely to the finance of social and welfare spending. The VAT seems to fill this bill in Western Europe.

*Conclusion*

The introduction of a subtractive VAT is basically the introduction of a general tax using net transactions or GNP as its base. A major tax on transactions is more than likely appropriate at the national level when 30 to 40 percent of GNP must be funneled through government to finance social security plus goods and services provided by the public economy. Also, a general transaction tax, and particularly VAT, provides export stimulation and import protection, which makes possible more national independence in setting expenditure policies. The payroll tax does not have these features, and it rests directly on costs of labor.

The bad social-impact reputation of a tax using transactions as its base can be only partially erased by numerous deductions and exemptions. In fact, it is perhaps unwise to attempt to change attitudes toward a transaction tax in this manner. There is no logical stopping place short of changing a "general" transaction tax into a "special product" excise tax.

General acceptance is more likely to be found in emphasizing improvement of general welfare through spending of collections.[19] European and particularly German and Scandinavian experience and the new British VAT seem to indicate that a high-rate tax on transactions becomes acceptable only in an informed democracy with citizens possessing a high social consciousness when, directly or indirectly, the revenues collected are associated with basic minimum-income protection.

The financing of an expanding basic social security, medical delivery, and welfare program from payroll, income, and profit taxes, all direct taxes, places a strain on a tax system limited to these taxes.[20] The introduction of a general transaction tax with substantial rates has overcome this difficulty in many Western European countries.[21]

## Payroll Tax versus VAT

Since 1975, the social security trust funds have been in deficit. In 1977 legislation was adopted to substantially increase the age base and the rates applied to this base by the federal payroll tax. This legislation will increase annual collections by about $25 billion in 1982, and the trust-fund deficits will have been turned around to a surplus of about $31 billion through higher taxes, increased interest receipts, and reduced benefits.

In order to bring about this social security financing shift, the federal payroll tax collections have been increased beyond what is desirable to continue a high level of employment. The combined rate (employee and employer) is not set at 12.26 percent, and the covered wage is $125,900. The law, to reach the goals set down in the 1977 legislation, provides a combined rate of 14.8 percent by 1982 and a wage base of $31,000. The goals established by Congress should be reached, but this could be done while payroll tax collections are being reduced. The adoption of a VAT along the lines of the Tax Restructuring Act of 1980 (H.R. 7015) would make this possible. If this is not done social security taxes must move upward as shown in table 4-2.

### Payroll Tax Coverage and Avoidance

The payroll tax uses only wages as its base. Tax payment can be decreased by the worker through arranging to work as a contract producer. The

**Table 4-2**
**Payroll Rates and Wage Base**

| Year | Taxable Wage Base ($) | Payroll Tax Rates[a] (Percent) |
|------|-----------------------|--------------------------------|
| 1977 | 16,500 | 5.85 |
| 1978 | 17,700 | 6.05 |
| 1979 | 22,900 | 6.13 |
| 1980 | 25,900 | 6.13 |
| 1981 | 29,700 | 6.65 |
| 1982 | 31,800 | 6.70 |
| 1986 | 40,200 | 7.15 |

Source: Helmut Wendel, *Technical Analysis Paper* (Washington: Congressional Budget Office, 1978), pp. 5-9.
[a]Rate is levied on the wage base twice—once for the employer and once for the employee.

worker can also reduce his liability by becoming a part of the ownership group. The first payroll tax-reduction technique is very popular with truckers. The second one works well under the conditions frequently found in the home-construction industry where workers often form a partnership with much of the work carried out by the members of the partnership.

The self-employed worker is encouraged by the U.S. payroll tax even when he decides to be covered by the tax. Prior to 1981, the self-employed person electing to be covered by the payroll tax paid 135 percent of the basic rate, or the regular employee rate times 1.35. After 1981, the relative self-employed rate is up somewhat, but remains 25 percent below the combined rate.

There are under the federal social security law other payroll tax-avoidance opportunities. For example, all federal-government employees and the federal government are exempted from the payroll tax. Also state and local governments can opt to be excluded as can welfare groupings, domestic help, and so on.

These avoidance opportunities and exemptions began to acquire major decision-making and economic importance when the combined payroll tax rate became 4.4 percent on the first $6,600 of wages back in the mid-1960s. Earlier the basic payroll tax rate and base over a thirty-year period had gradually increased from the combined 2 percent inaugural rate on $3,000 of covered wages. Currently the maximum annual payroll tax payment is $3,176. The employer writes the check for the full amount with one-half included as taxable income of the employee. The law permits employers to pay the workers' share as well as their own. When this is done, both employer and employee gain. The worker's salary is decreased, but payroll taxes are no longer a portion of his income tax base; therefore income taxes are reduced. The employer gains because the salary base on which he must pay is reduced.

The growth in the taxable wage base, from $16,500 in 1977 to the current $25,900 level, and projected levels to $40,200 in 1986 arise largely from wage-inflation projections. Rate increases are needed to keep revenues high enough to finance benefits in line with CPI increases. Rate increases will not be required when total wages received are included in the wage base used by the payroll tax, and the age distribution of those covered is stabilized.

*VAT Coverage and Rate*

In addition to including all wages in its base and not just some arbitrary individual wage level, VAT also includes profits, net interest, and rents. The base expansion if VAT were adopted would vary by industry and the coverage of a particular VAT. In aggregate, wages are about two-thirds of national income. Therefore, a VAT rate down by about one-third (and without taking into account other elements that generally increase the VAT base) would provide revenues equal to a payroll tax. Other elements mentioned above work to decrease the payroll tax base, but would not have a similar effect on the VAT base. One estimate sets the VAT rate necessary to replace employer current payroll taxes at 5.92 percent.[22] The 10 percent VAT proposed in the Tax Restructuring Act of 1980 (H.R. 7015) provides for a reduction of the combined payroll tax rate by 3.6 percentage points. This is done by funneling into social security financing $50 billion of the $115 billion that the 10 percent VAT along the lines outlined would provide.

The VAT revenue estimates implicit in H.R. 7015 point to a VAT of about 11.5 percent as necessary to bring in revenues equal to what could be provided in 1980 by a payroll-tax combined rate of 12.26 percent. The relatively high normal rate for a H.R. 7015 type of VAT to match payroll collections arises from exemptions and zero rating included in the legislation.

*Attitudes toward Tax Base Used*

Payroll taxes and also income and profit taxes, for some inexplicable reason, are not generally seen to be taxes on necessities or taxes on luxuries, as are transaction taxes such as VAT. The corporate profits and wages of a firm making necessities purchased largely by the poor can be taxed just as the profits and wages of a firm making and selling luxuries without arousing citizen protests of regressivity. Politically this attitude makes possible the levy of a full tax rate on payrolls of firms producing and marketing necessities. However, VAT, at least as set down in H.R. 7015, does not do this, and this is also generally true in Europe.

The base used by VAT tends to get reduced, and rather substantially, because it includes sales of products and services to both the rich and the poor. The base of the payroll tax is reduced, but to a lesser extent, by cutting the coverage of the employer-employee relationship. The use of an additive rather than the European subtractive type of VAT has shown in Michigan to have some of the coverage advantages of a payroll tax, while still enjoying a broader base than covered wages only. The additive-VAT base tends to get reduced somewhat by the exemption of small businesses and of businesses that are relatively intensive users of labor. This is true to a lesser extent of the subtractive-type VAT.

The payment of the payroll tax is definitely associated with the cost of labor and the take-home paycheck. This is not true of VAT.

The payroll tax is a labor cost. Therefore, it decreases the attractiveness of hiring more workers and reduces the employer's willingness to raise wages. The relationship of the tax to wages is clear-cut and immediate and cannot help but affect decision making along the lines outlined above.

### Allocation of Economic Burden

The European type of VAT is paid as purchases are made and is not directly related to anything the purchaser can control. The VAT collected is an add-on cost to be covered by price, and again the relationship is general, not labor-related. The VAT is much less likely to trigger wage action by the employee than the payroll tax.

The employee is hurt by lower wages when the payroll tax is deducted. Also, when VAT is collected on purchases, some prices will increase and very few prices will fall. These are today's economic impacts of fiscal action to protect the employee from poverty in case of illness or old age. Where the workers' union is strong, some of this cost will be shifted to employers and customers. Where unions are largely nonexistent and the demand for the service or the good is highly elastic, a good portion of both taxes will be carried by workers. If supply is inelastic (as, say, with land), a good portion of the tax will be carried by the owners of the product or service possessing an inelastic supply.

Because one-half is paid by the wage receiver and one-half by the business wage payer, analyses of the payroll tax tend to perceive some difference in the incidence between the two halves. The VAT avoids this particular difficulty, but because it is paid along the production line by a number of firms facing different supply and marketing conditions, much uncertainty exists as to VAT's incidence.

The general conclusion of Robert J. Gordon, and others, including the pioneer researcher John A. Brittain, is that it is also true that sensible conclusions about the economic burden of the payroll tax are hard to come by.[23] The general conclusion that about 70 percent of the total payroll tax is passed forward after a four-quarters interval may not be any more accurate than the others, but it does not try to treat the employer portion differently from the employee share.[24] Of course, for the payroll tax to be passed forward in generally higher prices, the money supply must permit it, just as in the case of any general price increase. Those who argue that the burden of taxes depends on microeconomic variations between labor markets and supplies are most likely right. However, that approach arrives at very few answers.

If the payroll tax is not generalized in higher prices, then it is carried by only covered workers and employers through some reduction of their surpluses. Economic units not falling in these categories would not be burdened by the tax, except to the extent that the payment is not met out of the surpluses and therefore requires higher prices.

The original social security costs more than likely were allocated in about the fashion described above. Today, with the combined rate at 12.26 percent and the salary base of $25,900, the price impact is greater. Tax payments of this magnitude, even after a generous allowance for inflation, in most cases cannot be absorbed readily. Prices and wages must be increased to include the portion of the new cost that is not shifted to land and through capitalization reduces the cost of this production factor. The portion of the payroll tax currently capitalized in lower resource values is apparently not large.

## Burden Shift

The retired person pays no payroll tax, but the cost of social security will be in the prices he pays. He would also pay VAT in the prices he pays. *The worker under current financing procedures is somewhat worse off than he would be under VAT. Today he is paying part of the payroll tax as a reduction of wages and again in higher prices.* The wage earner therefore would be acting to his own economic advantage if he favored VAT to finance social security. Also, the worker would benefit from VAT because it would stimulate exports and adjust import prices. This would increase the demand for domestic labor services.[25]

## Conclusion

The payroll tax is not such a bad tax that it should be eliminated at the federal level. Wages, however, cannot be the base for continuing rising tax rates. Wages are often taxed under the payroll tax, federal income taxes, and state income taxes and sometimes to finance urban activities. Action to avoid this very heavy burden based on one concept of ability to pay results in cash payments, barter arrangements, plus manipulated contract and ownership organization of work activity.

By including all added value, VAT treats businesses in a neutral manner and can provide substantial revenues without developing unmanageable administration difficulties.[26] The economic burden being carried by the payroll tax is already too high, but more revenues are needed if the actuarial deficit is to be held in check.[27] Introduction of a VAT along the lines of H.R. 7015 that will permit reduction of the combined payroll tax rate by 3.6 percentage points seems to be an appropriate compromise development.[28]

## Federal Government Using VAT
## to Finance Revenue Sharing

The idea of the federal government's providing substantial revenues to state and local governments arose out of ideas developed in the 1960s by Walter Heller and others around him. These block-grant types of financial aids were legislated to have a minimum number of expenditure restrictions. Federal funds would be available for distribution to state and local governments based on a formula including need and tax effort. The justification for these grants was based on belief that the revenue system in place at the federal level was much more productive than that of the state and local governments.[29]

### *Business Cycle*

The belief expressed in the 1960s that the federal revenues would be in surplus and the states in need proved to be incorrect. The data in the late 1960s demonstrated that the weak fiscal partner was the federal government, not the states.

The federal government has experienced a surplus once since 1963. The year was 1969. The $3.2 billion surplus of 1969 was funded by a $25 billion deficit in 1968. On the other hand up until 1980, state and local governments as a group have been running surpluses every year. The last state and local government deficit was recorded in 1967.[30] Therefore, if the federal government were to finance a substantial revenue-sharing program to reduce economic inequity, it would have to sharply increase revenues or negotiate large expenditure decreases.

A basic study completed by Bert Hickman with data for 1946-1958 concluded that the federal government was an economic destabilizer, not a stabilizer.[31] This is the situation because of rather violent federal-spending shifts arising usually from changes in defense-spending levels. Another important element in the federal economic destabilizing impact arises on the revenue side. The corporate income tax and the personal income tax collections move sharply with shifts in the level of economic activity. The source of much of the personal income taxed at progressive rates is profits, as is true of the corporate income tax. Profit levels are very volatile—falling sharply in a recession and climbing rapidly in a boom period or when price inflation is strong. State and local revenues and expenditures, on the other hand, are somewhat more stable than the general economy.[32]

If the federal government is to be an effective stabilizer of the economy, it must act to stabilize its revenues and do what is possible to stabilize expenditures. In its revenue-stabilizing effort, the reduction of the federal government's reliance on income and corporate profits taxes can be most helpful. *The introduction of a major VAT would stabilize federal revenues and, as a result, give revenue sharing a greater ability to stabilize the economy.*

The unstable revenue system of the federal government results in large federal-budget deficits in a recession. These deficits force the federal government into the money market to gain needed funds. One result of this relationship between federal borrowing and the level of economic activity is to increase the difficulties encountered in efforts to reduce interest rates and, therefore, to stimulate investment and, through the multiplier effect, the economy. Again, the stability of the collections from a major VAT would be very helpful.

## Sharing VAT Collections

Revenue sharing has been developed to accomplish general fiscal and economic goals and not to finance particular activities.[33] The revenues set aside in the federal budget to be used for revenue sharing are allocated only in a very general way to the geographic area where the funds were collected. The amounts allocated are determined by a formula that includes three elements: population, relative income, and tax effort. A local-government area with a large population earning relatively low per capita incomes and making an unusual effort to finance their local-government services will receive maximum revenue-sharing funds. Income equalization, not the return of funds collected to their source, is the basic goal of revenue sharing. In addition, the program singles out large cities for particularly favorable treatment.

As pointed out above, it is quite obvious the federal government does not have an excess of revenues to share. In fact, some estimates establish a federal deficit of $2.67 trillion in the social security program alone.[34] The term *sharing revenues* in any ordinary meaning implies that revenues have been jointly administered and now they are to be distributed on some agreed-upon allocation based on the geographical area or group of people from which the funds were raised. This is currently not the way revenue sharing operates—but it could be.

The use of a major federal-government VAT with the funds returned to the sources of the productivity would be a VAT utilizing the *origin* basis to distribute revenues assessed. This would be genuine revenue sharing of a stable revenue source that could be used efficiently in the local-government budgetary process. Also, the VAT used in this fashion could be used to pay refunds to exporters and would permit collection of a border tax on imports equal to the VAT rate and on a base including customs duties, freight, and insurance.

*Basis of Allocation*

In staying with the concept of returning VAT collections to local and state governments, table 4-3 provides data for 1967 and 1977 of state personal income and retail sales. These data are used to allocate $30 billion of collections from a federal VAT. Table 4-3 provides data that are useful in developing a procedure for generally allocating a portion of the collections of a national VAT to the state where the economic activity took place. A

**Table 4-3**
**Division of $30 Billion of VAT Collections among the States on the Basis of 1967 and 1977 Personal Income and Retail Sales**

| State | Percentage of Personal Income | | Amount of VAT Revenues (Millions of Dollars) | | Percentage of Retail Sales | | Amount of VAT Revenues (Millions of Dollars) | |
|-------|------|------|------|------|------|------|------|------|
|       | 1967 | 1977 | 1967 | 1977 | 1967 | 1977 | 1967 | 1977 |
| Alabama | 1.23 | 1.37 | 369 | 411 | 1.33 | 1.5 | 399 | 450 |
| Alaska | 0.16 | 0.29 | 48 | 87 | 0.13 | 0.3 | 39 | 90 |
| Arizona | 0.71 | 0.99 | 213 | 297 | 0.80 | 1.1 | 240 | 330 |
| Arkansas | 0.66 | 0.79 | 198 | 237 | 0.82 | 0.9 | 246 | 270 |
| California | 11.29 | 11.45 | 3,387 | 3,435 | 10.80 | 11.29 | 3,240 | 3,360 |
| Colorado | 1.00 | 1.24 | 300 | 372 | 1.06 | 1.4 | 318 | 420 |
| Connecticut | 1.87 | 1.66 | 561 | 498 | 1.63 | 1.4 | 489 | 420 |
| Delaware | 0.31 | 0.30 | 93 | 90 | 0.30 | 0.30 | 90 | 90 |
| Florida | 2.75 | 3.74 | 825 | 1,122 | 3.31 | 4.3 | 993 | 90 |
| Georgia | 1.84 | 2.01 | 552 | 603 | 1.99 | 2.2 | 597 | 660 |
| Hawaii | 0.39 | 0.45 | 117 | 135 | 0.35 | 0.50 | 105 | 150 |
| Idaho | 0.29 | 0.34 | 87 | 102 | 0.37 | 0.40 | 111 | 120 |
| Illinois | 6.57 | 5.78 | 1,971 | 1,734 | 6.21 | 5.4 | 1,863 | 1,620 |
| Indiana | 2.57 | 2.44 | 771 | 732 | 2.68 | 2.5 | 804 | 750 |
| Iowa | 1.38 | 1.31 | 414 | 393 | 1.62 | 1.4 | 486 | 420 |
| Kansas | 1.12 | 1.10 | 360 | 330 | 1.11 | 1.1 | 333 | 330 |
| Kentucky | 1.24 | 1.36 | 372 | 408 | 1.28 | 1.5 | 384 | 450 |

**Table 4-3** (*continued*)

| State | Percentage of Personal Income | | Amount of VAT Revenues (Millions of Dollars) | | Percentage of Retail Sales | | Amount of VAT Revenues (Millions of Dollars) | |
|---|---|---|---|---|---|---|---|---|
| | 1967 | 1977 | 1967 | 1977 | 1967 | 1977 | 1967 | 1977 |
| Louisiana | 1.45 | 1.53 | 435 | 459 | 1.53 | 1.7 | 459 | 510 |
| Maine | 0.42 | 0.41 | 126 | 123 | 0.47 | 0.5 | 141 | 150 |
| Maryland | 2.03 | 2.07 | 609 | 621 | 1.87 | 2.0 | 561 | 600 |
| Massachusetts | 3.09 | 2.78 | 927 | 834 | 2.95 | 2.6 | 885 | 780 |
| Michigan | 4.69 | 4.60 | 1,407 | 1,380 | 4.55 | 4.4 | 1,365 | 1,320 |
| Minnesota | 1.80 | 1.87 | 540 | 561 | 1.93 | 1.9 | 579 | 570 |
| Mississippi | 0.72 | 0.79 | 216 | 237 | 0.81 | 0.90 | 243 | 270 |
| Missouri | 2.22 | 2.11 | 666 | 633 | 2.44 | 2.2 | 732 | 660 |
| Montana | 0.31 | 0.31 | 93 | 93 | 0.37 | 0.40 | 111 | 120 |
| Nebraska | 0.71 | 0.69 | 213 | 207 | 0.82 | 0.70 | 246 | 210 |
| Nevada | 0.26 | 0.33 | 78 | 99 | 0.29 | 0.40 | 87 | 120 |
| New Hampshire | 0.34 | 0.37 | 102 | 111 | 0.38 | 0.50 | 114 | 150 |
| New Jersey | 4.13 | 3.87 | 1,239 | 1,161 | 3.66 | 3.40 | 1,098 | 1,020 |
| New Mexico | 0.40 | 0.46 | 120 | 138 | 0.44 | 0.60 | 132 | 180 |
| New York | 11.08 | 8.93 | 3,324 | 2,679 | 0.38 | 7.0 | 2,814 | 2,100 |
| North Carolina | 1.97 | 2.17 | 591 | 651 | 2.14 | 2.3 | 642 | 690 |
| North Dakota | 0.26 | 0.27 | 78 | 81 | 0.32 | 0.30 | 96 | 90 |
| Ohio | 5.41 | 5.01 | 1,623 | 1,503 | 5.25 | 4.9 | 1,575 | 1,470 |
| Oklahoma | 1.06 | 1.18 | 318 | 354 | 1.18 | 1.3 | 354 | 390 |
| Oregon | 0.98 | 1.10 | 294 | 330 | 1.08 | 1.3 | 324 | 390 |
| Pennsylvania | 5.96 | 5.46 | 1,788 | 1,638 | 5.64 | 5.2 | 1,692 | 1,560 |
| Rhode Island | 0.48 | 0.42 | 144 | 126 | 0.45 | 0.40 | 135 | 120 |
| South Carolina | 0.93 | 1.07 | 279 | 321 | 1.00 | 1.2 | 300 | 360 |
| South Dakota | 0.28 | 0.27 | 84 | 81 | 0.33 | 0.30 | 99 | 90 |
| Tennessee | 1.50 | 1.64 | 450 | 492 | 1.70 | 1.9 | 510 | 570 |
| Texas | 4.80 | 5.77 | 1,440 | 1,731 | 5.30 | 6.3 | 1,590 | 1,890 |
| Utah | 0.43 | 0.50 | 129 | 150 | 0.45 | 0.6 | 135 | 180 |
| Vermont | 0.19 | 0.19 | 57 | 57 | 0.23 | 0.20 | 69 | 60 |
| Virginia | 2.05 | 2.33 | 615 | 699 | 1.98 | 2.3 | 594 | 690 |
| Washington | 1.75 | 1.82 | 525 | 546 | 1.76 | 1.9 | 528 | 570 |
| West Virginia | 0.68 | 0.74 | 204 | 222 | 0.68 | 0.8 | 204 | 240 |
| Wisconsin | 2.13 | 2.12 | 639 | 636 | 2.14 | 2.12 | 642 | 630 |
| Wyoming | 0.15 | 0.20 | 45 | 60 | 0.17 | 0.20 | 51 | 60 |
| | 100.00 | 100.00 | 30,000 | 30,000 | 100.00 | 100.00 | 30,000 | 30,000 |

Source: *State Government Tax Collections in 1978*. Bureau of the Census, U.S. Department of Commerce, January 1979; *State Government Tax Collections in 1968*, Bureau of the Census, U.S. Department of Commerce; *1967 Census of Business*, vol. 1, U.S. Department of Commerce, January 1971, p. 14.

procedure for the distribution of revenues that would reach goals other than that of general economic activity used here could be established and administered without sending costs through the roof, and without prying into state and local government expenditure and tax-collection priorities.

In the example for which data are gathered, the federal government shares with the states $30 billion of its VAT collections. This amount is distributed on the basis of Department of Commerce calculated personal income allocated to the states and retail sales sited in each state. The portion of the $30 billion of federal VAT collections that would be allocated to each state on the basis of personal income or on the basis of retail sales makes a very substantial difference in only a few states. Nevada, for example, would receive significantly greater revenues if retail sales rather than personal income were used in making the allocation. In the case of Hawaii, somewhat surprisingly, the VAT allocation based on retail sales in 1977 would be only $15 million greater than if based on personal income. If it were considered desirable to use the allocation of VAT back to the states to work toward a more equal per capita revenue base among the states, a population adjustment could be included in the formula.

The use of all or a portion of the collections of a VAT, for allocation back to the geographic area of the origin of the economic activity, is an application of the origin concept of taxation. The origin principle teaches that revenues belong where the production took place. Personal income and retail sales are used here as a proxy for production included in the VAT base. The value of production taking place within a state can be estimated from manufacturing census data. Estimates can also be made of wholesale, jobbing, and transportation activity. More than likely their use to adjust retail sales data to establish the portioning of a national VAT would, because of inaccuracy, have a haphazard effect on the amount originally allocated to a state when the distribution is made on the basis of allocated personal income or retail sales.

Under this procedure of VAT allocation on the origin principle, each state would establish how the portion of VAT allocated to it would be used. If the federal government felt strongly that VAT and retail sales should not be collected from the same base and that poor states should benefit more than the more prosperous, then the sharing of VAT could be based on a formula that would give a flat per capita amount and an additional amount based on retail sales level or personal income. Finally, some of the distribution of VAT would be established by the portion of total state and local revenues raised from general and selective retail sales tax. The smaller the percentage of total taxes collected that were based on transactions, the greater the allocation to the state of revenues from the federal collections of VAT.

Financing particular projects, as is common now, would be another way to use VAT collections to finance federal government aid to state and local governments. The funds would be allocated by some type of formula to finance medical, transportation, and education expenditures, as examples. If these federally encouraged programs included definite provisions for sunset actions and general evaluation as well as an assigned portion of VAT, an improved federal approach to the stimulation of an expanded and uniform level of a particular service would be brought into existence.

*Conclusion*

Potential exists for the use of VAT collections in such a way that desired tax reforms are initiated at the state and local levels. A national VAT, by combining revenue source with type of expenditure subsidy, can develop a more responsible approach to federal grants to state and local governments. This opportunity has not been fully explored by European VAT-using countries. In Germany, however, VAT collections are distribued to local governments on the basis of population. The United States would become, to a degree, an innovator in the expansion of utilizing a broad-based tax such as VAT to improve the allocation efficiency of government resources.

## Full-Employment Policy

The greatest U.S. crisis of underuse of human potential took place between 1930 and 1939. Times were bad, but so were they in 1974. Prices in the 1930s were comparable with those of the panic years of the 1870s, but this was not true in 1974. Stagflation was coined to express the 1974 conditions.

Unemployment in 1929 was estimated to be only 3.2 percent. By 1933 the percentage of the labor force out of work was calculated to be 25.0 percent. In 1975 the unemployment rate was 8.5 percent; approximately the same level was reached in 1980. Unemployment in the United States in the 1930s was not licked until the factories added labor to fill European World War II munition orders, and men were needed for our expanding armed forces.

Early in January 1942, the National Resources Planning Board issued a statement favoring government action to keep full employment after the war. Congress feared this policy would require planned inflation and the Board was ordered dissolved. Nevertheless, on January 11, 1944, President Roosevelt proclaimed "the right to a useful and remunerative job" as the first of a new economic bill of rights.

The 1944 Republican candidate for President declared, "If at any time there are not sufficient jobs in private employment to go around, the government can and must create job opportunities, because there must be jobs for all in this country."[35] This goal of jobs for all and the government as an employer of last resort was widely discussed as a desirable postwar policy. However, the words *full employment* were not used in the Employment Act of 1946. It was not until 1976 that federal legislation aiming at full employment and using the words *full employment* as a goal was adopted. The legislation is titled "The Full Employment and Balanced Growth Act." The legislation is most frequently called the Humphrey-Hawkins bill. The bill states in section 107 that if any inflationary problems should arise in efforts to gain full employment, the President should come up with a plan to handle it.[36] The bill in section 104 gives the President the mandate to establish national priorities. The entire philosophy of the legislation is to establish adequate powers in the Presidency to permit the federal government to act as an employer of last resort. The legislation does not attempt to establish budgetary impacts or to recommend measures to increase the ability of the tax system to meet the needs of business and government.

*Economic Planning*

The provisions of the Employment Act of 1946 or the Humphrey-Hawkins bill do not bring forth specialized economic machinery to maintain a high level of employment. Thus, the goal of the most active advocates of full-employment legislation has not been realized. Rather, *the intent of the federal government to set policies that maximized employment was set, and this remains true.*

After thirty-four years, Congress has not developed economic machinery to eliminate the "waste of unemployment" and the "shortage of purchasing power." The unforecasted severe inflation of 1973 and 1979 demonstrated for all the need for a new approach to economic analysis. "Economic models based on closed systems with investment and consumption neatly combining to generate income no longer work."[37] To arrive at reasonable forecasts, the tenders of these models must rely on substantial "hands-on" manipulation.

*Real Wages*

Since 1969 the median income (as many receiving income below as above) in current dollars was $9,277; in 1979 it was $18,467. It looks as if the median income has very nearly doubled. But has it? After income and payroll taxes are deducted, the median income in 1969 was $7,947; in 1979 it was $15,546. Median income after income and payroll taxes has not done quite as well through the ten-year period as the before-tax median income. The after-tax median income adjusted for inflation between 1969 and 1979 actually decreased. In 1969 dollars, the after-income-and-payroll-taxes median real income had decreased from $7,947 in 1969 to $7,800 in 1979.[38]

Under VAT, payroll, income, and corporate profit taxes would be reduced and revenues stabilized. The need for expanded Federal Reserve credit to cover sharp reductions in tax receipts would decline. These developments would increase money-supply stability while more than likely reducing unemployment because labor relative to machines and fuel would cost less.[39]

*Conclusion*

The forces active in the economy are affected by many elements that cannot be forecasted with confidence. The stability and neutrality of VAT provide a substantial revenue base helpful in financing needed economic stimulants, while not requiring shifts in policy based on a forecast of future economic activity.

**Notes**

1. John J. Carroll, *Alternative Methods of Financing Old-Age Survivors and Disability Insurance* (Ann Arbor: Institute of Public Administration, University of Michigan, 1960), p. 5.

2. Robin Barlow, Harvey E. Brazer, James N. Morgan, *Economic Behavior of the Affluent* (Washington: Brookings Institution, 1966), p. 7.

3. Franco Reviglio, "Social Security: A Means of Savings Mobilization for Economic Development," mimeographed (Washington: International Monetary Fund, 1966), p. 36.

4. Richard W. Lindholm, *Value Added Tax and Other Tax Reforms* (Chicago: Nelson-Hall, 1976), pp. 182-186.

5. L.J. Kotlikoff, "Social Security and Equilibrium Capital Intensity," *Quarterly Journal of Economics* 93 (May 1979):233-254.

6. Committee on Ways and Means, U.S. House of Representatives, "Explanation of the Tax Restructuring Act of 1980" (H.R. 7015) (Washington: GPO, 1980), pp. 4, 9.

7. Carl G. Urh, *Sweden's Social Security System* (Washington: Social Security Administration, 1966), Research Report no. 14; and the Conference Board, *Road Maps of Industry*, no. 1774, December 1975.

8. Old-age pensions, mother pensions, child care, unemployment benefits, health insurance, sick benefits, prenatal and maternity benefits, and low-income benefits. The federal government now supports three aged pensions programs: the regular contributory program, Old Age and Survivor Insurance (OASI); allowance to aged persons not receiving pension from private sources, Old Age Benefits (OAB); and means-tested allowance to needy aged persons, Supplemental Security Income (SSI). The SSI is the newest, and it cost $5.2 billion in 1975, about 10 percent as much as OASI. "Old Age Pensions: Level Adjustment and Coverage," *OECD Observer*, no. 77 (September-October 1975):19-23.

9. "Everyone wishes to be generous to old age: nearly everyone resents paying increased national insurance contributions." Davies T. Windsor, "Pensions for the Future," *New Society*, April 28, 1966, p. 13.

10. J. Henry Richardson, *Economic and Financial Aspects of Social Security* (Toronto, Canada: University of Toronto Press, 1960), p. 62.

11. Ibid., p. 65.

12. James A. Brittain, *American Economic Review*, 61 (March 1971):123, concludes ". . . that labor bears the tax . . . that its burden on low income groups is greater than generally realized. It also implies that its impact on income distribution is typically regressive. The qualities of the payroll tax offer a solid basis for proposing that this form of taxation be curtailed or eliminated." Norman B. Ture, in *The Value Added Tax: Facts and Fancies* (Washington: Heritage Foundation, 1979), p. 60, does not believe VAT is superior to the payroll tax in financing social security.

13. E. Deran, "Changes in Factor Income Shares under the Social Security Tax," *Review of Economics and Statistics*, 49 (November 1967):627-630; and R.F. Hoffman, "Factor Shares and the Payroll Tax: A Comment," *Review of Economics and Statistics*, 50 (November 1968):506-508.

14. Arnold C. Harberger, "Taxation, Resource Allocation, Welfare," in *The Role of Direct and Indirect Taxes in the Federal Revenue System* (Washington: Brookings Institution, 1964), pp. 33-42.

15. Richard W. Lindholm, "The Value Added Tax: A Short Review of the Literature," *Journal of Economic Literature* 8 no. 4 (December 1970):1178-1189.

16. G. Schmolders, *Turnover Taxes* (Armsterdam, Netherlands: International Bureau of Fiscal Documentation, 1966), p. 15.

17. Ibid., p. 71.

18. Data as provided in International Monetary Fund, *Government Finance Statistics Yearbook*, vol. 3 (Washington, 1979).

19. "When pension goals are realized, the disposable income of pensioners will eventually be about 70 percent of that of childless couples in similar earnings brackets." Uhr, *Sweden's Social Security System*, p. 135.

20. Jonathan Spivak, "Putting a Lid on Social Programs," *Wall Street Journal*, December 31, 1975, and "Halfway on Social Security," editorial, *Wall Street Journal*, January 26, 1976; comment, *Citibank Monthly Letter*, "Social Security—The Cost that Won't Quit" (August, 1980) pp. 8-10.

21. H. Wendel, *Aggregate Economic Effects of Changes in Social Security Taxes*, Technical Analysis Paper (Washington: Congressional Budget Office, 1978); and Henry Aaron, "Advisory Report of Social Security," *Challenge*, March/April 1980, pp. 12-16; and Joseph G. Simanis and John R. Coleman, "Health Care Expenditures in Nine Industrialized Countries, 1960-1976," *Social Security Bulletin* 43, no. 1 (January 1980(:3-8.)

22. Ture, *The Value Added Tax*, p. 58.

23. Robert J. Gordon, Brookings Papers on Economic Activity, vol. 1 (Washington: Brookings Institution, 1971), p. 122; John A. Brittain, *The Payroll Tax for Social Security* (Washington: Brookings Institution, 1972).

24. George L. Perry, Brookings Papers on Economic Activity, vol. 3, 1970.

25. Ture, *The Value Added Tax*, p. 60.

26. Richard W. Lindholm, "New Tax Directions for the United States" (Committee on Ways and Means, U.S. House of Representatives, 94th Cong., 1st Sess.) (Washington: GPO, 1975), pp. 8-11.

27. E.K. Browning, "Why the Social Insurance Budget Is too Large in a Democratic Society," *Economic Inquiry* 16 (January 1978):139-142.

28. James W. Wetzler, "The Role of a Value Added Tax in Financing Social Security," *National Tax Journal*, 32 no. 2 (September 1979):334-345; W. Vroman, "Employer Payroll Taxes and Money Wage Behavior," *Applied Economics* 6 (1974):189-204.

29. Walter W. Heller, *New Dimensions of Political Economy* (Cambridge, Mass.: Harvard University Press, 1966), pp. 88, 118.

30. Richard W. Lindholm, "The Embarrassing State Surpluses," *The Tax Executive* 31 (October 1978):27-33.

31. Bert G. Hickman, *Growth and Stability of the Post-War Economy* (Washington: Brookings Institution, 1960), p. 215.

32. Robert W. Rafuse, "State and Local Fiscal Behavior over the Post-War Cycles," in R.A. Musgrave, *Essays in Fiscal Federalism* (Washington: Brookings Institution, 1965), pp. 63-121.

33. Richard P. Nathan, Allen D. Manuel, and Susannah E. Calkins, *Monitoring Revenue Sharing* (Washington: Brookings Institution, 1975), particularly chapter 3.

34. The social security deficit of $700 billion is inflation-adjusted to present-value terms. The undiscounted total is $2.6 trillion. Michael Boskin, *Wall Street Journal*, January 21, 1980, p. 17.

35. Governor Thomas E. Dewey, September 21, 1944.

36. Murray L. Weidenbaum "The Case against the Humphrey-Hawkins Bill," *Challenge*, September/October 1976, p. 22.

37. John Cobbs, "The Limits on Economic Advice," *Business Week*, November 10, 1973, p. 36.

38. Median for all families with one earner employed full-time year-round as reported by U.S. Department of Commerce, Bureau of the Census, for 1967 to 1977; 1978 and 1979 are estimated by the Tax Foundation.

39. G. Brennan and D.A.L. Auld, "The Tax Cut as an Anti-Inflationary Device," *Economic Record* 44 (December 1968):520-525.

# 5

## Preserving International Competitiveness

### Overview

The second and third sections identify the generally accepted reasons why nations find VAT helpful to them in their efforts to maintain a sound international posture. The fact that the United States has seen fit not to adopt a major VAT has encouraged the outflow of capital from the United States and the retention abroad of earnings from foreign operations. In addition, the failure of the United States to utilize VAT has made more probable production abroad for sale to third-nation buyers of products of U.S. businesses. All these economic forces, which are set in motion by the failure of the United States to harmonize its tax system, work to reduce U.S. employment and the investment of U.S. businesses' profits in the United States. Consideration is also given to the use of subsidies to permit domestic industries to meet import competition.

The fourth section brings to the surface the VAT-price relationships closely associated with international trade. The point considered is whether the refund of VAT on exports encourages exports. Consideration is given to the difference in the effect on prices of a VAT and a CIT.

The fifth section presents a brief historical description of the development of the concept of the destination principle. It is this principle which provides the theoretical support for the treatment given by GATT to indirect taxes on goods entering international commerce. The discussion points out that the current very different treatment GATT accords direct and indirect taxes did not exist in the mid-1920s as a settled doctrine. In 1926 the United States, Canada, and Czechoslovakia levied retaliatory import duties on French exports benefiting from exemption of domestic indirect taxes. The historical practices summarized demonstrate strong support for the levy of countervailing duties on products benefiting from the refund of any type of domestic tax because the product was exported.

The sixth section discusses the decline in the relative value of the dollar during the past ten years. The analysis concludes that a dollar with a falling international value is a very expensive way to strengthen the foreign side of the U.S. economy.

The concept of the destination principle becomes a part of the discussion again because the principle includes the idea that tax justice requires that those who pay the tax should benefit from the expenditure of the col-

159

lections. Therefore importers of products should not pay a tax levied by the producer nation and spent in the producing nation. In other words, a justification for the current GATT treatment of indirect taxes, such as VAT, is provided. Support is also provided for the refund of all domestic taxes levied on exports. The acceptance of this domestic-tax-refund-on-exports position results in a nation with the relatively largest public sector having the largest refund and therefore, on this basis at least, the best international competitive position.

The current different GATT treatment of taxes placed within the destination-principle concept (indirect) and those within the origin-principle concept (direct) affects export and import decisions. A result of this situation is a reduction in the efficiency with which production and trade are carried out in the world.

The seventh section takes cognizance of what should be considered in setting import duties and border taxes. The 1979 multilateral trade negotiation (MTN) is seen to be an effort largely aimed at a continuation of the reduction of tariffs carried out under the Kennedy round fifteen years earlier.

The lowering of tariffs, as provided for in both the MTNs, increases the effect of internal revenues on the movement of internationally traded goods and services. As the sensitivity of international activities to domestic taxes is increasing because of lower tariffs, the impact of the manner in which internal revenues are raised is also increased because of the higher level of these tax collections. Both forces work toward greater need for internation tax-system harmonization. For the United States this points toward a strong international-based reason to adopt VAT.

The eighth section demonstrates the type of complications and difficulties that the United States is certain to encounter when its domestic taxes are not in basic harmony with those existing in other comparably developed industrial nations. The analysis is based on the U.S. experience with the Domestic International Sales Corporation (DISC).

The conclusion of the analysis of the last section and of chapter 5 is that the general area of the U.S. taxation of international business has been a disaster. A general major U.S. tax based on transactions would be a very useful rectifying step.

## Balance of Payments and
## Tax Harmonization

The value-added tax has proved itself in Europe. A result has been a relative increase in the portion of total government revenues arising from this multilevel transactions tax. The development has relieved the revenue pressure for higher and higher corporate and individual income taxes. More than likely, VAT will also make it politically easier to retain general indirect taxation as the major revenue raiser in Europe. The net effect will be that pressures for Eurpean use of direct taxation will decrease, and unfavorable attitudes toward indirect taxation, particularly of the multistage type, will also decrease. In turn this will permit more generous treatment of profits and incomes under the direct tax rates of EEC member states.

A number of undesirable results for the United States can be associated with this tax situation: (1) It makes it more difficult for the United States to enjoy its economic potential. (2) It causes the rebirth and continuation of international economic barriers. (3) Free World liquidity is reduced through foreign reluctance to hold dollars, increasing the possibility of international financial crises.

*Crisis Development Pattern*

United States' international-payments difficulties set into motion by U.S. tax disharmony cause the following chain of events: The lower profits taxes in the EEC member states than in the United States make it attractive for U.S. capitalists to invest in the EEC and retain reserves outside the United States and for EEC capitalists to refrain from investing in the United States— causing negative international balances on capital accounts. The tax refund available to exporters from EEC member states, but not available to exporters from the United States, and the border taxes assessed by EEC, but not by the United States, combine to reduce U.S. international balances on trade accounts.

The United States, by shifting its national tax system toward the existing and evolving tax system of EEC member states, can escape the "national tax disharmony syndrome." But this is not the only possible escape route. The United States could freely float the dollar, withdraw from GATT, and freely change its tariffs to compensate for border taxes and tax refunds, or severely restrict foreign investment of U.S. savings. The alternatives to moving toward tax harmonization are not attractive, but to a degree we have been following a number of them during the past several years.

The Europeans and particularly the EEC member states also have alternatives. They could revalue their monetary units upward relative to the U.S. dollar. They could abandon the trade advantages possessed by indirect taxes. They could prohibit foreign investments in their country. Some of the alternatives have the same basic unattractiveness of a reduction of freedom in international transactions, as is true of the U.S. alternatives. Others run counter to the basic competitive nature of international transactions between national groupings.

*Conclusion*

A very reasonable conclusion to draw from this analysis is that international economic freedom and Free World economic growth would be well served by a basic change of the U.S. tax system toward the existing and evolving European model. This would require a substantial reduction in the portion of U.S. federal-government receipts arising from direct taxes and an increase in indirect taxes in effect. To do this would more than likely involve legislation providing for the gradual introduction of a national value-added tax similar to H.R. 7015. At the same time, low- and middle-income receivers would enjoy lower income and payroll taxes. The corporate income tax could also be reduced. The U.S. tax system would be largely harmonized with that of the EEC member states. The adoption of H.R. 7015 (1980) would largely bring this about.

The tax differences between the United States and Europe are sufficiently sharp to warrant new U.S. legislation. However, the U.S. tax legislation with an international impact that has been recommended and adopted has not been aimed at a general harmonizing of the U.S. tax system with the tax system existing and evolving in Europe, except in an incidental way. Instead, the aim has been to develop procedures such as quotas, minimum import prices, antidumping duties, and DISC to prevent unbearable strain on basic U.S. industries. The Europeans cannot be expected to shift their tax system toward the U.S. approach as they are enjoying very substantial benefits from the present relationship.

## International Investment

The VAT develops an environment favorable to new investment by making it fiscally possible to reduce CIT and capital-gains taxes. There is little doubt that the level of taxes, and particularly those on profits and capital gains, is an important determiner of the location of investments. Taxes must always be an important part of the investment decision.[1]

All nations are anxious to increase the level of domestic investment. Frequently this results in special favors being granted to new investments that are not generalized to existing operations.[2] In the United States we are familiar with this type of industrial-development competition between states and communities. At the international level, the reduction of tariffs during the past fifteen years and the greater freedom in the transfer of funds among nations have increased the impact of the domestic tax environment.

*Use of Domestic Subsidies*

The apparent current development of subsidies to domestic producers so they can meet import competition impairs GATT tariff findings. In many cases reciprocal tariff reductions were granted to increase access to foreign markets. If subsidies to domestic producers for the local market counter these negotiated tariff-reduction agreements, then the aims of the GATT procedures are undermined. Protection has moved from tariffs to subsidies for domestic producers. The procedure prevents loss of domestic markets to foreign producers. In doing this, domestic investment of savings is encouraged to meet domestic demand for the product, and if VAT is used as a major revenue source, exports can meet foreign competition through refunds of VAT without violating GATT understandings.

Another way to encourage new international investment is to grant domestic tax exemptions and capital subsidies.[3] In order to make certain these subsidized international investments continue to produce foreign exchange after the flow of foreign exchange arising from the original investment is ended, company performance requirements are established.

These performance requirements frequently require a determined level of local content in the product manufactured and marketed. Another frequent requirement sets a level of exports to be met. For example, the Mexican Automotive Decree sets export-expansion requirements. In Spain a variety of incentives have made Ford's Fiesta that nation's largest foreign-exchange earner.

A basic underlying ingredient of this development is the growth of taxation as a portion of the GNP of industrialized countries. Tax favors can be much larger and, therefore, more attractive. This impact, as mentioned above, has combined with reduced trade and foreign-exchange barriers to make international investment location much more an area needing established ground rules. New international understanding somewhat along the lines of GATT may be needed to limit the rise of incentives and performance requirements to attract investment and to control their marketing and use of foreign products in established performance requirements.

## Trade Restrictions

The current growth of antidumping assessments is an attempt to prevent the international investment stimulants from working themselves out. The use of restrictions after the investment is made is very likely to be much more costly than if an original limit on international investment stimulation had existed. Sometimes the investment stimulation only amounts to the removal of formerly applied restrictions, for example, the expansion of the right to withdraw earnings from the country of their source. These developments toward greater freedom that also encourage investment should not be treated by the ground rules like a tax holiday grant, for example.[4]

*Conclusion*

The pressures for uniformity of the investment climate act to develop a favorable climate for harmonization of taxes. The VAT is widely used by the industrial nations of the world and is certainly a good possibility for use as the basic revenue measure that would be utilized in a relatively uniform fashion by the nations of the world, perhaps largely as it is currently used in Western Europe. The United States, because it has discussed but has not adopted a VAT, is a major area where advocacy of this approach to taxation and investment harmonization should develop.

## Manufacturer's Tax

The manufacturer's tax has been a mainstay of Canadian national-government revenues since 1924 when it replaced a gross-turnover tax that had been introduced in 1920. Through the years, the rate of the Canadian manufacturer's tax and the dedication of the revenues collected have varied.[5]

*Canadian Experience*

The Canadian experience with a manufacturer's tax that is collected by the national government alongside provincial RSTs has, on the whole, been good. The tax applies to value at one level only of all goods not exempted that are made or imported into Canada. The list of exemptions gets longer every year as one pressure group after another is able to lobby through Parliament the exemption desired. Despite the extended exemption-listing growth, the Canadian manufacturer's tax provides about 10 percent of national-government revenues.

The fact that Canada came into the current underemployment, government transfer-payment environment with a broad-based manufacturer's tax at a 12 percent basic rate has been most helpful in economy-managing efforts. About one-fourth of the manufacturer's tax collections go to the Canadian Old Age and Security Administration. This has put a sound financial base under the Canadian social security program. In addition, the original high rate and the inclusion of a large portion of the sales of manufacturers have permitted stimulation of the economy while at the same time reducing the tendency toward wage and price inflation inherent in monetary or fiscal stimulation.[6]

*Strengths of Manufacturer's Tax*

The manufacturer's tax has many of the helpful characteristics of a VAT. Within the boundaries of this discussion, for instance, a manufacturer's tax, by being refunded on exports and collected as a border tax on imports, increases the competitive position of the Canadian producers of nonagricultural products. Also, like VAT, a manufacturer's tax can be levied without serious disturbance of a productive state and local government retail sales tax.

### Advantages of VAT

The Canadian manufacturer's tax is not separately quoted on the invoice. One reason is, of course, that payment is not needed by anyone as a deduction in arriving at manufacturing taxes due. This also means the tax, like property or payroll taxes, becomes a part of the cost of production. This observation leads to the great advantages of VAT over a manufacturer's tax, which have caused Canadians to generally agree that they will be introducing a VAT as a matter of international economic defense if for no other reason.

The relative strengths possessed by VAT over a manufacturer's tax can be summarized under three headings. All three get down to the fact of reduced revenue and the rationale for selecting manufacturing for higher taxation.

1. The revenue per percentage point of tax rate in the United States of a manufacturer's tax like the one in Canada is about $2.5 billion. The revenue from a U.S. value-added tax with food, housing, medical costs, and intergovernment expenditures exempt is about $9 billion per percentage point.
2. The coverage of only manufacturer's sales causes the tax payment to be concentrated in the few manufacturing regions of the nation.
3. The exclusion from the tax of all productive activities other than manufacturing reduces the efficiency of the market in the allocation of resources to meet the demands of consumers.

### Avoidance of Retailing

The manufacturer's tax, by avoiding the retail level, escapes nearly all possibility of becoming confused with the retail sales tax. This same relationship would exist with a VAT that did not include the retail level. The VAT, as developed in France, was originally of this type. However, the EEC, when developing a uniform tax for its member states, opted for a VAT that included retailing.

Because of the problems that exist when the VAT base includes retailing, a U.S. value-added tax, when introduced, might exclude retailing. If this were done, the base would be reduced by about 15 percent, or down to $7.6 billion per percentage point.[7] After excluding retailing, VAT would continue to raise about three times more per percentage point of tax than would a manufacturer's tax. This greater productivity of VAT over a manufacturer's tax, even when retailing is excluded, permits use of a rate one-third that of a manufacturer's tax to meet any given revenue goal.

*Foreign Trade*

There is much to be said in favor of the use of a broad tax base and low rates. For example, problems of avoidance and evasion are reduced; so also are impacts that would push business decisions away from the efficiency provided by the competitive market. On the other hand, in the particular situation under consideration, higher rates limited to only manufacturing have a national advantage. The taxes collected under these higher rates, under the destination principle of GATT, can be refunded on exports, and they set the level to which border taxes may be assessed on imported manufactured goods.

*Setting the Taxable Base*

The single-level manufacturing tax suffers from valuation problems more severe than those of the RST or the VAT. The price set by a manufacturer to a related firm is likely to be below an arm's-length price, and a large portion of manufacturer's sales are of this type. Common ownership or affiliation among buying, transporting, and selling enterprises is prevalent.[8]

It is not unusual for a manufacturing firm to sell its entire output at reduced prices to wholesalers and specialized distributors that are affiliates. These affiliates later negotiate sales at the true market price. The operation results in a substantial reduction of the manufacturer's tax base and lower taxes.

Nevertheless, the Canadian manufacturers' tax has proved to be a steady and substantial revenue raiser. The administrative discretion developed in setting the true manufacturers' sale price has worked. The price established for taxation is a compromise between a price that includes transportation, delivery, finance charges, installation costs, and the like and a price limited to the product's price on the dock, ready to be placed in a crate and loaded.

A somewhat analogous problem arises in the administration of VAT on goods and services used in the business of the producer. These goods are not sold and do not develop a VAT liability, but the VATs included in purchases of services and goods used in the production process are deductible from a sales total that did not include the producer good being used by the production firm. The result is a subsidy of own-produced capital goods under the conventional subtractive VAT.[9]

## Conclusion

The use of a one-level tax, whether at the manufacturing or the retail level, creates serious administrative problems as the rate is set high enough to produce substantial revenues. When a tax is levied on sales at all levels—gross turnover tax—the cascade effect hurts specialized and smaller businesses. Also the amount of tax to be associated with a product exported and exempt from the tax is most difficult to calculate. The characteristics of a typical VAT avoid most of these shortcomings of a single-level or an all-level gross sales tax.

VAT, by being a net turnover tax, allows for the credit on tax due of VAT paid as the good and service went through the prior production, transportation, and marketing processes. VAT, however, includes gross sales at all levels of all goods and services. VAT, therefore, avoids the problem of evasion that exists when only one or two of the economic process levels is included in the tax base.

The GATT permits treatment of taxes allocated to the indirect category of taxes, a quite different international treatment from those categorized as direct taxes.[10] Direct taxes are not refundable, but indirect taxes are. Also, border taxes may not be levied on imports to compensate for domestic direct-tax collections.

Indirect taxes on exports can be refunded, and border taxes of an equal level may be assessed on imports. The same treatment is accorded to VAT as to special excise taxes or gross-turnover taxes; GATT assumes that all indirect-tax collections are reflected entirely in the price of the goods. This position does not differentiate between general and specific indirect taxes. The approach flies in the face of accepted indirect-tax theory.[11]

Basically the tax-rebate-on-exports conclusion of GATT rests on two assumptions: (1) in some way the general price level can increase through the imposition of a general excise tax, but this is not true if special excises are levied on selected products (price linkages is denied); (2) the levy of direct taxes depresses the return to the factors of production and does not result in price increases to permit maintenance of after-tax income levels.

## Historical Perspective on the Destination
## Principle and Turnover Tax

As it developed in France in the post-World War I period under the Poincaré National Union Government, the turnover tax did not provide for the exemption of exports. The 1926 rates applied to domestic sales were 1.3, 2, and 2.5 percent. The tax on exports was at 1.3 percent on nonluxury exports and 12 percent on luxury exports.[12]

In 1922 France moved toward some use of replacement or production taxes to supplement or replace turnover taxes on certain products. "Under the turnover tax, exports received only a 2 percent exemption, all sales previous to the last one remaining taxable." The replacement taxes provided for the exemption of exports made directly by the manufacturer.

The French Ministry of France reported in 1926 that the United States, Canada, and Czechoslovakia had considered the exemption of exports from the full turnover tax to be dumping and, in consequence, had levied retaliatory import duties.[13] This argument carried the day when combined with a severe decline of the international value of the French franc and an overriding need for revenues. In 1927 international economic and fiscal conditions had righted themselves, and France suspended its tax on exports.

### Destination Principle

It is clear that in the days when the turnover tax was first spreading through Western Europe, the fact that the tax was an indirect tax was not related to the international treatment it received. Exports were both exempted and subject to a special tax, depending on economic circumstances. Also, no provision was made to refund to exporters more than the turnover tax collected on the last transaction. Finally, the trading nations of the world in 1926 saw the exemption of exports from the full turnover tax to be dumping, which made the application of countervailing import duties appropriate.

The situation today, fifty-five years later, lacks some of the forthrightness displayed among the Western nations between 1922 and 1926, as they stabilized their economies after the serious disruption of World War I.[14] Between then and now, tax savings and their effects on competitive prices have been subjected to erudite analyses that cloud the issue.

### Acceptance of French Refund

France and her trading partners in the 1920s basically accepted the simple position that a tax was a cost that had to be paid out of receipts. If the cost could be reduced, so could prices, and a competitive position would be improved. *If exporters were excused from paying taxes that were normally paid by domestic producers, then exports were being subsidized, and that was that.*

One of the great weaknesses of economic analysis has been the failure of models to include government as an element of an operating economy with costs that must be met. The manner in which this cost is paid can vary widely. It can be done in a way that either reduces risk and investment in the private sector or increases costs of certain designated goods and services. But whatever the procedure, the payment must be made out of current production. This is said with the full realization that the manner of collection may affect the level of economic activity.

## Institutional Impacts

A difference in the effect of a collection or payment because of the level of the source of the collection, or benefactor of the payment, is not unique to government. A worker paid by the piece may be more productive than one paid by the hour. An investor may be less adventuresome if a large portion of gains must be paid in taxes, but no subsidy is forthcoming if a loss is incurred. These interrelationships are obvious, but difficult to quantify.

The manner in which a levy or payment is made affects its impact on all the complicated interrelationships of the economy. Just exactly how these work themselves out can only be guessed.[15] Of course, this impact varies with the economic environment. Therefore, the best that can be done is to look at all payments, whether for wages, raw materials, or taxes, as costs that must be covered in prices charged by the individual or business firm. How each firm raises the money to make necessary payments varies somewhat from case to case, but basically the money comes from the sale of goods and services.

## Conclusion

As used in Europe, VAT is a net-turnover tax. The history of the development of the turnover tax in France and the attitude toward the tax by Western nations during the period of the evolution of the cascade-turnover tax demonstrate that the refund of the tax on export sales was not accepted as a necessary part of the use of the tax. For a while France, in fact, levied a higher rate on the export sale than on domestic sales. Later a partial refund and the exemption of the export sale developed in France. Other nations saw this to be an export subsidy and responded with antidumping duties. *There is strong historical support for the levy of countervailing duties on products benefiting from a refund of VAT.*

## Dollar Trouble and International Imbalance

In August 1971 the U.S. dollar was devalued. A forecast widely made had the United States benefiting from a dollar that freely floated to its true lower level relative to other currencies. The lowered value of the dollar would decrease the international price of U.S. goods, making U.S. products more competitive both at home and abroad. This has happened as forecast in some instances and for brief periods, but the basic favorable relationship expected has not fully developed.

*General Considerations*

The depreciation of the value of the dollar has accompanied inflationary pressures in the United States. It was only for a brief period that U.S. exports were stimulated by the depreciated dollar. Very soon the domestic inflation expanded because of generally higher-priced imports. When this happened, prices of internationally traded U.S. goods rose, and the trade benefits of the lowered exchange rate for the dollar evaporated.

Sometimes the unhealthy and higher inflation rate in the United States than in Germany and Japan is blamed on the relative decline in the growth of U.S. productivity and on the high oil prices. Some of the fault surely rests on these characteristics of the current economic scene; however, other causes must be examined. After all, our economy's rapid movement toward an increased emphasis on the service industries, where productivity increases are less than in agriculture and manufacturing, is an element in the picture. Also, in comparing oil costs in the United States with those in Japan and Germany, it must be kept in mind that the net import of mineral fuels is a higher percentage of GNP in Japan and Germany than in the United States. *What we have here is a demonstration that a falling dollar exchange rate with other currencies is a very expensive and undesirable procedure for improving the international side of the operations of the U.S. economy.*

A dollar that is declining in value relative to other currencies is also increasing the relative domestic-currency cost of scarce and necessary U.S. imports. A depreciating exchange rate is too blunt an instrument to be used to affect international economic relationships. The use of taxes such as VAT which can be used as a border tax and also as a tax refund if desired, but also not used when advantageous, possesses useful superiorities.

An important advantage of the use of VAT is its selectivity. A shortcoming is that adjustments are limited under GATT to the legislated domestic level of the indirect tax being refunded or added as a border tax. This shortcoming may actually be a strength because it forces realization by all that fiscal adjustments to favor exports and to hold back imports are limited. This realization will cause a weakening of the tendency to favor domestic rather than foreign customers. This is helpful. Furthermore, the realization of an approaching end of the stimulants causes domestic producers to get down to business in adapting their product line to foreign demands and working with labor to increase domestic productivity.[16]

## International Negotiations

The United States in 1979 completed the Tokyo round of general trade negotiations. The operation was along the lines of the Kennedy round of fifteen years ago. The fifteen-year period between the Kennedy and Tokyo negotiations was filled with international economic changes. Most of them, even including devaluation of the dollar (or perhaps, more correctly, the revaluation of the currencies of the major industrial nations), were seen as possibilities in 1964. This, however, was not true of the OPEC oil embargo and monopoly.[17]

The economics of border taxes, the value-added tax, the destination principle, and the relationship of each to the other, the topic of this section, were also only dimly perceived in 1964. United States negotiators failed to give a high priority to the manner in which indirect taxes are treated under GATT understandings. The new studies of the incidence of the corporate profits tax and business indirect taxes were not yet digested. Amazingly, this continues to be largely true in 1980.

Today, OPEC oil prices and billions of foreign-exchange earnings by oil-export nations dominate international economic discussions. Under these conditions, consideration of the harm to freedom of trade and foreign-exchange earnings of the destination principle (that is, of tax refunds on exports) and of border taxes on imports looks a good deal like nit-picking. On the other hand, it is also generally recognized that if a better job had been done to maintain established international competitive positions, the need to make today's nearly impossible big decisions on how to stablize the dollar without stifling investment with tight money would be more realizable.

International tax harmonization and domestic-tax incidence is an area that was passed over lightly in both the Kennedy and Tokyo rounds. The Kennedy round neglected the domestic-tax aspects of international commercial operations. This failure more than likely speeded up the deterioration of international economic relationships that have proceeded through the years. And, now again, the dominance of potential international impacts of the oil cartel and the high price of gold may cause the day-after-day impact of border taxes levied on U.S. exports to be neglected.

## Fundamentals of the Destination Principle

The destination principle, and its justification of border taxes and tax refunds on exports, owes a considerable portion of its acceptability to the theory that benefits of the expenditure of tax collections are neutral and to the concept of the forward shifting of indirect taxes. The tax refund on exports is justified because the revenues that would be collected from the tax if it were not refunded would not be available to finance government expenditures to benefit the consumer importers. Therefore, by combining these government-expenditure benefit ideas with forward-shifting concepts, the collection of the same taxes on goods exported as on goods used domestically amounts to the collection of higher taxes on exports than on goods consumed locally. When exports are taxed by the exporting nation, taxes are paid on imports by citizens of a nation not benefiting from the consumption of public goods financed with taxes paid.

In this very complex fashion, one can reason that the collection of the same taxes on goods produced, but exported, as on goods domestically produced and consumed amounts to the collection of higher taxes on exports than on goods not exported. Consumers of imports, through forward shifting of taxes not refunded on exports, finance services enjoyed by the residents of the exporting nation. On the other hand, border taxes paid by importers provide funds to finance services that can be enjoyed by those paying the taxes.

### Destination Principle and Encouragement of the Public Sector

If the destination principle is utilized by all nations relative to all their taxes, then as far as the free flow of trade is affected by taxes, the producer utilizing the least private resources and producing in the nation with the largest public sector will be supplying all users, if resources are used approximately as efficiently in all economies. Under these conditions, other nations using the product will levy border taxes equal to the taxes borne by the imported products when they are produced in the importing country. The border tax allocates to imports the costs of production met by government spending in the importing nation (and not the higher amount) that, under the conditions assumed here, are spent by the nation of export.

The tax refund on exports and the border tax on imports, administered in this fashion, encourage the use of government-provided resources to meet worldwide needs for the traded product. Under these conditions, if the traditional and most efficient producer were a large relative user of private resources, the competitive advantage of the most efficient producer would decline. In turn this would reduce the efficiency of worldwide production.

### Encouragement of Efficient Producer

In the European Economic Community's tax-harmonization program, it is proposed that the destination principle for indirect taxes be abandoned between member states, but continued between member states and third countries. The new situation, because it makes indirect-tax rates and procedures considerably more uniform within the EEC than under the current situation, has been thought of as a move toward greater tax harmonization. The new indirect-tax uniformity could generate less as well as more trade between member states and a less or more efficient use of resources than that which existed when considerable variation in indirect taxes existed and the destination principle was uniformly utilized.

For example, if the nation exporting product X were an efficient producer and possessed a highly developed public sector financed with indirect taxes, and if the principal importer were a nation with a relatively low-level indirect tax, then the condition before harmonization would have been more favorable to nondomestic consumers than would be true under harmonization with uniform indirect-tax rates. Under the complete tax harmonization, the low-tax nondomestic consumer of product X would no longer benefit from a larger refund of indirect taxes than was assessed as border taxes. If the demand for product X in the importing nation were rather elastic, imports would decline and the number employed in the production of X in the formerly relatively high user of indirect taxes would decline. On the other hand, if the former relative use of indirect taxes of the exporters and importers of product X were reversed, employment and consumption would be stimulated under complete harmonization.

## Trade between a Nation Using the Origin and a Nation Using the Destination Principle

The use of the tax-origin principle (no refund of taxes on exports and no border taxes) nearly exclusively by one producing area and a very considerable use of the tax-destination principle by another are a closely paralleling situation to that which is developing between the United States and the EEC. Under this fiscal relationship, exports will be stimulated from the destination-principle country to the origin-principle country, but not on the basis of most efficient resource use. For trade to be in balance, under conditions of unchanged terms of trade, factor or production costs, including taxes, will have to be considerably less in the origin-principle country than in the destination-principle country; that is, labor and capital will receive less per unit of export. This relationship finds reflection in exchange rates, and the currency of the origin-principle country will be relatively undervalued. This in turn encourages foreign investment in industries meeting domestic demand in the origin-type tax country and at the same time relatively high-cost domestic producers because of higher-priced imports.

This tax-caused economic relationship between predominantly destination- and predominanlty origin-principle countries is summarized below.

If the cost of product X is $C + T$ (where $T$ equals taxes and $C$ is all other costs) and these costs are equal in two countries A and B, and if both countries use the origin principle relative to taxes, each country will produce the product X it requires. Whether this situation corresponded with that of best allocation of factors relative to product X is not determinable because we do not know what other uses could be made of factors used to produce X in countries A and B.

If the situation is changed only in that A utilizes the destination principle and B keeps the origin principle, then the cost of X produced in A becomes $C$ to B while the cost of X to A users remains at $C + T$. The cost of X produced in B remains $C + T$ to domestic users and foreign users. Under these conditions, the consumers of X in B begin to purchase their X in A rather than from domestic producers.

Taxes paid by producres of X for local consumption in countries A and B have not been changed, but their relative international competitive position has been affected. Country A, by utilizing a tax system capable of using the destination principle and by taking advantage of this opportunity, has improved its international economic competitive position. Country A will be selling X cheaper, and B will be offering X at the same price; but A will be adding a border tax to this price. Consumers of X in B will purchase more from A, and consumers in A will purchase less of X from B.

The price that country A pays for products from B will increase its tax receipts because of the collection of a border tax. In turn, its tax receipts are reduced by the refunding of taxes on its new market for X in B. The higher price A pays for imports will tend to reduce its consumption of imports, and the lower prices of exports will tend to stimulate exports. Balance can be restored by reducing the value of the monetary unit of B, which is another way of saying reducing what can be purchased abroad, for an hour of labor in B. This situation cannot be remedied by increasing hourly wages in B, for this would counter the cure of devaluation adopted in B to meet the new competitive conditions arising from A's introduction of a tax system that can make use of the destination system.

*Conclusion*

The economic and philosophical bases of the destination principle are founded on a complex group of tax and expenditure incidence assumptions. These have become less acceptable through the years as the result of findings of new studies.

The application of the destination principle causes an unequal impact of a given tax level on international economic competitive conditions. The elimination of the destination principle does not change the difference in the cost impact of a given tax collection level or that arises from different expenditure efficiencies, or from variations in the impact of the tax itself and the administrative procedures related to the accumulation of capital and general economic efficiency. *The destination principle is an unnecessary additional element restricting freedom of economic exchange. In addition, it acts to encourage high-cost production and to interfere with free choice of fiscal measures by the electorate of the various nations of the world.*

Its elimination should be a basic element in GATT consideration of taxes in relation to general export subsidies and compensatory border taxes.[18] The impact on costs and prices of direct and indirect taxes is seldom determined on the basis of which of these two categories the tax falls into. Therefore, different treatment based on this tax characteristic is generally not justified.[19]

## Optimality in the Taxation of U.S. Imports

The U.S. imports are not liable for general border taxes, as are the imports, for example, of the member states of the Common Market. Border taxes of the United States are limited to the special product excise taxes used by the federal government. Of course, as U.S. imports move into the distribution stream, they are subject to the same state and local sales taxes as domestic commodities. However, U.S. imports are never subject to a major general national levy, as are the imports of the nations using a value-added tax.

The U.S. imports are in many cases the products of foreign affiliates of U.S. businesses. The degree of U.S.-centered control that is exercised over these foreign business affiliates who export to the United States varies considerably. Also, the competitive conditions prevailing in the markets of the world affect the level of U.S. imports from all foreign suppliers.

Today with the large and expensive imports of petroleum products, the U.S. imports of manufactured products have fallen to about 50 percent of the total.[20] These manufactured imports are dominated by the automobile category. The imports of raw materials have been generally of growing importance, and as foreign producing units of petroleum and minerals come under the control of the nations in which they are located, the profits from these activities are drained away from U.S. business control. This reduces U.S. business capital available for investment.

### Multinational Trade Negotiation

The recently completed multilateral trade negotiation (MTN) at Geneva utilizes the rate base provided by the Kennedy round of fifteen years ago.

The Kennedy round reduced the tariffs which the United States collects on imports of nonagricultural products of Common Market member states by $2,094 million. The EEC tariff reduction granted on U.S. imports was about $700 million less.[21] An interesting aspect of these data is that the nonagricultural-sector products granted 50 percent tariff reduction were nearly $500 million greater on U.S. imports from the EEC than on EEC imports from the United States. The EEC reductions of 1 to 24 percent on imports from the United States were over $600 million more than on U.S. imports from the EEC.

The very aggregate data quoted here clearly demonstrate the large-percentage tariff reductions on imports made by the United States and the small tariff reductions on imports made by the Common Market member states. These tariff changes were being made at the same time as EEC member states were adopting VAT as a replacement for their cascade-turn-over taxes and expanding the revenues arising from this source. So we had a condition here where U.S. tariffs on EEC exports were being reduced more than EEC tariffs on U.S. exports. In addition, EEC border-tax rates were being increased. The situation in 1980 after the Geneva-Tokyo round is not greatly different. For example, the United Kingdom in mid-1979 subtantially increased VAT rates.

*Tax Disharmonization*

The optimality of the location of production activity is affected by the restriction of imports by quotas, tariffs, or border taxes. The new situation that arose out of the development of a changed relative position of imports competing on the U.S. market reduced the optimality of production and marketing decisions in both the United States and Europe. The United States became a much more desirable market in which to sell EEC-produced goods. On the other hand, the EEC became a much more difficult market in which to sell U.S.-made goods.

A large portion of this changed situation can be traced to the reduction of the relative importance of U.S. tariffs and an increase in the absolute height of EEC border taxes. The reduction of location efficiency caused by tax disharmonization results in higher real costs.

The destruction of the portion of the Bretton Woods agreement establish-ing fixed or negotiated exchange rates against the U.S. dollar or gold arose from many causes. One basic cause, however, was the inability of the United States to purchase all the imports offered on the U.S. market to earn dollars to meet the varied national needs of the nations of the world. When the U.S. imports became as large as exports, the end of the line had been reached. The high-profit U.S. market could not measure up to Bretton Wood, expecta-tions, and direct controls on the outflow of funds were introduced.[22]

*Adjusting through VAT*

The reversal of the international commercial world initiated on August 15, 1971, requires the United States to operate very largely as all other countries do. This means that imports enter the United States on the same basis as they enter the other industrial nations. Basically that is what the earlier Kennedy round and the recent Geneva negotiations were all about. The international-trade role of VAT in this scenario is to ease the adjustment period.

The VAT makes it easier for companies adjusted to produce primarily for the domestic market to maintain the competitive position needed to produce and sell the exports required to purchase imports. The VAT can also lend a hand to those already exporting to some extent, but whose heart is really not in it. The help provided by VAT, along with the lower income taxes that its use makes possible, provide tax favors on exports comparable to those available when foreign production is exported to third-country importers.

*Conclusion*

The VAT is sometimes seen as an expensive way to purchase imports, for the tax favors turn out to be a large portion of estimated increased exports. When a comparison of this type is made, the analyst is assuming that some unnamed procedure can be used to purchase imports at a lower short- and long-term cost. When money units are quoted as establishing both the cost and the value of imports, the analyst is assuming that the domestic currency can be used to purchase imports when it has not been "accredited" by a certain quantity of exports. The U.S. analyst was able to think along these lines during the twenty-five-year Bretton Woods period. Since August 15, 1971, a new approach has been required, and VAT may just be one of the best procedures for use by a considerable portion of the business community in operating under the "new rules."[23]

## DISC and Distortions of International Capital Movements[24]

The investment abroad of U.S. savings has increased as opportunities in Europe expanded and as the need for offshore sources of additional raw materials, particularly petroleum, grew. For a time during the late 1960s and early 1970s, controls and a special tax on foreign-sourced interest and dividends were imposed to reduce the level of foreign investment by U.S.

nationals. Also, the 1962 and the 1975 revenue acts have acted to discourage the investment abroad of U.S. savings by increasing the speed and height of tax collections in incomes arising from foreign business ventures.

## Capital Inducements

The attraction of investment funds to an area to increase employment and tax-paying ability has gone along part and parcel with emphasis on economic growth. Although low-income countries undoubtedly have greater need for outside investment of funds in productive undertakings, they have not been alone in the scramble. All sections of the planet have considered themselves in need of additional capital investments. Of course, this has meant that nations considering themselves to be in need of additional capital for one reason or another have provided capital from their own inadequate supply to meet the capital needs of another area.

This movement of capital takes place generally when the owner feels that his earnings are maximized by this type of action. The granting of special incentives to attract capital or the placing of a special burden on the earnings of capital can distort use and location of capital. Examples of these two types of allocation distortions are provided by Ireland and the favors it grants to U.S. capital[25] and the high corporate profits tax on repatriated earnings levied by the United States.[26]

The Irish policy has resulted in the attraction of substantial U.S.-sourced investments. The profits from these operations are exempt of corporate income taxes, but are considered as appropriately taxed when expatriated to Holland and can from this point benefit from deduction of full Dutch corporate income taxes[27] when transferred for investment or as dividends.[28]

Between 1969 and 1975, foreign investment by affiliates of U.S. companies grew from $11.8 billion to $29.6 billion.[29] These were earnings which were generally subject to only the corporate income taxes of the country in which they operated. Profits of U.S. affiliates are invested abroad partially because their return to the United States for investment would make them subject to the difference between the corporate profit taxes paid and those applicable under the U.S. corporate income tax.

In both the special Irish situation and that of foreign affiliates of U.S. companies generally, distortions of capital movements have arisen out of the manner in which the U.S. corporate profit tax operates. Of course, the types of capital-use decisions made were also affected by the level of foreign tax rates and the manner in which they were applied. Nevertheless, the way in which the United States taxes businesses tends to dominate because of the large relative importance of the U.S. multinational-corporation development and the overall size of the U.S. economy.

*DISC Producer Loans*

The role of The Domestic International Sales Corporation (DISC) in the reduction of capital-movement distortions arises from its encouragement of investment in the United States of earnings arising from foreign operations. In addition, the very fact of lower corporate income taxes on exports passing through DISC reduces the attractiveness of capital export from the United States.

In order to qualify for DISC tax benefits, a DISC must invest its tax-deferred income into the export portion of the business. As a matter of fact, DISC is a counterinducement and somewhat reduces the impact of capital-use distortions arising from both foreign and domestic tax practices.

The procedure for doing this investing is detailed under the procedures for making producer loans. The approach taken places very elaborate controls over the calculation of when a producer loan is a legitimate use of DISC-retained and tax-free earnings to expand investment dedicated to the expansion of exports.

The legislation and the regulations are basically aimed at avoiding the use of DISC-retained earnings to purchase capital dedicated to exporting while at the same time export-related capital is being reduced at some other point of the operations of the corporate group. In other words, retained earnings of DISC to be used within the provisions of the legislation providing for producer loans must cause an increase in the control group's capital (after tax allowed depreciation) used to carry out export activities.[30]

The DISC legislation does not contemplate the reduction of the distortion in the investment of capital as one of its goals. However, the legislation definitely does this in a negative way; that is tax favors are withdrawn if export assets or other export expansion expenditures are not made with DISC income. Apparently, the complications of the procedures and the need for operating funds in the international area have prevented the producer-loan procedure from having a major impact. Unfortunately, Treasury reports of DISC operations do not include information dealing with producer loans. Therefore, reliance must be placed on interview information and articles published by tax practitioners.[31]

The business community reports very bad experience with the DISC producer-loan provision. For example, the loan could become unacceptable if inventories for foreign export were drawn down or if accelerated depreciation reduced the value of the asset acquired with the loan, while additional export-related assets had not been acquired with funds other than those arising from producer loans.[32]

The DISC legislation's attempts to avoid rechanneling funds to finance exports from conventional sources to new uses, because of the reduced export need arising out of the availability of producer loans, are so cumbersome and filled with so many uncertainties that apparently producer loans are seldom used. On top of these limitations concerned with making certain producer loans result in a real increase in export-related assets, the DISC legislation limits the quantity of loans that can be made to one borrower. This effectively prevents using producer loans to start up a new export operation. But, if this were not enough, the law also provides that producer loans may not be made to a borrower until the borrower has completed one taxable year.

Another aspect of the regulation of the use of producer loans concerns the treatment of foreign investment attributable to producer loans. These amounts lose their DISC tax protection and are treated as deemed distributions, and therefore are fully taxable. Here we have an approach that may have some potential for reducing the misallocation of capital due to tax inducements available abroad. For example, all U.S. corporate groups and affiliates could be granted a tax reduction on taxable income that would vary with the portion of total new investments made in the United States. The result would be an immediate tax break to all corporate groups operating largely in the United States, plus tax inducement to continue to operate domestically.[33]

*Conclusion*

The general area of the taxation of international activities of U.S. business has been a disaster. A principal cause of the difficulty has arisen from the need to make adjustments for international business with a national tax system that does not possess a general major transactions tax.

The enactment of DISC attempted to encourage exports and investment in the United States to produce goods to meet foreign demand. The legislation provides for corporate income tax savings if certain conditions are met. The legislation is complex, and its impact has not been great. In addition, it is doubtful if the procedure stays within the general principles of GATT.

**Notes**

1. C. Fred Bergsten, "Toward Greater Cooperation in International Investment Policies" (Washington: Department of the Treasury, February 28, 1980).

2. Ernst and Whinney, "Investing in the United States," *International Series*, April 1980.

3. James R. Gallagher, "Republic of Ireland Taxation," *The Tax Executive* 26 (January 1974):149-160.

4. Peggy B. Musgrave, "Direct Investment Abroad and the Multinationals: Effects on the U.S. Economy," Committee on Foreign Relations, U.S. Senate, August 1975.

5. John F. Due, *The General Manufacturer's Tax in Canada* (Toronto, Canada: Canadian Tax Foundation, 1951).

6. Gregory V. Jump and Thomas A. Wilson, "Tax Policy Options for Increasing Employment without Inflation," *Canadian Tax Journal* 20, no. 2 (March-April 1972):144-153.

7. U.S. Department of Commerce, *Business Statistics—1977* (Washington: GPO, 1978), p. 10.

8. U.S. Treasury Department, "Federal Manufacturer's Wholesale and Retail Sales Taxes," *Hearings Revenue Revision of 1942* 1: 351.

9. Clara K. Sullivan, *The Tax on Value Added* (New York: Columbia University Press, 1965), pp. 237-238.

10. Article XVI, sec. B4 of GATT bans the remission "of direct taxes or social welfare charges on industrial or commercial enterprises." This means that a flat-rate corporate income or payroll tax may not be retailed as allocated to exports but a VAT or a manufacturer's tax could be rebated.

11. See Uranla K. Hicks, *Public Finance*, 1955, pp. 248-251; Harry Gunnison Brown, *JPE*, April 1939, pp. 254-262; M. Kryzaniak and R.A. Musgrave, *Shifting of the Corporation Income Tax*, 1962; and Earl R. Rolph, *JPE*, April 1952, pp. 102-117.

12. Carl S. Shoup, *The Sales Tax in France* (New York: Columbia University Press, 1930), pp. 43-44, and *Public Finance*, pt. 2 (Chicago: Aldine, 1969); A.G. Buehler, *General Sales Taxation* (New York: The Business Bourse, 1932), p. 101.

13. Ibid., p. 188.

14. Robert Murray Haig, *The Public Finances of Post-War France* (New York: Columbia University Press, 1929); Edgard Allix and Marcel Lecercle, *La Taxe sur le Chiffre D'affaires* (Paris: Rousseau, 1927).

15. Ray M. Sommerfeld, Hershel M. Anderson, and Horace R. Brock, *Introduction to Taxation* (New York: Harcourt, Brace & World, 1969), p. 40.

16. Ken Messere, "A Defense of Present Border Tax Adjustments," *National Tax Journal* 32, no. 4 (December 1979):481-492.

17. Richard W. Lindholm, "Review of *Fiscal Studies No. 15*, 1977," authored by National Bureau of Economic Research, *Journal of Economic Literature*, September 1978, pp. 1049-1051.

18. Organization of Economic Cooperation and Development, "Changing to VAT," *OECD Observer*, February 1970.

19. A.B. Atkinson and J.E. Stiglitz, "The Design of Tax Structure: Direct Versus Indirect Taxation," *Journal of Public Economics* 6 (1976):55-75.

20. *Economic Report of the President, 1979* (Washington: USGPO), p. 296.

21. *Report on United States Negotiations, 1964-67* (Trade Conference Office of the Special Representative for Trade Negotiations, 1967), vols. 1, 2.

22. Gerald M. Meier, "The Bretton Woods Agreement—Twenty-Five Years After," *Stanford Law Review* 23 (January 1971):252-253.

23. Clyde Hartz, "The New GATT—Successor to the Kennedy Round," *Business Economics* 14, no. 3 (May 1979):5-8.

24. EEC Council Resolution of February 10, 1975, on measures to be taken to combat international tax evasion and avoidance to accomplish, among other things, a reduction of distortions of capital movements. *European Taxation* 15, no. 2 (February 1975):67.

25. Gallagher, "Republic of Ireland Taxation."

26. *IMF Survey* 4, no. 10 (May 26, 1975):152.

27. This practice of assumed full tax payment is called *tax sparing*.

28. Gallagher, "Republic of Ireland Taxation."

29. *IMF Survey*, p. 152. Total U.S. investment in nonresidential structures and producers' durable equipment was $94.1 billion in 1974.

30. L.S. Ullman, *Bulletin for International Fiscal Documentation* 26, no. 10 (October 1972):379-381.

31. Interviews carried out by author during summer and fall of 1974.

32. Jane G. Gravelle and Donald W. Kiefer, "Deferral and DISC: Two Targets of Tax Reform" (Washington: Congressional Research Service, 1978), pp. 21-28.

33. Paul R. Kahan, "Computing DISC Taxable Income," *The Tax Executive* 31 (April 1979):240-250.

# Index

# Index

# About the Author

**Richard W. Lindholm** is currently professor and dean emeritus at the University of Oregon. He has previously held academic posts at Michigan State University, The Ohio State University, Texas A&M University, The University of Texas, and the College of St. Thomas.

Dr. Lindholm has been consultant to the finance departments of the state governments of Minnesota, Texas, Ohio, Michigan, and Oregon. In addition he has served as a specialist in government finance to Pakistan, South Vietnam, Korea, Papua New Guinea, and Turkey. During 1975 and again in 1979, Dr. Lindholm was employed as consultant to the U.S. Committee on Ways and Means and to its chairman, Congressman Al Ullman.

Dr. Lindholm is the author of ten books in the area of taxation policy, including *Introduction to Fiscal Policy*, *Public Finance and Fiscal Policy*, and *Value-Added Tax and Other Tax Reforms*.